PAUL
and TIME

PAUL
and TIME

LIFE IN THE
TEMPORALITY OF CHRIST

L. ANN JERVIS

Baker Academic
a division of Baker Publishing Group
Grand Rapids, Michigan

© 2023 by L. Ann Jervis

Published by Baker Academic
a division of Baker Publishing Group
Grand Rapids, Michigan
www.bakeracademic.com

Printed in the United States of America

Library of Congress Cataloging-in-Publication Data
Names: Jervis, L. Ann, author.
Title: Paul and time : life in the temporality of Christ / L. Ann Jervis.
Description: Grand Rapids, Michigan : Baker Academic, a division of Baker Publishing Group,
    [2023] | Includes bibliographical references and index.
Identifiers: LCCN 2023009232 | ISBN 9781540960788 (cloth) | ISBN 9781493438082 (ebook) | ISBN
    9781493438099 (pdf)
Subjects: LCSH: Bible. Epistles of Paul—Criticism, interpretation, etc. | God (Christianity)—
    Eternity. | Time—Religious aspects—Christianity. | Death—Religious aspects—Christianity. |
    Paul, the Apostle, Saint.
Classification: LCC BS2655.E7 .J47 2023 | DDC 227/.06—dc23/eng/20230526
LC record available at https://lccn.loc.gov/2023009232

Baker Publishing Group publications use paper produced from sustainable forestry practices and post-consumer waste whenever possible.

23   24   25   26   27   28   29   7   6   5   4   3   2   1

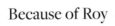

Because of Roy

Contents

Foreword

In his famous commentary on Galatians, J. Louis Martyn argued that the essential question being asked in that letter was, What time is it? His answer to that question invigorated a debate concerning Paul's conception of the Christ-event and whether that was, in relation to time, "linear" or "punctiliar" in character. But the question also invited another: How did Paul understand time? The great merit of Ann Jervis's argument in this book is to press that second question and to challenge the unreflective habits of Pauline scholars, who routinely describe Pauline eschatology as combining "the already and the not yet," such that the believer now exists in the "overlap" or "tension" between the old age and the new. Such language is so common among interpreters of Paul that they rarely stop to ask what sense it makes: How can two time periods "overlap"? How can the future be "brought into" the present? When Barth and Bultmann wrestled with the theological meaning of New Testament eschatology, they did not fall into the trap of figuring eschatology as a new period of time on a chronological continuum. But in subsequent decades, scholars of Paul have failed to give this matter the attention it deserves or to reflect carefully enough on their own language. In some hands, the notion of living simultaneously in "two ages" has given the impression that the resurrection has won only a limited victory over sin and death and that believers are currently battling to establish a reality that is half complete. Following recent reexamination of Barth's theology of time, a few Pauline scholars (e.g., Jamie Davies and Douglas Campbell) have raised questions about the time conceptuality employed by Paul and by his interpreters. But no one has made the meaning of time a central topic in the interpretation of Paul—until now, in this wide-ranging, provocative, and highly significant treatise by Ann Jervis.

Jervis's central thesis is that Paul understands the Christ-event not as the inauguration of a new time (a "new age") or as the intrusion of timelessness ("eternity") into the world of time but as the enclosure of one *kind of time* (death-time, or time determined by decay) within another *kind of time* (life-time, or the life of Christ). These two kinds of time are not periods of time in the normal sense, one following the other. Moreover, the difference between them is qualitative, not quantitative: Christ-time is not "more" time, since its unstoppability is but one feature of its superabundance. Crucially, although Christ may be said to live time, that temporality is not chronological or constrained "within" time, which is why believers who have lived after Christ may be said to have been crucified with Christ in a way that defies our normal understandings of past, present, and future. Equally importantly, union with Christ is not partial or incomplete, as if the believer lives a bifurcated life, partly in the realm of death and partly in the realm of life. On Jervis's reading of Paul, the believer lives completely and exclusively in the life of Christ. As Paul says, "the world has been crucified to me, and I to the world" (Gal. 6:14 NIV). In those terms, life in Christ is not a matter of both-and; it is straightforwardly either/or. The suffering, mortality, and temptation experienced by the believer are not, for Jervis, a sign of living still partially in the "present evil age." All such things have been enveloped, embraced, and taken over into the life of God in Christ and are therefore experienced by the believer "in Christ" and not in spite of him.

The great virtue of this book is to make us question our habits of language and thought and to confront us afresh with the strangeness of Paul's theology. Jervis draws on features of the philosophy of time, from Aristotle to our post-Einstein present, and she is also alert to those (relatively few) interpreters of Paul who have wrestled with his remarkable theological statements concerning time. In important ways, she insists, Paul simply marches off the map of our human conceptuality of time; if we domesticate him to fit our concepts, then we have failed to appreciate how radical he is. By highlighting the totalizing character of Paul's claims, Jervis questions the notion that Paul countered enthusiasts by his "eschatological reserve," a reading beloved of interpreters in the Lutheran tradition. Indeed, in certain respects her reading of passages in the "undisputed" letters of Paul brings them into close proximity with statements in Colossians and Ephesians, which are normally taken to be signs of an un-Pauline or over-realized eschatology. In these and in many other respects, her work throws a lot of Pauline cards into the air, allowing them to fall in unexpected places.

Each chapter here deserves careful attention and close exegetical scrutiny because, if Jervis is right, we need to think a lot harder about how to understand Paul's claims. Gnostic readings of Paul latched onto many of the features of Pauline thought that Jervis highlights, while Bultmann's existentialist reading provided a way to think about the anthropological consequences of inhabiting Christ's time in faith. If, for various reasons, neither of those options seems attractive to us today, we need to ask how we might express theologically what it means to live (inescapably) within human time, in our present enthrallment to entropy, while joined to a life reality that is not encompassed by, but itself encompasses, our chronic condition. If, as Jervis memorably puts it, for those in Christ death is not fatal, how is this to be believed, hoped, and practiced in a community that is shaped by such good news? Surprising, even shocking on first read, Jervis's book forces us to ask if we have read Paul aright at an absolutely central point, and it requires us to seek new patterns of thought in his wake. For that, we should all be heartily grateful.

John Barclay

Preface

The work of this book is a departure from much of my other writing. Rather than hoping to understand Paul more clearly by including historical description, I look at his writings synthetically. I am sure that if time and space permitted, and readers' patience allowed, this book would have been stronger if I included arguments based on historical situatedness at each point where I interpret Paul's words. I have not done this, mostly because it would have been an unwieldy project to produce and to read. This is not necessarily a loss, however, nor do I think that it downgrades my interpretations of particular texts. Something may be lost, but something is also gained by hearing together Paul's words from his various letters, written over several years, to and from different circumstances. In this way, we may gain a greater sense of the vision that guided his initiatives and responses as the apostle navigated the new waters God opened to him in Jesus Christ. It is because of this approach to getting to know Paul's thought that I do not include disputed letters, though occasionally I note comparisons with them.

At the outset it must be acknowledged that though this is a book about Paul and time, time as a category is not something Paul discusses. I may then seem to be imposing a category on the apostle's writings or trying to tease out something from material that is really concerned about other matters. However, Paul is fundamentally and centrally concerned about life and death, which themselves are temporal categories. Life and time are metonymies, for one without the other is impossible; to conceive or experience one is to conceive or experience the other. Death, on the other hand, is the destroyer of life and of time. To speak of death is to speak of the opposite of time.

One of the things I struggled with was allowing myself to seek and suggest what Paul meant, whether or not it made sense of Christian experience. I pushed myself to hear Paul even when what I heard was not explanatory of my experience or observation of living the Christian life. What I have found most challenging is the idea that those in Christ are exclusively in Christ. As I perceive the consequence of Paul's conception, those invested in his words cannot blame the ongoing present evil age for suffering, sinning, or physical death; neither can they use it to explain such things. If I take this idea and its consequence on board, it makes my work as priest and preacher much more challenging. While I am used to understanding and presenting the prevalence of raw and wretched suffering or destructive sinning or the deaths of loved ones as due to forces at war with our good God, Paul asks me to dig deeper. Maybe there is an understanding of the Christian life other than that of living in the overlap of the ages. If I try to see things through Paul's eyes (at least as I have glimpsed them), I find God to be stranger than I already believed: the one who defeated destructive forces by submitting to them on the cross. As I read Paul, the nature of God's victory through Christ is even more unexpected. Through the cross and resurrection, God diminishes God's foes, leaving as an option their illusory temporality—which leads only to the destruction of life and so time—while announcing that this option will end. God permits God's foes a limited range of influence, allowing humanity to choose to exist in the illusory dead-end temporality grounded in defeat (what I term "death-time"); which is in reality non-time. Those who choose this temporality live there and there alone, though in the end this temporal option will be no more, and all will finally be in God.

Is God's willingness to tolerate God's foes for the sake of humanity's freedom a kind of love that verges on the incomprehensible?

On the other hand, through the crucified, risen, and exalted Son,
God opens to humanity God's temporality—the only real time—
through which all things, even suffering, the human propensity to
sin, and physical death, are transformed to and for life. The good
news is that, in Christ, God offers God's own life (what I call "life-
time") in which, as is the case for Christ, the pains and challenges
of human life are reframed and transformed. This also can be seen
as a sign of God's love—the opportunity to live as God's Son and
to learn in the face of suffering, the temptation to sin, and mortality
that nothing separates us from God's love.

The Shape of the Book

I introduce this book by discussing the critical centrality of our
assumptions and convictions about time (and eternity) in our interpretations of Paul. This centrality is clear when we survey, as
I do in chapters 1 and 2, the two most influential understandings
of Paul's view of time: the salvation historical and apocalyptic interpretations. These two quite different hypotheses about Paul's
interpretation of Christ's life, crucifixion, resurrection, and exaltation are founded on particular understandings of Paul's temporal structure. Interestingly, despite their differences, both salvation
historical and apocalyptic readings rely on a common conviction
that Paul inherited a two-age framework, which he had to modify
in order to make sense of the fact that Christ was resurrected but
the faithful were not. Paul fit Christ's resurrection into his inherited
schema by reworking it: the two ages are not sequential but rather,
because of Christ, now overlap. Believers are those who live in the
overlap of the ages.

In chapter 3, I point out several problems with this common view
and propose that Paul does not think that believers live in the overlap of the ages but instead that they live exclusively in Christ. This
recognition has consequences for our understanding of how Paul

conceives of believers' temporality. Being joined to Christ is to live in a temporality entirely distinct from that of the present evil age. I term time in Christ as "life-time," and time in the present evil age as "death-time." These are not alternative appellations for the old and new age: one is an age and the other a being.

Chapter 4 begins a discussion of the temporality of union with Christ, offering the idea that union with Christ means living Christ's time. The discussion starts with a description of what I take to be a commonplace understanding of time. It proceeds to the claim that Paul thinks of Christ as living God's temporality, which is life-time: time that is not only endless but in which there is only life. I relate Barth's understanding that God's life and God's time are inextricable to my understanding of Paul's conception of divine time. I propose that the apostle thinks of God living eventful temporality that produces change, especially between God and God's creation. God, however, does not live tenses the way humans do, for in God's temporality the past, present, and future are not discrete or sequential. I then turn to a description of Paul's two types of time: life-time, which is the only real time, and death-time, which is time shaped by its end.

Chapter 5 explores the time of the exalted Christ, discussing Christ's past, present, and future. Paul describes Christ's past and present in terms that indicate change and therefore temporality. Christ's future, however, is largely revelatory of his current life. What is still to come for Christ is that his present tense will be revealed. Apart from the unique reference to Christ's handing over his reign and being subjected to God, the future events in Christ's life do not create change in his life—except insofar as he reveals that life. While believers' future will be changed when they have access to Christ's present—they will receive incorruptibility—for Christ, the eschatological events are a publication of Christ's present.

Chapter 6 explores two significant passages in which Paul speaks of eschatological events, one from 1 Corinthians 15 and the other from Romans 8. While these passages are usually understood to be about the future for both believers and Christ, I read them differently: the events described are future for believers but largely not so for Christ. These passages indicate that Paul understands what is to come in human chronological time as the revelation of Christ's present reality. Moreover, these passages indicate that by living in Christ's time, the faithful live presently in the victory of Christ's resurrection and in the glory that is now.

In chapter 7 I spell out the relationship between being in Christ and temporality. I briefly analyze the temporal implications of several scholarly proposals about what Paul means by union with Christ. I then turn to a rereading of Paul's eschatology in light of my interpretation that union with Christ is union with Christ's time.

Chapter 8 explores how my interpretation affects our understanding of the meaning of suffering, physical death, and sin in Paul. I propose that the apostle does not see these as symptoms of the still unvanquished evil age but as transformed by and fitting with being in Christ.

In the book's conclusion I reflect on the matters raised by my reading and underscore some of the foundational pieces of my thinking.

Acknowledgments

The idea for this book germinated over decades. The seed was planted in the first year of my doctoral work under Richard N. Longenecker of blessed memory. For some now-forgotten reason, in Dr. Longenecker's course on Jewish apocalyptic, I read Oscar Cullmann's *Christ and Time*. I was intrigued but not convinced. Over the next busy years of doctoral work and then teaching, combined with family life and church work, the idea lay dormant. It was not until over half a decade ago that I was able to get back to pondering the idea of time, and given my long-standing fascination with Paul, there was nothing for it but to write on Paul and time.

I have been exceptionally fortunate in the support I have received. My work was supported by a social science and humanities research (SSHRC) grant from the Canadian government. This significant grant allowed me to hire a superb research assistant, Carolyn Mackie. Carolyn's attention to detail, professionalism, and kindness is matched only by that of Adrienne Jones of Graham Library, University of Toronto. Both, particularly during the COVID-19 lockdown, made it possible for me to keep reading, thinking, and writing. My friend Ann McRae heroically read the final proofs under time pressure. Thank you, Ann.

I have also received invaluable direction from Bryan Dyer at Baker Academic and from Dave Nelson when he held the position of acquisitions editor at Baker Academic. In the lonely early days, when I couldn't find anyone else who was thinking about Paul and time, Dave was a great encourager. Michael Thomson, now an editor at Wipf & Stock, also believed that this project was worth doing, and I thank him. The strong guiding hand of Melisa Blok, editor at Baker Academic, accomplished the hard work of getting the manuscript into as readable a form as possible and even made the often painful editing process close to delightful (no irony intended). Melisa is a treasure, and I consider that over the course of our working together we developed into friends. Thank you, Melisa.

Gradually, I found my tribe, as it were, or it found me. Judith Newman introduced me to scholars in Jewish studies who were thinking about temporal matters. I am immensely grateful for her friendship and belief in the project when it was in its infancy. Through her I met Loren Stuckenbruck, Matthias Henze, and Grant Macaskill, all of whom inspired me to think broadly and creatively and who got me involved in the Enoch seminar. I have also benefited from the scholarly companionship of Jamie Davies. After a paper I presented at the 2018 Society of New Testament Studies conference, we discovered that we were both restless with standard interpretations of Paul's understanding of time. I thank him for his generosity in reading a draft of this book. Jamie's perceptive comments helped me dig deeper.

My friend and former colleague Andrew Lincoln has, over the years, faithfully read and discussed the ideas that form the foundation of this book, and recently read a draft. The fact that he doesn't completely agree with me even while encouraging me has been immensely important. My friend Susan Eastman, whose important work on Paul takes a different road, also graciously read and interacted most insightfully with the manuscript. Other scholarly friends have been generous in reading or engaging with portions of the work: Beverly Gaventa, Terry Donaldson, Joe Mangina, Douglas Campbell, Paul Gooch, Stephen Chester, Alexandra Brown, and Nate Wall. I am also grateful for conversation in the apocalyptic theology group organized by Phil Ziegler and the interest and support of colleagues at Wycliffe College, University of Toronto.

I am very grateful to John Barclay for writing the foreword. John has long been a model to me of rigorous, insightful, and gracious scholarship. I am honored by his words.

Many others have helped along the way by believing in the work and, some of them, by praying for me. If you are reading this page, you know who you are. I will name a couple in particular: David Townsend, who bolstered my confidence more than once, and Pam Jolliffe. Pam has been by my side since early teen years, offering wisdom, fun, and practical help. A testament to her love is that, even though she does not live in the world of scholarship or the church, Pam read this book in its entirety and with engaged curiosity.

Family members, especially Dylan, Allana, Bronwen, and Tracy, have supported this endeavor, at times with bemusement, but always with charity. This book is dedicated to my husband, Roy Hogg, whose extraordinary love flows from his life in Christ.

Introduction

Thinking about Time

———

It is impossible to meditate on time and the mystery of the creative passage of nature without overwhelming emotion at the limitations of human knowledge.

Alfred North Whitehead, *The Concept of Nature*, 48

Whether or not we have had opportunity to explore the matter of time philosophically and/or scientifically, we are intensely aware of it. In our daily lives we regularly hear or say that "time flies" or that we are "out of time" or "just in time." Temporal motifs and assumptions frame not only our daily lives but also our reading of Paul. Our study and interpretation of Paul involves conceptions and assumptions about time.[1]

Time is a feature in Pauline interpretation both because Paul worked with conceptions of it and because his interpreters do as well. That is, this book assumes both that interpreters bring conceptions about time into their interpretations of Paul and that Paul brought understandings of time into his interpretation of God's

1. Harink demonstrates this excellently in "Time and Politics in Four Commentaries."

work in Christ. Among other things, I hope this book encourages interpreters to be open to the possibility that their conceptions about time and Paul's may not be the same.

I wish to raise our consciousness about the fact that the matter of time is integrally involved in our Pauline interpretation. What we interpreters think about time and what we presume Paul thinks about time both deeply affect our reading and understanding of the apostle. In the first two chapters, I will illustrate this by describing the two dominant theological interpretations of Paul: salvation historical and apocalyptic.

The most obvious way time is involved in our interpretation is the standard practice of noting that our "time" is different from that of the apostle's. Those of us who think Paul's words may be potent today will also imagine how we might translate concepts and allusions from his time two thousand years ago to our own time. In addition to the matter of time emerging in the recognition of different historical time periods, interpreters understand implicitly or explicitly that time is intrinsic to Paul's thought, and so to our understanding of the apostle's words. We will see the broad strokes of this when we look at the salvation historical and apocalyptic interpretations of Paul. Even apart from these frameworks, we (knowingly or not) discuss time when interpreting Paul.

The most obvious area where this is the case is in interpretation of the apostle's eschatology: Did Paul think that the end of time was going to come in his lifetime or that it had already partially come? In fact, time is intrinsic to most, if not all, aspects of Paul's thought. Investigation of his Christology inevitably involves temporal matters. For instance, in discerning Paul's understanding of the cross, resurrection, and exaltation, we may ask whether he thinks of Jesus as still the crucified one subsequent to his being seated at God's right hand. When seeking to understand Paul's conception of God, we recruit ideas about time. For example, does Paul think that God lives a timeless or a time-full life, and how is God's life affected (or not) by God's sending the Son into human history? Trying to apprehend Paul's soteriology necessarily involves the matter of time: Does Paul think that the revelation of the righteousness of God in the gospel is still happening in our time, or was it over and done with in the events of Christ's incarnation, death, and resurrection? Comprehending Paul's ethics also necessarily engages temporality: By participating in Christ, do people progress over time to become like Christ, or are they already changed into Christ's siblings once they believe? Such questions are a tiny percentage of the vast number of questions that are regularly asked of the apostle. Here I wish simply to demonstrate that these questions, like a myriad of other Pauline perplexities, involve the matter of time—both interpreters' claims about Paul's temporal notions and, relatedly, their own assumptions about time.

This book's primary aim is to offer a fresh understanding of how Paul thinks of time. Admittedly, Paul does not ruminate on time as an abstract concept, as have philosophers and theologians. Nevertheless, he, like the rest of us, works with notions about time. I will propose that he conceives of two types of times (it should be noted that these two types of time are not, as will become clear, two ages) and that these types provide the fundamental framework for his interpretation of the significance of Jesus Christ.

As with most things, when we seek to understand another, we do so best if we first understand ourselves. In what follows I attempt a general description of notions about time that we may bring to our reading of the apostle—whether these be unconscious assumptions or influences from our education or experience. This description may not fit you. If not, I hope it stimulates thinking about what conceptions of time you do bring to your interpretation and whether or not you assume that Paul shares them.

Thinking about Time

Unless we have been trained as physicists to think about time mathematically, I venture that most interpreters of Paul conceive of time as an entity of some sort, whether actual and separate from us or internal to our being. Some of us may have questioned whether time is objectively real or whether the concept of time is just the way we humans make sense of reality.[2] We may have wondered, along with Augustine, whether time "is an extension of the mind itself."[3] That is, we may have wondered if there actually is an objective entity that we name "time," or if time is a feature of human consciousness. Heidegger puts it that in the "ordinary conception, there is a remarkable vacillation as to whether the character to be attributed to time is 'subjective' or 'Objective.'"[4] We may know that Kant is famous for claiming that time (along with space) is something internal to humankind's way of knowing, and that therefore it is subjective.[5] We might be aware of J. M. E. McTaggart's theory that time is unreal. Using philosophical logic and postulating two series of time (the A and the B series), McTaggart claims to have proved that "nothing is really in time."[6]

I suspect that the majority of Paul's interpreters operate with an objective view of time, thinking that it actually exists. We may, in fact, think of time as single, universal, and transcendent. That is, our notion about time may be that time is a container for events. It is the frame that contains events and is itself unaffected by the events it contains. We may think of time as separate from space[7]—a separate entity that just keeps on going.

This manner of thinking about time is Newtonian. Distinguishing between what he calls common or relative time, like hours and days, the duration of which is measured in terms of motion, Newton claims that there is an absolute time: "absolute, true, and mathematical time, in and of itself and of its own nature, without reference to anything external, flows uniformly and by another name is

2. Parmenides (born circa 515 BCE) appears to have questioned time's objective existence. See M. Wright, *Cosmology in Antiquity*, 126.
3. Augustine, *Confessions* 11.26. All English translations by Pine-Coffin.
4. Heidegger, *Being and Time*, 457. "Objective" is capitalized in original translation.
5. Kant writes: "Time . . . has subjective reality with regard to internal experience: that is, I really have the representation of time and of my determinations in it. Time therefore is to be considered as real not so far as it is an object, but so far as it is the representation of myself as an object. . . . Time is nothing but the form of our own internal intuition" (*Critique of Pure Reason*, 33).
6. McTaggart, *Nature of Existence*, 22.
7. Cf. Aristotle, *Physics* 6.2. See Hawking, *Brief History of Time*, 18.

called duration."[8] Consequently, "the flow of absolute time cannot be changed."[9]

We may know of Aristotle's understanding of time as that which allows us to measure motion and rest from motion, while not being identical with motion.[10] And we may also be aware that Augustine agrees with this aspect of Aristotle's understanding of time: time and motion are not the same thing.[11] Moreover, we may know that both the Philosopher and the Theologian understood time to exist.[12]

In addition to conceiving of time as objectively real, we may think that time itself flows,[13] and, if so, we typically conceive of it as moving forward in one direction. Those of us influenced by Jewish and Christian thought may think of time teleologically. Time flows ahead toward a God-ordained goal.[14] Even apart from a religious consciousness, the conventional, modern Western view of time is that it is linear; before and after are conceived of as before and after on a line. Heidegger is probably right that the ordinary conception of time is that it is "an endless, irreversible sequence of 'nows' which passes away."[15] The sequential or linear concept of time is, of course, distinct from the understanding of time as circular. In Western discussions

---

8. Newton, *Principia*, 408.

9. Newton, *Principia*, 410. More than one philosopher of time has postulated that the invention of the mechanical clock contributed to the conviction that there was an absolute, objective time. See Fagg, *Becoming of Time*, 19.

10. Aristotle, *Physics* 4.12.

11. Augustine, *Confessions* 11.21–27.

12. Aristotle, *Physics* 4.13; Augustine's claim that God created time (*Confessions* 11.13) must entail the conviction that time is real.

13. See Barrett's intriguing elucidation and expansion on Heidegger's view of time. Barrett proposes that the flow of time is with us and we are within it ("Flow of Time," 354–76).

14. Regarding a Christian view of time, S. G. F. Brandon writes of "Time as the field in which God's beneficent purpose majestically reveals itself" (*History, Time, and Deity*, 3). (Brandon capitalizes occurrences of the word "time.") Johann Baptist Metz comments that "*time with a finale*, this oriented time, unknown to either the Greek-Mediterranean or the Near Eastern cultural worlds, became the root of the understanding of the world as history" ("God," 29 [italics original]). See, however, the contrarian position of Marc Brettler, who argues that eschatology does not predominate in the Hebrew Bible, and when it does, it does not speak of the end of time. "Those who depict biblical time as linear, with the 'end of time' as a goal or *telos*, are misreading the text" ("Cyclical and Teleological Time," 122).

15. Heidegger, *Being and Time*, 478. This is not, however, how the person who lives with what Heidegger calls "resoluteness" exists. Such authentic being "assigns itself time and allows itself time" (463).

of the concept of time, there is a long-standing distinction made between circular and linear views of time. The ancient Greeks and Eastern thinkers are typically portrayed as regarding time as a circle, related perhaps to the cycle of the seasons and the planets. Both Plato and Aristotle assume the circularity of time.[16]

Augustine strongly critiques the cyclical conception of time: "Some philosophers have . . . introduce[d] cycles of time, in which there should be a constant renewal and repetition of the order of nature; and they have therefore asserted that these cycles will ceaselessly recur, one passing away and another coming."[17] This is not the biblical view, according to Augustine, for God, "though Himself eternal, and without beginning, yet He caused time to have a beginning."[18] For Augustine, the rectilinear view of time accords with Scripture.

Those of us who conceive of time as linear almost certainly think of it sequentially; there is the past, then the present, and then there will be the future. These tenses follow each other as if on a line. We may also have recognized that though we think about time in a linear fashion, this way of thinking does not accord with our experience. As Augustine has famously put it, "There are three times, a present of things past, a present of things present, and a present of future things. Some such different times do exist in the mind, but nowhere else that I can see. The present of past things is the memory; the present of present things is direct perception; and the present of future things is expectation. If we may speak in these terms, I can see three times and I admit that they do exist."[19]

And yet, while it is common to think in terms of the three tenses, things are more complex than that. Again, Augustine: "How can . . . the past and future, *be*, when the past no longer is and the future is not yet? As for the present, if it were always present and never moved on to become the past, it would not be time but eternity. If, therefore, the present is time only by reason of the fact that it moves

16. See Plato, *Timaeus*, esp. 37–39; Aristotle, *Physics* 4.14: "Even time itself is thought to be a circle."
17. Augustine, *City of God* 12.13.
18. Augustine, *City of God* 12.14.
19. Augustine, *Confessions* 11.20.

on to become the past, how can we say that even the present *is*, when the reason why it *is* is that it is *not to be*?"[20] We may have contemplated, as William James does, "that what is past, to be known as past, must be known *with* what is present, and *during* the 'present' spot of time."[21] This recognition may have led us to imagine a more fluid relationship between past, present, and future. Perhaps it has caused us, along with Augustine, to consider whether in fact the flow of time is only in one direction: from the past, through the present, to the future. Perhaps the Bishop of Hippo is right that time "can only be coming from the future, passing through the present and going into the past. In other words, it is coming out of what does not yet exist, passing through what has no duration, and moving into what no longer exists."[22]

We, in the post-Einsteinian world, are almost certainly also aware of the critical discoveries in physics about the nature of time: that time is a dimension that bends, for it is interactive with and interdependent on the physical properties of the universe.[23] This understanding of time is, of course, theoretical and mathematical and not information that most of us use in our daily lives or in our reading of Paul. Nevertheless, being reminded of it may loosen our assumptions and free us to imagine that time's nature (if we choose to think that time exists) may be other than our conventional notions. For instance, recognizing time as a dimension of reality that is inextricably connected to space (space-time) means that we can envision the past and the future in spatial terms: the past is below the present and the future is above. Moreover, if time is relative and warped, rather than being Newton's mathematical regular perfection, then

20. Augustine, *Confessions* 11.14 (italics original).

21. James, "Perception of Time," 381. The intriguing relationship between humans' organization of time in terms of the three tenses and their actual experience of time has been pondered by, among others, the French phenomenologist Eugène Minkowski. He proposes that the "passage of the past into the present does not have a linear character" since only atomistic features of the past make themselves present in the present ("Presence of the Past," 515). Heidegger describes the pull of the future in the present for those who live with resoluteness (*Being and Time*, 370–80).

22. Augustine, *Confessions* 11.21.

23. For a review of proposals about time by Einstein and those after him, see Fagg, *Becoming of Time*.

we make room for imagining time being changed and transformed when it has contact with forces of reality.

Thinking about Eternity

We may take it for granted that in addition to time there is another mode of temporality—the life of God—which we typically call "eternity." Like many before us, we may think that one way to understand eternity is to think of it as the opposite of time: time is not eternity. The second edition of Karl Barth's Romans commentary famously works with the idea of the binary opposition of time and eternity.[24] This hard distinction between time and eternity has a long pedigree going back at least to Plato: eternity, unlike time, is unmoving and unchanging. Plato believed that time was created by "the father and creator" as a way for creatures to have access to a copy of the eternal ideal.[25] "Eternity itself rests in unity," while time, which moves in a circular fashion, is its image.[26]

The long-standing understanding of eternity is that it is timelessness.[27] Augustine thought of eternity (that is, the life of God) as absolutely without time—at least not time that is in any way similar to human experience of time. "In eternity nothing moves into the past: all is present."[28] Eternity is "a never-ending present."[29] Eternity is simultaneity—there is no past, present, and future in God's life. Eternity is *nunc aeternitatis*. In this sense, eternity is timelessness.

As influential as Augustine's conception of eternity is Boethius's: "A perfect possession all at once of limitless life."[30] Though Bo-

24. Citing Kierkegaard's phrase, Barth writes about "'the infinite qualitative distinction' between time and eternity" (*Romans*, 10).
25. Ephraim Radner puts it well: the idea derives from Plato that "time is how eternity is apprehended by creatures" (*Time and the Word*, 89).
26. Plato, *Timaeus*, 37–38.
27. See Brian Leftow, who seeks to defend God's timelessness against modern arguments that this cannot be the case if we believe God to be an agent or person who acts in the temporal world (*Time and Eternity*). See, on the other hand, William Lane Craig, "God, Time, and Eternity," which is one of the more accessible arguments in favor of divine temporality as the nature of eternity.
28. Augustine, *Confessions* 11.11.
29. Augustine, *Confessions* 11.13.
30. Quoted from Placher, *Narratives of a Vulnerable God*, 31 (Placher's translation).

ethius's definition has typically been understood to define eternity as timelessness, William C. Placher's wise interpretation is that "Boethius's eternity is neither simply time like that of creatures indefinitely extended nor a timelessness altogether unrelated to temporal duration."[31] This is the case, according to Placher, because Boethius equates eternity with life, and life necessarily involves time. Perhaps, then, Boethius sought to understand eternity as a different kind of time: "Past, present and future come together in a meaningful whole, moving from, to and always in, God."[32]

Anselm of Canterbury understands God to be beyond all time and God's eternity as "limitless life existing all at once, wholly and perfectly."[33] Eternity is more than eternal duration, for there is no past or future in God's eternity, though all past, present, and future is contained in God. As Katherin A. Rogers writes, "There is no suggestion that He simply *knows* past, present, and future. The clear import is that all of these times are equally there 'in' God."[34]

Another notion of eternity is that it is infinite duration.[35] In biblical studies, this view was made famous by Oscar Cullmann, who held that in the New Testament the opposition is not between time and eternity but between limited and unlimited time.[36]

The classical view of eternity was broken open in part by challenges to the traditional view of God. In particular, Hegel's philosophy of

31. Placher, *Narratives of a Vulnerable God*, 31.
32. Placher, *Narratives of a Vulnerable God*, 45.
33. Anselm of Canterbury, *Monologion* 24. Quoted from Rogers, "Anselm on Eternity," 5 (Rogers's translation).
34. Rogers, "Anselm on Eternity," 6 (italics original). Rogers also writes, "Anselm consistently describes things and events that exist in time as always there and present to God. It is not that propositions about them are known by God or that God knows them through knowing what He Himself intends to do. The things and events themselves exist in divine eternity" (7).
35. We might note that there is a distinction to be kept in mind between timelessness and duration. Though scholars like Eleonore Stump and Norman Kretzmann ("Eternity") argue that medieval understandings of eternity were that it was timeless yet possessing duration, their view has not achieved much acceptance. It is difficult to conceive of a timeless eternity, which is to say an eternity in which all time is at once, as also having duration.
36. Cullman, *Christ and Time*, 46. Antje Jackelén comments (not directly focusing on Cullmann) that the idea of eternity as "the simple infinity of a super-continuity" in effect flattens out time (*Time and Eternity*, 229). She also says that "total synchronicity in which everything is available nonstop" does the same (229).

the development of Absolute Spirit and Alfred North Whitehead's process theism brought into Western thinking concepts of God's eternity and its relation to time that unsettled classical views.[37] Theologians such as Wolfhart Pannenberg describe eternity (God) as both being and becoming, and they understand God to have a relation to time.[38] In contrast to the idea of eternity as non-change in distinction from time, which is full of change, Pannenberg proposes that the biblical idea is that eternity and time are not completely distinct. Rather, "eternity is the truth of time, which remains hidden in the flux of time. . . . Eternity is the unity of all time." Consequently, "eternity is God's time."[39] Robert Jenson thinks that time participates in eternity and that in regard to the biblical God, we should "speak of 'God's time' and 'created time,' taking 'time' as an analogous concept."[40]

Barth's later thinking on time seems both to affirm the classical view of the distinction between eternity and time[41] and to propose that God is temporal.[42] This puzzle has been studied by Barth scholars.[43] Some have dismissed Barth's understanding of eternity and time as confused. R. T. Mullins diagnoses what he terms the "Barthian Blunder": Barth both rejects the doctrine of divine timelessness and affirms it.[44]

Thinking about Paul's Thinking about Time

Some of the concepts just described may have influenced our perceptions of what we mean when we talk about time (and eternity). The awareness to keep top of mind as we move forward concerns

---

37. Whitehead, *Process and Reality*.
38. Pannenberg proposes, for instance, that the incarnation and resurrection were always in God, but until their temporal actualization they are not true (*Jesus—God and Man*, 320–22).
39. Pannenberg, *What Is Man?*, 74.
40. Jenson, *Systematic Theology*, 35.
41. "Time has nothing to do with God" (Barth, *Church Dogmatics* II/1, 608).
42. "God . . . is supremely temporal" (Barth, *Church Dogmatics* III/2, 437).
43. Hunsinger argues that Barth's doctrine of the Trinity is the key to the puzzle ("*Mysterium Trinitatis*").
44. Mullins, *End of the Timeless God*, xvii.

not only our own assumptions about time but whether we have assumed that Paul shares our assumptions. I hope that articulating some of the puzzles and presumptions in thinking about time may elucidate our own assumptions. I expect that, in the main, Pauline interpreters think of time as real, sequential, having forward motion, and distinct from eternity. If we have contemplated the problem of the present, asking whether the past and the future have any reality apart from the present, then we may or may not have brought this into our reading of Paul's thoughts on the past and the future.[45]

We now turn to the two most influential temporal structures that interpreters have built to make sense of Paul's thought. Time is not a new topic in Pauline studies; scholars have long recognized that understanding Paul's view of time is essential to understanding everything else he writes. Consequently, scholarly debate concerning Paul's view of time has a particular seriousness. Scholars rightly recognize that the framework—chosen or assumed—for organizing Paul's temporal thought deeply shapes how the apostle is understood. The prime competing views are typically labeled "salvation historical"[46] and "apocalyptic." Though recently there has been an attempt to proffer both-and positions,[47] one or the other of these

45. For instance, is the past actually in the present in a figural way, or is it simply in the present because that is the only way to know it?

46. Unlike for theological studies, in which the concept of salvation history is no longer much discussed (there is no separate entry for salvation history in the *Anchor Bible Dictionary* or *Theologische Realenzyklopädie*), for biblical scholars, especially scholars of Paul, salvation history remains a matter of concern.

47. We will see below that N. T. Wright thinks that he offers a mediating position. Michael Bird and Jamie P. Davies explicitly seek a middle way. In a study of Galatians, Bird contends that "Paul's apocalyptic gospel is necessarily salvation-historical by nature of the Jewish context of his eschatology and Christology. . . . Whatever rupture takes place within Israel's history, Paul—just like other Jewish seers—still envisaged an event proving God's faithfulness to Israel, even if the corollaries of this deliverance meant reconfiguring Israel's Torah and Israel's election around the Messiah in an innovative way" (*Anomalous Jew*, 167). In a study comparing the "apocalyptic Paul" to apocalypses, Davies writes, "In the light of the apocalypses . . . the . . . rejection of salvation-historical paradigms in favour of a 'punctiliar' liberation . . . is called into question by the importance attached to history in the apocalyptic literature" (*Paul among the Apocalypses?*, 200). He continues, "A genuinely apocalyptic approach to Paul, developed in the context of the mode of thought expressed in this body of literature, avoids . . . false antitheses. . . . In its eschatology, it affirms both 'irruption' and redemption history" (203).

two options is very typically the scaffolding on which scholars build their Pauline interpretations.[48] One sees the apostle as understanding time as linear, sequential, and teleological: the salvation historical view. The other understands Paul as conceiving of time as that which can be and has been invaded by God (eternity): the apocalyptic view.

48. Another significant voice is Giorgio Agamben, *Time That Remains*. Though he has an independent view, Agamben has some similarities to the apocalyptic interpretation. I will discuss him briefly below.

1

Paul's Conception of Time in Salvation Historical Perspective

The term "salvation history" is the most common translation of the German word *Heilsgeschichte*.[1] This word appears to have been introduced by Johann Christian Konrad von Hofmann in 1841 in a work titled *Weissagung und Erfüllung im alten und im neuen Testament*.[2] Hofmann uses the word to argue that there is a promise-fulfillment dynamic in the Bible. Scripture is a sequence of promise and fulfillment culminating in Christ. The fact that not everyone can see this progressive, saving revelation of God in history is not the fault of God. It is because insight into the truth of salvation history is available only to people of faith. The proponents of salvation history think that God directs history/time,[3] and more than that,

---

1. This word is also translated "sacred history" or "redemptive/redemption history."
2. Greig, "Critical Note."
3. I equate history and time in this description because that reflects the view of salvation historical thinkers. See, for instance, Gerhard von Rad, who writes that time in the Old Testament contains historical events: "Israel was not capable of thinking of time in the abstract, time divorced from specific events" (*Old Testament Theology*, 100). For some salvation historical interpreters, the idea of history as actual events in time and space is critical. For instance, when N. T. Wright speaks of history, he is referring to historical moments in time. He believes he can "place Paul in his actual (if complex) historical setting" (*Paul and the Faithfulness of God*, 1516).

1

that God directly acts in history/time. As one salvation historical advocate puts it, "The Bible . . . and Paul's writings . . . are a testimony, inspired by God, regarding a redemptive sequence of events (and their interpretation) related to and revelatory of the divine will and actions in the world. For that reason 'history' (*Geschichte*) is a fundamental dimension . . . for comprehending the 'salvation' (*Heil*) of the Christian gospel."[4]

Intrinsic to the idea of salvation history is that for those who believe in the biblical God, time/history is understood as God's creation and as being under God's control. Even though most people do not see it, in reality God's purpose is being worked out in human time. More than that, time is directed by God toward the goal God has for it. Central to the concept of salvation history is the idea of continuity. Continuity signals, even equates to, the faithfulness of God. God is continually and constantly interested in, invested in, and intervening in time because God is faithful to God's creation and to the purposes for good that God has planned for God's creation. Time/history is under God's direction, and it is unfolding as God determines; it has a goal. The biggest goal has been reached: Christ.

What salvation historical interpreters propose is that time/history cannot be truly explained by physicists, philosophers, or historians. Salvation historical thinkers regard God as the author and shaper of history. God directs events. God has a plan. God has a purpose for time and is directing it. Key words/concepts for salvation historical interpretation are "unfolding plan," "epochs," and "God's purpose."

Within the salvation historical interpretative framework, the Old Testament prophets are the premier recognizers of God's saving work in history. The prophets claim that disobedience to God will result in historical (political) consequences. Likewise, obedience to God will make a difference in human time/history. God directs history in response to the faithfulness of God's people—or sometimes

---

4. Yarbrough, "Salvation History (*Heilsgeschichte*)," 188.

despite their unfaithfulness. History/time is under God's control, and God can manipulate it to suit God's purposes.

God works with time not only by working with what people did or do but by offering new possibilities. God's work in history is not confined to working with what has been and what is. Through the prophets, God offers new things that are in continuity with the past—for instance, a new covenant or a new exodus.[5] God created time, and God can do with time what God wants. God is understood to be able to step into history and create something new, though the critical emphasis in salvation history is on the continuing faithfulness—the constant trustworthiness—of God, as *made evident in time*. Of course, it needs to be emphasized again that it is necessary to believe in God in order to see this. However, for salvation historical interpreters, the necessity of belief does not mean that God's direction of history is only a matter of belief; it is actual.

While it was in the nineteenth century that Hofmann gave a name to the idea of God's involvement in and direction of history/time, the concept of Heilsgeschichte was not itself new. Peter C. Hodgson notes that the Latin Christians Tertullian, Eusebius, Lactantius, Orosius, Salvian, and Gregory the Great all developed versions of salvation history.[6] Augustine shares a salvation historical template for reading Scripture, arguing against the pagan idea of eternal recurrence—the cyclical view of time—and emphasizing rather that there is an "eschaton," an end.[7] In *The City of God*, Augustine writes a story of salvation, telling of the creation of the world and of time and of the big moments in the history of God's salvation of the world. Particularly in books 15–18 of *The City of God*, Augustine describes seven stages of God's salvation. Yet for

5. See Klaus Berger's helpful entry "'Salvation History'" in *Encyclopedia of Theology*.
6. Hodgson, *God in History*, 18. Hodgson suggests that Tertullian Christianized "an essentially pagan view of salvation history—a view which, with its logic of divine governance, intervention, reward and punishment, and eventual triumph, was to have a far-reaching and fateful impact on Christian thought. It provided a frame of reference for reading the Hebrew scriptures" (15).
7. See Löwith, *Meaning in History*, 165.

Augustine the events of history are not most important but rather history's goal: damnation or salvation in the world to come. In history, God's purpose is worked out for the sake of the eternal city of God.[8]

What sets Augustine apart from modern salvation historical interpreters is his intense focus on eternity—the city of God. God's chief interest is not the earthly city—events in the human experience of time—but rather the heavenly city that God has determined since the beginning. Karl Löwith comments that in Augustine we do not find so much the idea of progress as the idea of pilgrimage toward.[9] Hodgson writes that for Augustine there is "no *history* of salvation but only an *eternal decree* and *telos* of salvation."[10]

Augustine's relativizing of the importance of history/time distinguishes his salvation historical framework from its modern usage, which understands the biblical writers' God to be concerned with events in history. The influential twentieth-century biblical scholar Gerhard von Rad proffered a nuanced and elegant view of the Old Testament's salvation historical framework. Von Rad proposed that, in distinction from surrounding cultures, the Hebrews understood "time as containing events."[11] Eventually Israel came to

> realise that her present was based on an earlier series of creative events, a somewhat involved historical development. . . . Israel came to realise that Jahweh had a definite plan for her, and her ancestors had made a long journey with him. . . . There was a long road, that is to say, a history, which led up to her formation. . . . The idea of history which Israel worked out was constructed exclusively on the basis of a sequence of acts which God laid down for her salvation. . . . It was God who established the continuity between the various separate events and who ordained their direction as they followed one another in time.[12]

8. See Dawson, "Christian View of History," 37.
9. Löwith, *Meaning in History*, 169.
10. Hodgson, *God in History*, 18.
11. Von Rad, *Old Testament Theology*, 100. See critique of von Rad in Momigliano, "Time in Ancient Historiography," 180, 183.
12. Von Rad, *Old Testament Theology*, 105–6.

Despite such a fine example of the modern salvation historical view of time—time as a forward-moving continuum that can
be filled by God-initiated events and directed by God toward a
goal—some have found the concept of salvation history deeply
problematic. As Martin Hengel (himself a proponent of salvation
history) puts it at the beginning of an article in which he argues
for a sophisticated version of salvation history, Heilsgeschichte "is
not in favour in modern theology."[13] Robert Yarbrough states that
"salvation history is a category that has fallen from grace in the
recent decades of new perspective popularity."[14] There are at least
two interconnected reasons for suspicion about the salvation history hypothesis: salvation history became an identity marker for
fundamentalism; and in its unsophisticated form, it cannot address legitimate philosophical concerns about history/time and
revelation.

Biblicism identified itself with the idea of salvation history. The
Chicago Statements on Biblical Inerrancy (1978) and Biblical Hermeneutics (1982) affirmed salvation history, seeing it as a necessary
companion to belief in the Bible's inerrancy.[15] It was essential to
fundamentalism that what the Bible describes were actual historical
events. And, since it deemed that the Old Testament in particular
regularly presents a cause-and-effect schema for the events it relates,
this means that the Bible claims a continual and progressive history
of God's saving activity in time/history. The theological and philosophical problems with this view of salvation history are myriad.
Among them is the idea that truth relies on objectively provable
facts. (If we can find Noah's ark, we have proven the truth of that
part of God's saving history.) As Hengel puts it, such a view is really
"a disguised rationalism which contradicts the nature of Scripture

13. Hengel, "'Salvation History,'" 229.
14. Yarbrough, "Paul and Salvation History," 339.
15. Article V on inerrancy states: "We affirm that God's revelation within the Holy Scriptures
was progressive" (International Council on Biblical Inerrancy, "Chicago Statement on Biblical
Inerrancy"). Article XIV on hermeneutics: "We affirm that the biblical record of events, discourses and sayings, though presented in a variety of appropriate literary forms, corresponds
to historical fact" (International Council on Biblical Inerrancy, "Chicago Statement on Biblical
Hermeneutics").

as the testimony of human faith to God's words and actions that create salvation."[16]

Another legitimate philosophical concern about salvation history is that it collides with the modern view of history—that history is a construction of the past governed by a particular viewpoint. In the modern context, salvation history is seen simply as a view of those who have certain beliefs about God and the Bible. It can have no relevance for secular understandings of history/time, and consequently the power and agency of God and the truth of the Bible—claims that are essential to the salvation historical framework—are diminished by virtue of being understood as simply the opinions of particular people. God is not the director of history; that is just the belief of a portion of humans. The Bible is not God's revelation about God's promises and their temporal fulfillments but the product of the beliefs of human communities.

Since the Enlightenment, humankind is understood to be the subject of history. God and revelation are seen as the province of individual believers. Albert Eichhorn, one of the founders of the history of religions movement, declared: "Science in its strictness and religion in its depth can no longer allow a special activity of God to be demarcated externally from everything else that happens in the world. The primal source of religion lies within the religious person."[17]

Moreover, the distinction between facts and the meaning of history is typically left unexplored in salvation historical interpretations. As philosophers of history regularly point out, relative to German, English has an impoverished vocabulary in this regard. *Historie* signifies the past as it actually happened. *Historie* can, then, be investigated by historical research. *Geschichte*, on the other hand, may refer to events in the past, but primarily it refers to the influence and effects of the past as they are understood in the present—the meaning of past events. For those who adhere to the concept of

16. Hengel, "'Salvation History,'" 243.
17. Quoted in Hengel, "'Salvation History,'" 235. Hengel lists several significant objections to the concept of salvation history on pp. 230–32.

salvation history, *Geschichte* in *Heilsgeschichte* is often understood as a conflation of *Historie* and *Geschichte*, with the emphasis being on the former. Typically, the essential discussion of the relevance of historical research for determining the meaning of history (*Geschichte*) is left unexplored. Further, modern salvation historical readings are almost certainly influenced by the relatively recent belief in evolution and progress, which, as Emil Brunner points out, is "sharply distinct" from the biblical view of time.[18]

On the other hand, salvation historical readers of Paul make their case on theological and ethical grounds: a salvation historical reading is a true reading of Scripture because it affirms God's ongoing faithfulness. This way of reading is deemed to be especially important in regard to understanding Paul. As Douglas Moo puts it, "A correct interpretation of Paul's theology demands recognition of a conceptual approach called 'salvation history.' . . . Paul starts from the assumption that God has accomplished redemption as part of a historical process."[19]

Salvation historical interpreters also claim that there is an implicit, if not explicit, anti-Judaism in other readings of Paul. Such interpreters argue that their way of reading, in which Paul is presented as thinking that Jesus Christ fulfills God's promises to the Jews, honors the Old Testament and Israel. In distinction from those who think that Paul had an apocalyptic encounter that was not presaged in Judaism, salvation historical readers credit their interpretation with honoring God's work with Israel.[20] Salvation historical readers of Paul claim the higher moral ground since their view does not discount the history of Israel. According to salvation historical interpreters, versions of the new perspective on Paul, which discount salvation history and depict Paul having a revelation of Jesus Messiah for which he is not looking, devalue Judaism. Salvation

18. Brunner, "Problem of Time," 88.
19. Moo, "Paul," 138.
20. On the other hand, the apocalyptic interpreter Douglas Campbell argues that the salvation historical reading is "dangerously vulnerable to supersessionism—the church will almost inevitably *replace* Israel, and the Jewish people" (*Quest for Paul's Gospel*, 38 [italics original]).

historical interpreters think that Paul sees "himself to be caught up in a salvation historical drama begun at creation, sustained through Old Testament epochs, fulfilled in Jesus' cross and resurrection, and consummated at some yet-to-be determined junction."[21] They use the fact that Paul cites the Old Testament as proof that Paul thinks God has a progressive and unfolding plan for history, for time.[22]

Representative Salvation Historical Pauline Interpreters

Among the several important scholars who might be mentioned here,[23] perhaps the most influential current proponent of a salvation historical reading of Paul is *N. T. Wright*.[24] While Wright speaks of his framework as covenantal rather than salvation historical, his claim that Paul thinks in terms of plot and plan is a version of the salvation historical hermeneutic. Wright speaks of a "process"[25] and declares that there is a *"single plan* [which] *always involved a dramatic break."*[26] In *Paul and the Faithfulness of God*, Wright claims that Paul thinks there is a *"single divine plan* to which God has been faithful."[27]

Though Wright presents himself as reading Paul in terms of both covenant and apocalyptic, both he and his critics make plain that his understanding of apocalyptic is at odds with that of apocalyptic interpreters of Paul. Wright opines that "'apocalyptic' . . . must, I believe, be retained as part of Paul's worldview—but it must be retained *within* the larger historical framework which we are exploring."[28] As anyone who has read even some of Wright's prodigious output knows, the historical framework that he explores is

---

21. Yarbrough, "Paul and Salvation History," 324.
22. Yarbrough, "Paul and Salvation History," 332.
23. See especially Richard N. Longenecker, *Paul, Apostle of Liberty.*
24. The names of scholars who take the salvation historical perspective are italicized. Scholars with whom salvation historical interpreters disagree are also discussed in this section. The names of these latter scholars are not italicized.
25. N. T. Wright, *Climax of the Covenant*, 236.
26. N. T. Wright, *Climax of the Covenant*, 241 (italics original).
27. N. T. Wright, *Paul and the Faithfulness of God*, 499 (italics original).
28. N. T. Wright, *Paul and the Faithfulness of God*, 461 (italics original).

the story of Israel, which culminates in Jesus the Messiah, who is "the fulfillment of the long purposes of Israel's God."[29]

Paul, according to Wright, fits his ideas into a narrative with a plot. Wright claims that "Paul's worldview had a strongly implicit and frequently explicit narrative."[30] Though Wright complexifies this idea by referring to three levels of narrative,[31] he presents Paul as regarding time as an ongoing, God-directed entity that God uses for God's plan. Wright claims that "the kind of Jew who became a Pharisee was implicitly aware of living in a *continuous story going back to Abraham, perhaps even to Adam, and on to the great coming day*."[32] According to Wright, Paul has a story undergirding his gospel—a narrative. Paul fits Christ into that story. Christ is the climax of the covenant, the answer to God's promises to Abraham.

One of the clearest windows onto Wright's perspective is the following statement: "At the heart of Paul's theology, holding together its many varied features in a single, supple, harmonious whole, we find his passionate conviction that the ancient divine solution to the world's problems had not been changed. The creator God would indeed save the world through Abraham's seed. Israel would indeed be the light of the world. But all this, Paul believed, had been fulfilled, *and thereby redefined*, in and around Israel's Messiah and the holy spirit."[33]

What is critical to Wright and what puts him squarely in the company of salvation historical readers of Paul is his conviction about "the rootedness of Christianity in history."[34] That is, the story that undergirds Paul's gospel is a story with real events visible in human time. Wright believes that when Paul refers to figures from Israel's religious history—for instance, Abraham—this is meant to call to mind the narrative that Israel is part of, reinforcing both the *historicity* and the continuity and forward motion of the story. Wright

---

29. N. T. Wright, *Climax of the Covenant*, 241.
30. N. T. Wright, *Paul and the Faithfulness of God*, 461.
31. N. T. Wright, *Paul and the Faithfulness of God*, 464.
32. N. T. Wright, *Paul and the Faithfulness of God*, 113 (italics original).
33. N. T. Wright, *Paul and the Faithfulness of God*, 772 (italics original).
34. N. T. Wright, *New Testament and the People of God*, 9.

describes Romans 9–11 as a "historical survey of how [God's] promises have been worked out."[35]

As with other salvation historical thinkers, Wright thinks Romans
9–11 is the text that clinches the argument.[36] Wright sees Romans
1–11 as about the faithfulness of God to God's promise to Abraham,
and Roman 9–11 in particular as about the "character and purposes
of God, and particularly his faithfulness to his promises."[37] Wright
argues that "the main subject-matter of Romans 9–11 . . . is the
covenant faithfulness of God, seen in its outworking in the *history
of the people of God*."[38]

Wright hears Paul in Romans 9–11 to be saying that all along Christ
was "the secret goal of Torah," that the Jewish law had "a specific
task and a particular period of time."[39] When that task is completed
and the period of time is over, the Torah "reaches its goal."[40] Wright
makes sense of the unexpected nature of Christ's cross and resurrection by saying, as mentioned above, that God's *"single plan always
involved a dramatic break."*[41] The crucified and risen Messiah is the
fulfillment of God's purposes for Israel. The Torah was always meant
to be temporary; Jesus "is the climax of the covenant."[42]

Wright is highly critical of apocalyptic interpreters of Paul,[43] and
they of him.[44] Apocalyptic Pauline scholars contend that Wright has

35. N. T. Wright, *Climax of the Covenant*, 241.
36. E.g., N. T. Wright, *Climax of the Covenant*, 231–51. For Oscar Cullmann, the influential
salvation historical biblical scholar of the last generation, Rom. 9–11 is evidence that Paul is
a salvation historian. As Cullmann reads these chapters, Paul explains the need for history to
continue after Christ. The time between Christ's cross and resurrection and Christ's return is
an "interval." In Rom. 9–11, Paul explains the necessity for this interval "in God's saving plan"
(*Salvation in History*, 254). God wants the fullness of the gentiles and unbelieving Israel to be
saved, and so God has allowed for an interval.
37. N. T. Wright, *Climax of the Covenant*, 235.
38. N. T. Wright, *Climax of the Covenant*, 236 (italics mine).
39. N. T. Wright, *Climax of the Covenant*, 241.
40. N. T. Wright, *Climax of the Covenant*, 241.
41. N. T. Wright, *Climax of the Covenant*, 241 (italics original).
42. N. T. Wright, *Climax of the Covenant*, 241.
43. For instance, N. T. Wright claims that J. L. Martyn's reading of Galatians sweeps "away
everything Jewish and replac[es] it with an entirely new context" (*Paul and the Faithfulness of
God*, 542). See Wright on apocalyptic interpretation in *Paul and His Recent Interpreters*, 135–220.
44. Beverly Roberts Gaventa challenges N. T. Wright's charge of de-Judaism or anti-Judaism on
the part of apocalyptic interpreters ("Character of God's Faithfulness," 78). John M. G. Barclay

not understood the nature of the apocalyptic that they see in the apostle. Apocalyptic for Paul cannot, as Wright proposes, be contained "*within* the larger historical framework."[45] Rather, according to apocalyptic interpreters, Paul is speaking about God's invasion into history—an invasion that is singular and without precedent.[46] Moreover, his critics contend that Wright has not understood the epistemological issue related to their view of Paul's apocalyptic. It is not only that a new thing has happened in Christ's death and resurrection but that a new way of knowing has been revealed.[47] Wright's use of the historian's toolbox, no matter how refined by his critical realism hermeneutic,[48] cannot address the kind of revealed knowledge that Paul claims.[49] Wright's focus on a continuous, God-directed story that takes place in human time is a model of modern salvation historical thinking. In this generation, it has been as influential and controversial as was Oscar Cullmann's presentation a generation ago.

Wright, in company with other salvation historical thinkers, pits himself against Rudolf Bultmann's Paul.[50] Bultmann famously argues against the importance of history for Christianity. He criticizes the idea of basing faith on historical fact. Instead, Bultmann argues, we should focus on the existential meaning of the Christ event. His famous idea that Christ has risen in the kerygma is a claim that faith stands apart from history. In Bultmann's view, Paul is not concerned with history because history is "swallowed up in eschatology."[51] The

---

describes Wright as "lampooning" rather than understanding apocalyptic readers of Paul, such as Martyn (review of *Paul and the Faithfulness of God*, 237).

45. *Paul and the Faithfulness of God*, 461. Jörg Frey rightly calls this a neutralizing of apocalyptic ("Demythologizing Apocalyptic?," 498). In Douglas Harink's analysis of N. T. Wright on Romans, he observes that "the apocalyptic-messianic character of Paul's gospel . . . is read as a significant feature of one climactic event (the coming of Christ) in the larger story, but not as constitutive of the very character of time itself" ("Time and Politics in Four Commentaries," 311).

46. Samuel V. Adams's challenge to N. T. Wright is "if history provides the interpretive matrix, then the actual impact of the irruption of God is minimized" (*Reality of God*, 238).

47. See Gaventa, "Character of God's Faithfulness," 76.

48. See N. T. Wright on critical realism and historical study in *New Testament and the People of God*, 31–46.

49. See Adams, *Reality of God*, esp. 240–47.

50. See also, for instance, Yarbrough, "Salvation History (*Heilsgeschichte*)," 188.

51. Bultmann, "History and Eschatology in the New Testament," 13.

present is an "eschatological present" in which individual people are to look at their "personal history" and see that in their present is the meaning of history. This calls for awakening to responsible decisions. Such is the "eschatological moment."[52]

Bultmann's claims are completely at odds with the idea of salvation history. For Bultmann, "the early Christian community understands itself not as a historical but as an eschatological phenomenon. It is conscious that it belongs no longer to the present world but to the new Aeon which is at the door."[53] Bultmann cites with approval E. Frank from *The Role of History in Christian Thought*:

> To the Christians the advent of Christ was not an event in that temporal process which we mean by history today. It was an event in the history of salvation, in the realm of eternity, an eschatological moment in which rather this profane history of the world came to its end. . . . For although the advent of Christ is an historical event which happened "once" in the past, it is, at the same time, an eternal event which occurs again and again in the soul of any Christian in whose soul Christ is born, suffers, dies and is raised up to eternal life. In his faith the Christian is a contemporary of Christ, and time and the world's history are overcome. The advent of Christ is an event in the realm of eternity which is incommensurable with historical time.[54]

Bultmann's Paul does not fit Jesus into an ongoing, God-directed historical plot rooted in God's call of Abraham. "For the person who stands within the Church the history of Israel is a closed chapter. . . . Israel's history is not our history, and in so far as God has shown grace in that history, such grace is not meant for us. . . . The events which meant something for Israel, which were God's word, mean nothing more to us."[55] Bultmann also opines that "eschatological perfection must not be understood as the perfection of a people's

---

52. Bultmann, *History and Eschatology*, 155.
53. Bultmann, *History and Eschatology*, 37.
54. Frank, "Role of History," 74–75, quoted in Bultmann, *History and Eschatology*, 153.
55. Bultmann, "Significance of the Old Testament," 31.

history" and that "Paul's view of history is not derived from his reflection on the history of Israel but from his anthropology."[56]

Among Wright's several critiques of Bultmann is the latter's project of reconceptualizing "the gospel *in a non-narratival form*, reducing it to the pure existential challenge of every moment."[57] Wright's vision of Paul's plotted gospel is diametrically opposed to this. Further, Wright reads Bultmann as separating himself and his gospel entirely from Judaism, resulting in "a radical *deJudaizing* . . . of Paul."[58] Wright sets himself in opposition to such an analysis, interpreting Paul to be presenting a story of Israel.

Likewise, *Oscar Cullmann*'s understanding stands against Bultmann's de-historicizing. For Cullmann, time is "the scene of redemptive history."[59] Christians conceive of time as a continuous process "which embraces past, present, and future. Revelation and salvation take place along the course of an ascending time line."[60] The early Christians thought of time as a straight line, unlike either the Greek idea of circularity for time or the metaphysical idea that salvation is beyond time. Rather, for the early Christians, revelation and salvation occur "in a connected manner during the continuous time process."[61]

Moreover, for Cullmann, there is a "mid-point" on the redemptive line that is a historical fact: the death and resurrection of Jesus Christ.[62] In distinction from Bultmann, who claims that "Christ being the end of the Law is at the same time the end of history,"[63] Cullmann thinks that history continues after Christ. Cullmann's *Christ and Time* is subtitled *The Primitive Christian Conception of*

56. Bultmann, "History and Eschatology in the New Testament," 12.
57. N. T. Wright, *Paul and the Faithfulness of God*, 457 (italics original).
58. N. T. Wright, *Paul and the Faithfulness of God*, 458 (italics original). See the critique of Wright's reading of Bultmann on this in Schliesser, "*Paul and the Faithfulness of God* among Pauline Theologies," 30. See also Bultmann, "History and Eschatology in the New Testament," 11–13, which evidences a more nuanced position than Wright allows.
59. Cullmann, *Christ and Time*, 32.
60. Cullmann, *Christ and Time*, 32.
61. Cullmann, *Christ and Time*, 32.
62. Cullmann, *Christ and Time*, 32–33.
63. Bultmann, "History and Eschatology in the New Testament," 13.

Time and History. Christ comes at the middle of salvation history, and there are future stages of salvation history. The church is in what Cullmann calls the "intermediate period" of salvation history.[64] The church and individual believers in the church must know that we are "on the way between the resurrection of Christ and his Parousia."[65] Cullmann posits that the "kerygma" that Paul received from the early church was already in a salvation historical framework: promise and fulfillment.[66] Paul understood himself called on the road to Damascus to be the one who, by preaching to the gentiles, carries out "this further development of the saving plan."[67]

Cullmann's presentation has several well-criticized flaws. James Barr rightly challenges him on his understanding and use of "aeon."[68] In addition, Cullmann has been criticized for overemphasizing chronological linearity in the Bible—one God-directed event following another in chronological time. Other readers of the Bible who are sympathetic to the salvation historical view will say that the Bible conceives of time not as a "line" but as several events. John Marsh calls them "kairoi."[69] Marsh also criticizes the idea that Christ is the midpoint on salvation's line: Christ is "not only the mid-point, he is the end."[70] According to Marsh, Cullmann's schema misses the biblical claim that "the final victory is achieved on the cross"[71]—we are not waiting for the final victory as Cullmann would have it.

Despite its problems, a version of Cullmann's articulation of salvation history has found an ongoing voice with *James D. G. Dunn.* Dunn credits Cullmann with his understanding of Paul's view of time.[72] As a disciple of Cullmann, Dunn claims that Hebraic thought (which Paul shared, though modified) understood time as a "a succession of ages"; "history was understood as an onward movement

64. Cullmann, *Christ and Time*, 154.
65. Cullmann, *Christ and Time*, 225.
66. Cullmann, *Salvation in History*, 250.
67. Cullmann, *Salvation in History*, 251.
68. Barr, *Biblical Words for Time*, 67–85.
69. Marsh, *Fulness of Time*, 175.
70. Marsh, *Fulness of Time*, 177.
71. Marsh, *Fulness of Time*, 178.
72. Dunn, *Theology of Paul*, 463n11.

or progression."[73] Dunn claims that the Hebraic idea is of a straight line that is "divided between the present age and the age to come."[74] Like Cullmann, he describes Christ as "the midpoint of history"[75] as well as "the end point of history."[76] "The single division of the time line, dividing present age from age to come . . . [has] been split into a two stage division. Messiah the end point of history had become also Christ the midpoint of history."[77] Another way to speak of this is "already–not yet."[78]

Dunn opines that Paul thought of Christ as "a preplanned climax to God's plan."[79] As a salvation historical thinker, Dunn uses words like "linear" and "process." He states that "salvation" is the "climax or end result of a process."[80] The climax, however, is not a clear end to the present age. The death and resurrection of Christ are not the end of Christ's work. That end is the parousia. Consequently, "those who share 'in Christ' and 'with Christ' are caught, as it were, between the two comings."[81] They live in eschatological tension because the ages "overlap" rather than follow each other sequentially. Dunn claims that believers live in "the epoch of overlap."[82]

Time in the Salvation History Proposal

Salvation historical interpreters of Paul emphasize that the apostle understood God to be a God who makes and keeps promises. For these interpreters a certain interpretation of Romans 9–11 is central

73. Dunn, *Theology of Paul*, 462.
74. Dunn, *Theology of Paul*, 462.
75. Dunn, *Theology of Paul*, 462.
76. Dunn, *Theology of Paul*, 463.
77. Dunn, *Theology of Paul*, 463.
78. Dunn, *Theology of Paul*, 466.
79. Dunn, *Theology of Paul*, 463.
80. Dunn, *Theology of Paul*, 493. In another place, Dunn proposes that Paul understood God's revelation to him on the Damascus road as "one which showed him how the ancient promises and hopes were to be fulfilled. It was new in that it focused on Jesus, but the new gospel was simply the new but also foretold way of completing the old purpose" ("How New Was Paul's Gospel?," 384).
81. Dunn, *Theology of Paul*, 468.
82. Dunn, *Theology of Paul*, 494.

(they read these chapters as about promise and fulfillment). They are dedicated to the idea that God's identity and trustworthiness are evidenced by the fact that God makes promises and fulfills them. This makes God a faithful God—for Paul (and for them). The chief evidence of God's faithfulness is Christ. Christ for Paul (and for salvation historical interpreters) is God's fulfillment of a promise.[83]

The claim that the future has come into the present time is a standard feature of salvation historical thinking (and, as we shall see, in a different way it is also a feature of apocalyptic interpretation of Paul), creating what Dunn describes as "eschatological tension."[84] Cullmann speaks of the *"the dialectic of present and future."*[85] Cullmann's version of salvation history is distinguished by his designating Christ as the midpoint on the linear line of salvation. This splits the period between creation and the parousia in two, with what is after the midpoint belonging to the new age even though the parousia has not come.[86] Salvation historical thinkers describe the peculiar situation of already–not yet as the two ages overlapping.[87] Cullmann speaks of the tension between "the decisive 'already fulfilled' and the 'not yet completed,' between present and future."[88] Dunn writes of Paul's "new departure" in envisioning an eschatological split between "a decisive 'already' and yet still a 'not yet.'"[89] Wright says that Paul's statement in Galatians that

---

83. Salvation historical interpreters consider that, for Paul, Scripture is about God's promises and their fulfillments. When Paul uses Scripture, then, he uses it as evidence for his presentation of Christ as God's fulfillment of God's promises. This understanding of how Scripture works for Paul appears to be a confirmation of the trustworthiness, and perhaps even the inspired nature, of Scripture itself. A compelling alternative to this is that of Francis Watson, who argues that for Paul "the relation between Torah and Christology is [not] one of narrative continuity" (*Paul and the Hermeneutics of Faith*, 501). See also my "Promise and Purpose," where I point out that in Rom. 9–11 and elsewhere in Romans, Paul does not in fact couple promise with fulfillment. I further suggest that Paul uses Scripture to give a glimpse not so much into the meaning of historical events as into the realm of God's life, into God's mind. For Paul, Scripture is a way that God communicates and a way to communicate about God.

84. Dunn, *Theology of Paul*, 461.

85. Cullmann, *Christ and Time*, 146 (italics original).

86. Cullmann, *Christ and Time*, 83.

87. See Dunn, *Theology of Paul*, 465.

88. Cullmann, *Salvation in History*, 172.

89. Dunn, *Theology of Paul*, 464.

Jesus the Messiah gave himself for our sins to rescue us from the present evil age makes it clear that Paul thinks in terms of two ages and that these ages overlap.[90] The age to come has come, but the old age continues. Believers live in the overlap of the ages. Wright speaks of Paul's "reworked eschatology."[91] Believers are "caught in the overlap of the ages."[92]

Time in a salvation historical context is an entity that God directs. It is sequential and linear. Salvation historical interpreters of Paul regard God as the director of history—that is, of time. God creates successive "epochs"[93] or, in Wright's presentation, a narrative (the story of Israel) that takes place in actual time. Salvation historical readers contend that Paul believed God was continually moving history toward a goal. Though now the goal has been reached, it will not be completed until Christ returns. God's focus is on shaping history to God's will and purpose. Humans can have faith in God because God works with and in history. God can work with time by bringing what is further down the line back into the present. This has resulted in the challenging (but perhaps also comforting) conception of believers' temporality as the overlap of the ages.[94]

---

90. N. T. Wright, *Paul and the Faithfulness of God*, 477.

91. N. T. Wright, *Paul and the Faithfulness of God*, 1048.

92. N. T. Wright, *Paul in Fresh Perspective*, 150.

93. E.g., Yarbrough, "Paul and Salvation History," 324.

94. I will suggest below, rather, that Paul is just as interested—perhaps even more interested—in claiming that humanity is brought into God's time than that God has come into human time. Moreover, I will challenge the idea that Paul thinks in terms of two ages.

2

Paul's Conception of Time in Apocalyptic Perspective

Interpreters of Paul who regard him as an apocalyptic thinker have at least one of the following two understandings of what Paul thought about time: subsequent to God's action in Christ, the present is discontinuous with the past, and/or time is an entity in which the future is pressing on the present. The present in much apocalyptic Pauline interpretation is a strange beast. It is defined neither by the past nor very much by itself. Whereas in commonsense understandings of time (and to some degree in the salvation historical view of time),[1] the present is defined by its location after the past and before the future, in the apocalyptic reading of Paul, the present subsequent to Christ is defined as severed from the past and pressed upon by the future.[2] The present, in other words, is almost unrecognizable as the present in any ordinary sense.

Here I will not take up the continuing question of the appropriate definition or the literary or social location of apocalyptic. This

---

1. Though salvation historical readers will also contend that the new age is inaugurated in the present, and so speak of "eschatological tension" (e.g., Dunn, *Theology of Paul*, 461).

2. However, some apocalyptic readers of Paul, such as Käsemann and Beker, seek to incorporate a salvation historical temporal understanding.

discussion has been ongoing, particularly leading up to and since the publication of volume 14 of the journal *Semeia*.[3] Neither will I take up the matter of whether, even granted a generally agreed upon definition of apocalyptic, it is useful to have such a definition or whether it limits observation. Nor will I engage with the discussion of whether interpreters of Paul who regard him as an apocalyptic thinker have rightly understood Jewish apocalyptic literature[4] and consequently have imbued the term "apocalyptic" with idiosyncratic meaning, in effect allowing "apocalyptic" to signal whatever the particular interpreter sees in Paul.

Here, I am solely concerned with how apocalyptic interpreters of Paul understand the apostle's conception of time. My focus is not on determining whether or not apocalyptic interpreters have correctly understood Jewish apocalyptic or Paul. Rather, at this point, my concern is to highlight their assumptions and claims about Paul's understanding of time. It must be stated that apocalyptic Pauline interpreters more often speak about two ages (the old age and the new; or the present evil age and the new creation) than they do about time. These interpreters regularly assume that Paul was working with a supposed Jewish apocalyptic concept of two ages. "Age" in apocalyptic readings of Paul is typically understood to be both a temporal term and a term indicating a reality with certain power structures. The significance of the change of the ages is primarily that the structure of reality has changed.

---

3. Collins, *Apocalypse*.

4. Among those who question Pauline scholars' claims about the nature of Jewish apocalyptic are the following: R. Barry Matlock examines what he calls "the roughness of fit" between apocalyptic readings of Paul and apocalyptic literature itself (*Unveiling the Apocalyptic Paul*, 15). Jamie Davies examines Jewish apocalyptic literature and questions Pauline scholars' simplified assumptions about it, which have, for instance, provided warrant for the idea of God invading the cosmos as an apocalyptic trope (*Paul among the Apocalypses?*, 201). Judith H. Newman questions whether eschatology is central to Jewish apocalyptic ("Participatory Past"). Newman's query, of course, undercuts the major reason that Jewish apocalyptic was brought into conversation with Paul—with Schweitzer's groundbreaking work on Jewish eschatology as the key to understanding the apostle. Emma Wasserman questions whether dualism and the expectation of a battle between suprahuman powers of good and evil is fundamental to apocalyptic—and so to Paul (*Apocalypse as Holy War*).

Time has a spatial dimension. When J. Louis Martyn, for instance, asserts that Paul's apocalyptic question is "What time is it?" Martyn claims that the apostle answers by saying that "the characteristic of the present time is . . . that it is the juncture of the new creation and the evil age."[5] The new creation and the evil age are distinguished by their structures of power. The difference between them is both temporal and structural/spatial. The evil age is passing and the other age is present and coming; one is fraught with anti-God powers, and the other is ruled by God. While Martyn speaks of a "before" and an "after,"[6] these prepositions are used both temporally and spatially. God has invaded the evil age (the before) with Christ and the spirit (the after). There are resonances with the idea in physics of time as a dimension; perhaps Martyn is implicitly envisioning "after" as above and "before" as below.

Such ideas downplay the commonsense understanding of time as an ongoing continuous entity organized in tenses. Apocalyptic interpretation of Paul does not primarily think of time as an entity that can be measured by change such that humans refer to it in order to organize their reality. (This distinguishes the apocalyptic reading from the salvation historical.)[7] Time is an entity that is joined to structures of power, thereby losing its normal meaning.

In what follows I offer a brief analysis of what a handful of pivotal and influential apocalyptic interpreters understand to be Paul's view of time.[8] If "time" permitted, I would also have included an analysis at least of the important work of Martinus C. de Boer,[9] Susan Eastman,[10] and Alexandra R. Brown.[11]

---

5. Martyn, *Galatians*, 102.
6. Martyn, *Galatians*, 99.
7. Although, it could be argued that Schweitzer thinks this way with respect to his idea that with the death and resurrection of Jesus the world-clock has advanced (Schweitzer, *Mysticism*, 113).
8. For a recent survey of apocalyptic interpreters, see also J. Davies, *Apocalyptic Paul*.
9. Especially de Boer, *Defeat of Death* and *Galatians*.
10. Especially Eastman, "Apocalypse and Incarnation" and "'Empire of Illusion.'" See also *Recovering Paul's Mother Tongue*, which is crafted on the basis that Paul had "apocalyptic convictions" (3).
11. A. Brown, *Cross and Human Transformation*.

Albert Schweitzer

Schweitzer deserves pride of place for influentially connecting Paul to Jewish eschatology.[12] Though around the same time Johannes Weiss described Paul's Messiah-faith as eschatological[13] and spoke of the "apocalyptic drama" that Paul portrayed in 1 Corinthians 15,[14] it was Dr. Schweitzer who most effectively injected into biblical studies the idea that Paul's thought had an eschatological framework. Schweitzer's conviction was that the way to understand Paul's distinctive idea of being in Christ was that Paul, like Jesus before him, had an eschatological worldview. "Paul preaches Christ-mysticism on the ground of the eschatological concept of the predestined solidarity of the Elect with one another and with the Messiah, as Jesus had done before him."[15] The difference between Jesus's preaching and Paul's is that Paul is preaching after the death and resurrection of Jesus. Consequently, "the hour in the world-clock" is different in the case of Jesus than that of Paul.[16] "World-time has been advanced by the death and resurrection of Jesus."[17]

Using primarily what he terms "the Apocalypses of Baruch and Ezra" and the eschatology of the prophets and of Daniel,[18] Schweitzer claims that Paul recognizes himself to be in a different eschatological landscape than his forebears because the Messiah has already come.[19] Though, like Jewish eschatology, Paul shares a "two-fold eschatology,"[20] he overlays it with "the new patch of the resurrection-and-transformation concept."[21] Paul's logic is that since Christ rose

12. Ernst Käsemann writes, "Since Albert Schweitzer, the problem of apocalyptic, its necessity, its meaning and its limits, [have been] cast disquietingly in [scholars'] path" ("Beginnings of Christian Theology," 101).

13. Weiss writes about "the eschatological Messiah-faith" (*History of Primitive Christianity*, 446).

14. Weiss, *History of Primitive Christianity*, 474.

15. Schweitzer, *Mysticism*, 113.

16. Schweitzer, *Mysticism*, 113.

17. Schweitzer, *Mysticism*, 114.

18. Schweitzer has been criticized for homogenizing Jewish eschatology. For analysis and critique, see Matlock, *Unveiling the Apocalyptic Paul*, 23–71.

19. Schweitzer, *Mysticism*, 76.

20. Schweitzer, *Mysticism*, 90.

21. Schweitzer, *Mysticism*, 95.

before the coming of the kingdom, so "participants in the Kingdom possess, like the Messiah, the resurrection mode of existence" before the coming of the kingdom. What this looks like is "being in Christ."[22] "Paul's conception is that, believers in mysterious fashion share the dying and rising again of Christ, and in this way are swept away out of their ordinary mode of existence, and form a special category of humanity."[23] For believers "the simple antithesis between Then and Now is no longer sufficient."[24] They are not still living "in the natural world-period (aeon)" but have "already entered upon the supernatural."[25]

The fact of Jesus's resurrection means that "it is now already the supernatural age. . . . We are therefore in the Resurrection period, even though the resurrection of others is still to come."[26] Consequently, "the natural and the supernatural world are intermingled." The transformation of the natural world "into the supernatural was in progress, as the transformation of a stage goes on behind the curtain."[27] Using another arresting image, Schweitzer says that "the immortal world is about to rise by successive volcanic upheavals out of the ocean of the temporal."[28] Christ's resurrection is "one island-peak,"[29] which has already irrupted into the temporal world. The peak that appears on the surface of the temporal indicates what is invisible—the large island that is its foundation. The island is those who are united with Christ. In "temporally separated upheavals," this island will grow until "all nature will take on immortal being."[30] At the general resurrection, "the whole continent of the immortal world will be visible," at which point the end comes, "when all things are eternal in God, and God is all in all."[31]

22. Schweitzer, *Mysticism*, 95.
23. Schweitzer, *Mysticism*, 96.
24. Schweitzer, *Mysticism*, 97.
25. Schweitzer, *Mysticism*, 97.
26. Schweitzer, *Mysticism*, 98.
27. Schweitzer, *Mysticism*, 99.
28. Schweitzer, *Mysticism*, 112.
29. Schweitzer, *Mysticism*, 112.
30. Schweitzer, *Mysticism*, 112.
31. Schweitzer, *Mysticism*, 112.

Schweitzer's conception of Paul's view of time is based on his understanding of time in Jewish apocalyptic literature. Like the majority of those he so profoundly influenced, Schweitzer thought that Jewish apocalypticism had a doctrine of two successive ages.[32] Schweitzer understood Jewish apocalyptic eschatology to be structured by two ages and thought of these two periods of time as characterized not only by being at different positions on the world-clock but also by being different "worlds"[33]—one immortal and the other not.[34] This view laid the generative framework for subsequent apocalyptic interpretation of Paul.

Schweitzer claims that because of Jesus's resurrection, which advanced the "world-clock" (presumably envisioning a forward temporal movement), Paul sees that this sequence has been usurped. Subsequent to Jesus's resurrection, the future exists in the present, at least for those who are in Christ.[35] Interestingly, unlike many subsequent apocalyptic interpreters, Schweitzer does not describe the situation of believers as one of *tension* between the already and the not yet. Rather, since "they are now assimilated to Jesus Christ . . . throughout the corporeity of the Elect who are thus united with Christ the springtime of super-earthly life has already begun. . . . These Elect are in reality no longer natural men, but, like Christ Himself, are already supernatural beings, only that in them this is not yet manifest."[36]

---

32. An important corrective to the simplistic view of Jewish apocalyptic as having a two-age/two-stage temporality should be noted: Loren T. Stuckenbruck has authoritatively demonstrated that there is ample evidence in Jewish apocalyptic literature for understanding that God has already intruded into history to defeat evil. The future ultimate defeat is guaranteed because of what God has done in the past ("Posturing 'Apocalyptic' in Pauline Theology," 253). "The present is shaped by both an eschatological past and a future that loops back as an *inclusion* to bring God's activity in history to its proper end" (256). Jews before Paul understood "themselves as living in a time between God's proleptic establishment of control over evil and the effective defeat of it at the end" (256).

33. Schweitzer appears to share Weiss's understanding of aeon as meaning not only a temporal period but a mode of reality (Weiss, *History of Primitive Christianity*, 604).

34. Schweitzer, *Mysticism*, 112.

35. See Schweitzer, *Mysticism*, 110, where it appears that Schweitzer thinks that the "supernatural" life has begun only for those who are "the Elect" (also 96).

36. Schweitzer, *Mysticism*, 110.

Schweitzer's view of Paul's conception of time includes the God's-eye view[37] of progressive expansion of the immortal into the temporal. Schweitzer envisions a developing manifestation of pods of reality that are already immortal. Looked at from God's vantage point, currently there is progress from the mixture of two ages to the final goal of all being in God. However, for those in Christ there is no such mixture. Such people are now supernatural and living in Christ; already–not yet is only from God's perspective. For those in Christ, time as an entity of change has in a fundamental sense ended. They live now as they will live forever.

Karl Barth

Another reading of Paul that has been immensely generative of apocalyptic readings is found in the second edition of Karl Barth's *Römerbrief*.[38] Though Barth does not identify his reading as "apocalyptic," many have found it, in the words of Douglas Harink, "*apocalyptically* charged."[39] There are, of course, many significant features of this remarkable commentary, but our focus is time. The context for understanding something of Barth's view of time in his Romans commentary is his famous endorsement of Kierkegaard's words about the infinite qualitative distinction between time and eternity.[40] Time is that which is not eternity and which eternity cannot enter. For Barth, time and eternity are as different as yes

---

37. Schweitzer does not put it this way, but that he thinks Paul knew about what is *invisible* in the temporal suggests that Schweitzer thinks Paul is looking at things from God's perspective.

38. Bruce L. McCormack rightly notes that Barth's commentary has been a significant influence on "those who read Paul as an 'apocalyptic theologian.' . . . Barth's commentary is regarded not only as a (largely) defensible piece of exegesis but as opening up an approach for understanding Paul which they too embrace" ("Longing for a New World," 144).

39. Harink, "Time and Politics in Four Commentaries," 296 (italics original). McCormack sees the 1922 *Römerbrief* as a mixture of what some later readers who see Paul as an apocalyptic theologian (e.g., de Boer and Martyn) will call cosmological and forensic apocalyptic, with the forensic element very much subordinated to the cosmological (McCormack, "Longing for a New World," 146). Jenson understands Barth's commentary to be "animated by an apocalyptic sensibility. . . . [It] established the *sort* of apocalypticism that would characterize much of the century's theology" ("Apocalyptic and Messianism," 5).

40. Barth, *Romans*, 10.

and no. Time, which Barth equates with history,[41] can never lead
to God. Eternity cannot exist in time but can only intrude on it,
thereby dissolving it and establishing time as something other than
what it was.

Barth emphasizes, indeed underscores, discontinuity between the
past and the present, the old world and the new world.[42] The old
world is the world of "time and of things,"[43] and it is "conditioned
by sin."[44] The new world does not exist beside the old: "The possibility of the one involves the impossibility of the other. . . . [By
the gospel] this world is dissolved by the dissolution whereby it is
established."[45] Barth continues, "The Gospel is the power of God,
the power of the Resurrection; it is the 'miraculous warfare.'"[46] At
the resurrection the new world is born.

Barth paraphrases Romans 1:16–17 in this way: "The Gospel is the
victory by which the world is overcome. By the gospel the whole concrete world is dissolved and established."[47] In the *Church Dogmatics*,
Barth will say that the cross of Jesus ended history: "Human history
was actually terminated at this point."[48] The death and resurrection
of Jesus Christ alter entirely the human situation.[49]

In the "apocalyptic jolt" that is Barth's second Romans commentary, there is less sense of tension between the future and the present
than subsequent interpreters of Paul as an apocalyptic theologian

41. Barth, *Romans*, 77.
42. Barth experts note the continuities and discontinuities between Barth's apocalyptic
understanding of time in his famous commentary and his later *Church Dogmatics*. Jenson sees
Barth in *Dogmatics* correcting the apocalyptic fixation in his Roman commentary on the absolute contrast between time and eternity. In *Dogmatics*, time and eternity do meet—in Christ
(Jenson, "Apocalyptic and Messianism," 10). Harink, on the other hand, suggests that Barth's
entire *Dogmatics* is shaped by understanding Paul as an apocalyptic thinker (*Paul among the
Postliberals*, 54).
43. Barth, *Romans*, 169.
44. Barth, *Romans*, 168.
45. Barth, *Romans*, 165.
46. Barth, *Romans*, 166. The interior quotation is from Luther, without attribution of the
source.
47. Barth, *Romans*, 35.
48. Barth, *Church Dogmatics* IV/1, 734.
49. Joseph L. Mangina describes *Church Dogmatics* IV/1 as "the Cross as Apocalypse"
(*Karl Barth*, 124).

typically portray.[50] Though we groan and wait,[51] as does creation, we "bear within us the eternal Future, which we know can never be realized in time."[52] Commenting on Romans 13, Barth writes that between the past and the future is "a 'Moment' that is no moment in time."[53] God's dissolution and establishment of all things in Christ's cross and resurrection has created, in the words of Barth's interpreter Douglas Harink, "the singular time of the gospel,"[54] not, in Barth's words, a "new, a second, epoch"[55] in which history goes on. God's action in Christ has rather performed a "transformation so radical that time and eternity . . . are indissolubly linked together."[56] Given Barth's claim about the radical distinction between time and eternity, this is perhaps meant to point to the degree of transformation that God accomplished in Christ more than to a dissolution of the distinction. They are linked, and so a new time is established.[57]

Commenting on Romans 8, Barth echoes Schweitzer's image (without attribution): "The vast ocean of reality, which now embraces and submerges the Island of Truth, subsides and is established so that only Truth remains: the Truth of veritable Reality! Time, immense and vast, from its first beginning to its furthest future, is Eternity! . . . I am . . . made a participator of the divine nature and of the divine life, with God, by His side and in Him."[58] We can know "the 'Now' which is time's secret," that is, the Resurrection.[59] Though "the victory and fulfilment and presence of the

50. Jenson, "Apocalyptic and Messianism," 10.

51. Given Barth's conviction that all humanity is saved in Christ (e.g., *Church Dogmatics* IV/1, 317), I hesitate to write "believers" and so use "we," as he does. In this regard he sharply diverges from Schweitzer.

52. Barth, *Romans*, 312.

53. Barth, *Romans*, 497.

54. Harink, "Time and Politics in Four Commentaries," 299.

55. Barth, *Romans*, 77.

56. Barth, *Romans*, 77.

57. Barth will speak of the "time which is beyond time" as "eternity in time" (*Romans*, 92).

58. Barth, *Romans*, 313. No reference is given to Schweitzer's image of the immortal world rising in volcanic upheavals out of the ocean of the temporal (Schweitzer, *Mysticism*, 112).

59. Barth, *Romans*, 313.

Truth is ours only by hope,"[60] hope allows us to see that waiting is our highest calling.[61]

In Barth's interpretation, there is little description of eschatological tension, of the already–not yet anxiety that later readers of Paul's apocalyptic typically describe. In his *Römerbrief*, Barth understands Paul's view of time to be that the future has come; the present is shaped by the future rather than in conflict with it. There is now a "time which is beyond time," "eternity in time."[62] The present is envisaged not as the inauguration of the new age in time, since, given the infinite qualitative difference between time and eternity, this would be impossible. "We . . . stand under the Cross, unable to do more than bear witness to the 'Now' of eternity which is ours, to the Day of Jesus Christ, which is no day, but the Day of Days, before and behind and above the days of our life."[63]

Admittedly, Barth conceives of some tension caused by knowing what has occurred and by waiting for the "existential occurrence of what has only apparently 'already' taken place, our expecting and looking for the eternal 'Moment' of the Appearance, the Parousia, the Presence of Jesus Christ."[64] Yet we are not waiting for a "temporal event," not a "historical . . . or cosmic catastrophe . . . a coarse and brutal spectacle."[65] We wait, rather, for our awakening when we step into a kind of time that knows we "stand at every moment on the frontier of time."[66] In that time we know "that the eternal 'Moment' . . . will not enter" into time, and consequently we will know that "each single . . . temporal moment" is the opportunity to love,[67] for acts of love come from the perception that "time shall be

---

60. Barth, *Romans*, 313.
61. Barth, *Romans*, 314–15.
62. Barth, *Romans*, 92.
63. Barth, *Romans*, 313. Jenson opines that Barth contributed to the unfortunate "reduction of biblical apocalyptic's new age to a timeless moment" (Jenson, "Apocalyptic and Messianism," 11). According to Jenson, it is a short step from this view of apocalyptic eschatology to Bultmann's existential interpretation (8).
64. Barth, *Romans*, 499.
65. Barth, *Romans*, 500.
66. Barth, *Romans*, 501.
67. Barth, *Romans*, 501 (italics removed). The original quotation contains a comma between "not" and "enter."

as eternity and eternity as time."[68] Whatever tension Barth admits is mild and anxiety-free relative to most subsequent apocalyptic presentations of the already–not yet.[69]

Barth claims that Paul thinks that in Christ we are in "the invisible New Age."[70] The kind of time that is chronological and sequential is an illusion. The kind of time that is true—time "qualified by the *Now!*"[71] which is not itself in time—is the kind of time that is on time's frontier.[72] Eternity may be known *in* time, but it is never *of* time. The intensity of living this time is not the intensity of being caught between the already and the not yet (between two ages) but the intensity of being fully awake and alive to love and to the presence of Jesus Christ.[73] We will necessarily love "in a succession of moments," but that we do love is because of our knowledge of the Moment.[74]

Here is a vision of Paul's view of time that is apocalyptic not because it, like Schweitzer's, sees Paul reworking a two-age Jewish apocalyptic template (in fact, Barth does not mention Jewish apocalyptic writings in his commentary). It is apocalyptic, rather, because of its challenge to the idea of progressive revelation and in the scale of its vision: eternity (God) has dissolved time in order to establish a kind of time in which humanity can peek over the edge of our time-boundedness and "dare to love the Unknown, to apprehend and lay hold of the Beginning in the End."[75] Barth's *Romans* is apocalyptic (as apocalyptic came to be understood in biblical and theological scholarship) in its claim that there is absolute discontinuity between what was and what God has done.[76] In Barth's

---

68. Barth, *Romans*, 497.
69. This may be connected to the fact that while Barth uses the rhetoric of battle in *Romans*, unlike many subsequent apocalyptic interpreters of Paul, his focus is not trained on a cosmic battle having been initiated by Christ's cross and resurrection.
70. Barth, *Romans*, 497.
71. Barth, *Romans*, 498 (italics original).
72. Barth, *Romans*, 501.
73. Barth, *Romans*, 501.
74. Barth, *Romans*, 498.
75. Barth, *Romans*, 501.
76. This radical discontinuity will be much nuanced in *Dogmatics*. Adams points this out in regard to *Dogmatics* IV/1, 170, where Barth places Jesus Christ in the framework of the history of Israel (Adams, *Reality of God*).

words from a writing other than *Romans*, the eschaton is "*not* the extension, the result, the consequence, the next step in following out what has gone before, *but* on the contrary, it is the radical break with all that has gone before, but also precisely as such its original significance and motive power."[77]

Ernst Käsemann

Käsemann is regularly credited with popularizing (against significant opposition) the idea of apocalyptic as foundational for early Christianity.[78] Käsemann spends almost no ink on comparing Jewish apocalyptic to Paul.[79] His understanding of apocalyptic thought is that it conceives of a battle between cosmic powers and God and that it is concerned with a people and the whole world, and not individuals. This understanding of apocalyptic is carried on and nuanced by subsequent Pauline apocalyptic interpreters.

In regard to time, Käsemann is adamant, against his teacher Bultmann, that Paul's eschatology is not an exclusively present eschatology. Rather, Paul's letters evidence "a compromise between present and future eschatology."[80] Proof of this is that Paul opposes his Corinthian converts' enthusiasm (that is, their belief that "the end of history . . . has already come to pass")[81] with "eschatological reservation."[82] Paul believes that "the day of the End-time has already broken,"[83] but there is still a future to be expected: the return of Christ, which will be the end of death's continuing reign. Käsemann is certain that Paul thinks that though believers participate in

77. Philip G. Ziegler's translation of "Der Christ in der Gesellschaft," 35; quoted from Ziegler, *Militant Grace*, 8.

78. See especially Käsemann, "Beginnings of Christian Theology" and "Primitive Christian Apocalyptic." In "Primitive Christian Apocalyptic," Käsemann directly responds to some of his critics, such as Gerhard Ebeling and Ernst Fuchs.

79. He does a small amount of comparative work in his Romans commentary (e.g., Käsemann, *Romans*, 308). He briefly mentions the Dead Sea Scrolls ("Primitive Christian Apocalyptic," 123).

80. Käsemann, "Primitive Christian Apocalyptic," 131.

81. Käsemann, "Primitive Christian Apocalyptic," 133.

82. Käsemann, "Primitive Christian Apocalyptic," 132.

83. Käsemann, "Primitive Christian Apocalyptic," 133.

Christ's death, they do not yet participate in his resurrection. Death still has dominion over them, whereas it does not have dominion over Christ. There is more to come.

Paul "modifies the apocalyptic scheme of the two aeons"[84] on the basis that now the cosmic powers are subject to Christ's lordship. Presently all the powers except the power of death are defeated in the church with the result that there are two realities—"the Church as the redeemed and the world as the unredeemed creation."[85] In other words, rather than two succeeding ages, there are now two opposing worlds.[86] Nevertheless, it is essential to Paul that his converts recognize that they are not yet at the end, but rather they are "still living through the pangs of the Messiah."[87]

Subsequent to Christ's death and resurrection, then, time is an entity that is known to have an end point and a final period before that ultimate end. The end has begun, but it has not arrived. That will only happen at the parousia. Käsemann does not ponder whether the present aspects of Paul's eschatology interrupt linear time in the way that later advocates of the apocalyptic Paul will when they speak of already–not yet. Käsemann's temporal framework is based on his understanding of what time means in apocalyptic. "The world has a definite beginning and a definite end, the course of history therefore takes a definite direction and is irrevocable, articulated in a series of epochs clearly distinguishable from each other."[88] For Käsemann time is sequential. The future is not an invasion or interruption of time but fits within the end-time period.

This goes toward explaining Käsemann's claim that Paul's theology is shaped by salvation history.[89] It is, however, a "deeply paradoxical"[90] kind of salvation history. It is a salvation history that is not "a process of historical development."[91] For in it the eschaton breaks in and

---

84. Käsemann, "Primitive Christian Apocalyptic," 134.
85. Käsemann, "Primitive Christian Apocalyptic," 134.
86. Käsemann, "Primitive Christian Apocalyptic," 129.
87. Käsemann, "Primitive Christian Apocalyptic," 136.
88. Käsemann, "Beginnings of Christian Theology," 96.
89. Käsemann, "Justification and Salvation History," 66; and *Romans*, 307.
90. Käsemann, "Justification and Salvation History," 68.
91. Käsemann, *Romans*, 316.

takes root in history,[92] which manifests itself, as we have seen, in two contrasting realms (the realm of Adam and the realm of Christ).[93] "The apocalyptic scheme of two successive aeons . . . is transferred to the present."[94] Yet there is also more to come: the essential return of Christ when Christ's lordship will be manifest. The eschatological is part of history, providing a "cohesion" that "leads from creation to Christ and the Parousia by way of the choosing of Israel and the promise."[95] The end of history and the end of this history are expected at the parousia.

Käsemann's suggestion that Paul modified the two-age apocalyptic idea with the idea that there are now two conflicting realities (the church and the world) fits within a linear understanding of time. In the end-time there are two realities, one obedient to God and one not. This will end at the parousia. Time is an entity that is progressing toward the end.

J. Christiaan Beker

Beker pushes forward the idea of Paul as an apocalyptic thinker.[96] In line with Käsemann, Beker claims that Paul's theology is apocalyptic and modifies Jewish apocalyptic's two ages in light of Christ's resurrection. Like Käsemann, Beker assumes a temporal continuum. Beker speaks of process—of God as an intervener in a process[97] and of the resurrection of Christ as beginning the process of transformation.[98] Beker refers to God's salvation history not only with the Jews themselves[99] but with all people.[100]

92. Käsemann, "Justification and Salvation History," 68.
93. Käsemann, "Justification and Salvation History," 67.
94. Käsemann, "Justification and Salvation History," 67.
95. Käsemann, "Justification and Salvation History," 68.
96. Beker, *Paul the Apostle*. Beker writes that he wants to "press" the apocalyptic understanding advanced by Käsemann, among others, "for a fresh understanding of Paul, because only a consistent apocalyptic interpretation of Paul's thought is able to demonstrate its fundamental coherence" (143).
97. Beker, *Paul the Apostle*, 19.
98. Beker, *Paul the Apostle*, 149.
99. Beker, *Paul the Apostle*, 243.
100. "God's salvation history reaches its eschatological stage in the creation of the one people of God, the one church of Jew and Gentile" (Beker, *Paul the Apostle*, 83).

Setting himself apart from Käsemann, Beker claims that while Käsemann saw apocalyptic as Paul's polemical doctrine against the enthusiasm of gentile believers,[101] apocalyptic is, rather, the "coherent center of Paul's theology";[102] "Paul is an apocalyptic theologian with a theocentric outlook."[103] Beker also criticizes Bultmann, whose realized eschatology, he contends, ignores the "not yet" of both the transformation of creation and God's final judgment.[104] Beker also finds mistaken Cullmann's placing of Christ at the midpoint of an ongoing process, for in Beker's view this effectively extends the eschaton indefinitely, making the end "a continuous and permanent variable."[105]

According to Beker, Paul, in thoroughly apocalyptic fashion, thinks in terms of promise and fulfillment, and of an ongoing battle between God and anti-God powers (in particular, death) that awaits consummation. The cosmic scope of Paul's vision means that there is not a church-world divide;[106] both the church and the world are waiting for the final triumph of God when creation will be transformed. While, because of Christ's resurrection, the apocalyptic future is present,[107] what Beker stresses is that "the Christ-event awaits a cosmic consummation."[108] The final triumph of God is assured, but it is not yet.

Beker's concept of Paul's view of time, like that of Käsemann, is linear. The temporal line means that the future can come into the present ("the incursion of the future into the present").[109] Christ's resurrection is "the appearance of the end in history."[110] Beker's main point—that for Paul the triumph of God is not yet consummated—rests on a linear understanding of time. God's triumph is somewhere

---

101. Beker, *Paul the Apostle*, 17.
102. Beker, *Paul the Apostle*, xiv.
103. Beker, *Paul the Apostle*, 362.
104. Beker, *Paul the Apostle*, 179.
105. Beker, *Paul the Apostle*, 355.
106. Although, Beker does describe the church as "the avant-garde of new creation in a hostile world" (*Paul the Apostle*, 155).
107. Beker, *Paul the Apostle*, 58, 153.
108. Beker, *Paul the Apostle*, 277.
109. Beker, *Paul the Apostle*, 145.
110. Beker, *Paul the Apostle*, 149.

down the temporal line. Life now is "the *dialectic* of cross and resurrection," which "will be embraced by the *sequence* of resurrection-
life *after* our cruciform life in the final victory of God."[111] Beker
presumes chronological, sequential, linear time as the nature of the
apocalyptic time with which Paul worked and does not contemplate
whether the presence of the end changes historical (chronological)
time.

J. Louis Martyn

Though Martyn's work is not without its critics,[112] and even his
admirers disagree with or are cautious about significant features
of his work,[113] his confident presentation of Paul's apocalypticism,
especially in Galatians, is indeed "a new benchmark for the interpretation of Galatians"[114] and is seen as "one of the greatest readings
of Paul."[115] It must be recognized that Martyn is indebted to his
student, Martinus C. de Boer, with whom I engage in a subsequent
chapter. Foundational for Martyn is de Boer's important proposition that Jewish apocalyptic thinking had two tracks, one forensic
and another cosmological.[116]

Martyn stresses both the discontinuity between the present and
the past and the discontinuity between the present and the future.
He stands against what he terms the redemptive-historical interpretation of Paul. The idea that Paul thinks in terms of a "historical line"[117] that has reached its climax in Christ is the view not of
Paul but of Paul's opponents in the gentile mission. Martyn dis-

---

111. Beker, *Paul the Apostle*, 207 (italics original).
112. N. T. Wright criticizes Martyn for, among other things, using "apocalyptic" in a way
that does not reflect what is evident in Jewish apocalyptic writings (Wright, *Paul and His Recent
Interpreters*, 170).
113. Richard B. Hays asks, "Can Martyn really maintain at the end of the day that Galatians,
as he reads it, does not lead inevitably to an anti-Jewish, supersessionist Christian theology?"
(Hays, review of *Galatians*, 377).
114. Cousar, review of *Galatians*, 4.
115. Barclay, review of *Galatians*, 5.
116. See de Boer, *Defeat of Death*.
117. Martyn, *Galatians*, 344.

tinguishes himself from Pauline interpreters who think of Paul "as a redemptive-historical theologian."[118] Paul thinks not in terms of developmental sequence. Rather than thinking of time in a linear fashion, Paul thinks that God has acted in a punctiliar way.[119] Presumably this means for Martyn that Paul thinks that God uses time by creating events at particular moments that are not tied together in a straightforward cause-and-effect manner. Time, in God's hands, is the entity in which God creates what God wants as God wants, such as two punctiliar events: the covenantal promise (Abraham) and the "singular and punctiliar seed (Christ)."[120] Martyn writes that the first event "refers"[121] to the second, but he does not ponder how.[122] What is important for Martyn in this regard is underlined by his affirmation of Philipp Vielhauer's statement that "the history of Israel as a sequence of events does not interest Paul in the slightest."[123]

Martyn's Paul has an understanding of the relationship between the past and the present that goes against the grain of commonsense temporal understanding. The past does not feed into the present. Rather, what is in the past can "refer" to the present but not by moving into it through the flow of time. God can determine which events in the past should now be in the present (and which should not be).[124] And when such an event is in the present, it is because God has placed it there. God's promise to Abraham in the past is now in the present in "the singular seed, Christ."[125] The past has come into the present not by flowing into it but through God placing the

---

118. Martyn, *Galatians*, 347. Among those Martyn names are J. Christiaan Beker and N. T. Wright.

119. Martyn, *Galatians*, 348.

120. Martyn, *Galatians*, 339.

121. Martyn, *Galatians*, 339.

122. That is, Martyn does not describe the referral as, for example, promise-fulfillment or typological.

123. Vielhauer, *Oikodome*, 218, quoted in Martyn, *Theological Issues*, 223n30.

124. Martyn's contention that Paul separates law and covenant is an incidence of something from the past (the law) no longer being part of the present. Martyn famously contends that "the true voice of God's scripture" is not law but the covenantal promise God spoke to Abraham (*Galatians*, 340). "The covenant is to be equated solely with God's promise to Abraham and thus sharply divorced from the Law" (341).

125. Martyn, *Galatians*, 349.

past in the present. This transgresses, of course, our typical understanding of time.

Integral to this understanding of the relationship of the past and the present is Martyn's conviction that God's invasion of the evil age indicates a radical distinction between the past with its structures, including the law, and God's present activity in Christ. On the basis of the claim that Paul thinks in terms of two ages, which, according to Martyn, is "a scheme fundamental to apocalyptic thought,"[126] he hears Paul as believing that there is a "disjunctive dualism"[127] between the two ages. One age does not morph into the other; rather, there is a dualistic disconnect between the two. When the new creation/new age comes into the present it is not because the past has developed into the present but because God has determined that the old age is finished and the new age is come.[128]

The character of time is that the present evil age, having been invaded by God sending Christ and the spirit into it, is "dynamically interrelated" to the new creation—which is another kind of time.[129] The new creation is a new reality with new antinomies and a new way of knowing, and it is also a new kind of time. "The basic characteristic of the present time is given, then, in the fact that it is the juncture of the new creation and the present evil age."[130] This juncture is the result of a radical disjuncture. There is a "radically new perception of time"[131] because the past—that is, the present evil age—no longer feeds into the present. The past has ended by virtue of God's rearrangement of everything about it through invading it with Christ and the spirit. Paul thinks there has been what Martyn calls a "punctiliar liberation" as opposed to a "gradual maturation."[132]

126. Martyn, *Galatians*, 98.

127. Martyn, *Theological Issues*, 178.

128. In his appreciative review of Beker's *Paul the Apostle*, Martyn criticizes Beker for understanding apocalyptic as structured by continuity (salvation history). Beker's view that God's final triumph takes place through a God-directed continuum of history goes against what Martyn sees as the fundamental dualism of Paul's apocalyptic thought (Martyn, *Theological Issues*, 178).

129. Martyn, *Galatians*, 66.

130. Martyn, *Galatians*, 102.

131. Martyn, *Galatians*, 104.

132. Martyn, *Galatians*, 389.

In terms of time, Martyn's claim of the God-initiated rupture between the past and the present that occurred in Christ's death and resurrection in effect brings the future into the present: the "eschatological subjection of the world has already begun."[133] We readers of biblical scholarship may be so used to such assertions that we do not hear what they claim about time. The eschaton is the future; that the future has begun in the present means that the future has come into the present.

For Martyn the new creation is the "after" that has invaded the "before," the present evil age.[134] This invasion changes the present into a different reality with, as Martyn emphasizes, different antinomies. Yet the present evil age continues. Its structures, for instance the Flesh, are now challenged because the new creation has invaded it. And so, for instance, the Spirit is now at war with the Flesh.[135]

Martyn's (and others') claim that Paul thinks that the two ages exist at once indicates a particular understanding of the apostle's view of time: the present and the future coexist. The fact that the present is not understood as being changed into the future by virtue of entry into the future but rather is conceived of as an entity at war with the future (and with which the future is at war) relies on a strange conception of time. The future does not come after the present but can be in the present, and when it is in the present it does not change the present into the future. The present and the future can exist in the same moment. This is counter to our ordinary understanding of how time works: a continuous succession of past to present to future. It is also different from our experience of time in which the present moment almost always contains both the past and the future, though (in a healthy, functioning human) the present is the clear context for remembering the past and anticipating the future. In conventional temporal understanding, neither the past nor the future are understood to actually be *in* the present. In regard to time, this vision of Paul as an apocalyptic thinker understands him

133. Martyn, *Theological Issues*, 113.
134. Martyn, *Theological Issues*, 121.
135. Martyn, *Theological Issues*, 121.

to think that the past is discontinuous with the present and that the future and the present exist now at the same time.

Beverly R. Gaventa

Gaventa understands Paul's theology to be "apocalyptic theology," a designation that indicates "the unimaginable size of God's actions on behalf of the entire cosmos, including humanity itself."[136] According to Gaventa, Paul sees that creation is enslaved to anti-God powers and that, in Christ, God has invaded this dire situation. A battle has ensued, with God fighting against the powers that enslave God's creation.[137] The result is an antithesis between Christ and new creation, on the one hand, and the cosmos, on the other.[138] Christ's crucifixion does not win the battle, but it does unmask the powers and signal their inevitable defeat.[139] In this sense, Christ's crucifixion "inaugurates a new age."[140]

On the basis of Romans 8, Gaventa hears Paul as thinking that "creation continues to be sold into slavery, despite the resurrection of Jesus Christ and the new life of believers."[141] Nevertheless, God's intervening work in Christ means that the powers "cannot and will not prevail."[142] Gaventa's apocalyptic Paul sees that at the cross God initiated a battle against enslaving anti-God powers. Liberation for God's creation, including humanity, is "not complete."[143] The sign of the ongoing battle is the continued presence of Sin and Death.[144]

While there is an implicit understanding of discontinuity between what went before Christ's cross and what comes after, what Gaventa

136. Gaventa, *Our Mother Saint Paul*, 84.
137. Gaventa makes the case that even Romans is saturated with military imagery ("Rhetoric of Violence").
138. Gaventa, *Our Mother Saint Paul*, 108.
139. Gaventa, *Our Mother Saint Paul*, 122.
140. Gaventa, *Our Mother Saint Paul*, 103.
141. Gaventa, *Our Mother Saint Paul*, 60.
142. Gaventa, *Our Mother Saint Paul*, 60.
143. Gaventa, *Our Mother Saint Paul*, 81.
144. Apocalyptic interpreters of Paul regularly capitalize Sin and Death (and often Flesh) in order to signal their understanding that Paul conceived of these as powerful suprahuman entities capable of controlling humanity. I tend to do the same when describing views of scholars who read Paul apocalyptically.

understands this to mean temporally is unclear.[145] Gaventa focuses on what she reads as Paul's conviction of an ongoing God-initiated battle against anti-God powers that has not yet ultimately been won. Gaventa appears to presume that Paul works with a linear understanding of time. Though she speaks of God's apocalypse "taking place in the present,"[146] this refers not to God's final victory but to God's invasion of creation. The "apocalyptic drama"[147] proceeds sequentially: the death of Christ is God's invasion of enslaved creation, which liberates humans from Sin, changing believers into God's children. These children of God "await their ultimate final redemption."[148]

Douglas A. Campbell

Campbell's massive *The Deliverance of God* has as its subtitle *An Apocalyptic Rereading of Justification in Paul*. For all Campbell's rethinking of the Protestant interpretation of Paul on justification in favor of an "apocalyptic rereading," Campbell does not spend much time defining "apocalyptic." For him it appears to mean an understanding that subsequent to Christ there are two opposing reigns: one is the reign of God through Christ, and the other is the reign of "more sinister figures."[149] What Campbell calls "non-Christian reality" is a reality of enslavement to Sin and Death.[150] The only solution to this state of enslaved oppression is for God to rescue humanity, and God does this out of love.[151] The result is "fundamentally transformational," a work of the spirit allowing people to live not in the flesh but in Christ.[152] Campbell states that "the unconditional,

145. Gaventa insists that while Romans may be about God's covenant faithfulness to Israel, it is primarily about declaring that all people, including Israel, are, since the death and resurrection of Christ, "within a conflict" in which God is reclaiming the world for Godself (*Our Mother Saint Paul*, 122–23).

146. Gaventa, *Our Mother Saint Paul*, 81.

147. Gaventa, *Our Mother Saint Paul*, 140.

148. Gaventa, *Our Mother Saint Paul*, 135.

149. Campbell, *Deliverance of God*, 63.

150. Campbell, *Deliverance of God*, 63.

151. Campbell, *Deliverance of God*, 65–66.

152. Campbell, *Deliverance of God*, 64.

revelatory, transformational and liberational aspects of this event mean that it is appropriately described as 'apocalyptic.'"[153]

It is not until Campbell's second big book, *Pauline Dogmatics: The Triumph of God's Love*, that he offers significant reflection on the temporal implications of such an apocalyptic reading of Paul's soteriology.[154] Campbell draws on *Sachkritik* in this regard, essentially attempting to demythologize Paul's temporal understanding on the basis of a modern scientific one. Campbell accepts Einstein's description of time as a field, rather than a line or a constant that "moves along steadily."[155] Campbell states that "Paul himself did not understand this view of time."[156] Nevertheless, according to Campbell, it helps to explain what he sees as tension in Paul's thought between the claim that believers have resurrected, spiritual minds while living in bodies that die. Paul believes that the resurrection of believers "is, in some sense," present; it "has begun."[157] Second Corinthians 5:17 indicates that Paul thinks "a resurrection of sorts has taken place."[158] Understanding that time is not linear but, rather, a field reconfigures the tension inherent in the partiality of resurrection for believers. It is not that this tension needs to be resolved, and one day it will be; rather, there is no future in the perfection of time into which the dead enter.[159]

According to Campbell, it should be understood that God did not create time, though God upholds it. Time is "an interim ordering structure, upheld by God."[160] Campbell suggests that Paul himself thinks in terms of interim arrangements, which are not part of God's "elected created order"; according to Campbell's reading

153. Campbell, *Deliverance of God*, 66.
154. Between *Deliverance of God* and *Pauline Dogmatics*, Campbell published two smaller books, *Framing Paul* and *Paul*.
155. Campbell, *Pauline Dogmatics*, 157.
156. Campbell, *Pauline Dogmatics*, 161.
157. Campbell, *Pauline Dogmatics*, 105.
158. Campbell, *Pauline Dogmatics*, 105.
159. Campbell, *Pauline Dogmatics*, 163.
160. Campbell, *Pauline Dogmatics*, 582. Campbell relies on T. F. Torrance's proposal about "ordering structures," which are not part of God's original intention (Torrance, *Space, Time and Resurrection*, 185). These ordering structures serve to keep chaos in some sort of check (Campbell, *Pauline Dogmatics*, 580).

of Paul, the Mosaic dispensation is one such interim ordering arrangement.[161] Campbell considers, then, that it is not too far a leap to think that Paul would be comfortable considering that time also has a temporary function.

The basis of this fascinating reevaluation of the apostle's understanding of time, and of time itself from a theological perspective, appears to be that time is separate from God. Campbell speaks of God "as being 'above' the field of time."[162] Though he affirms Barth's conception of God living a perfection of time in which all past, present, and future is at once,[163] Campbell does not tease out whether this can be described as time. It is rather the perfection of time.[164] He does speak of "another type of time altogether—the resurrected time . . . the new, perfect time."[165] Campbell, however, barely explores this idea on the basis of Paul's letters. He merely distinguishes between "the old time" and perfect time.[166]

It appears that Campbell assumes that time is not of God: it is not created by God, God is above it, and God does not live time—or, better put, God does not live our kind of time, "old time." Campbell admits that Paul does not make these claims, but nevertheless, "some of his positions give us permission to extrapolate from his stated positions to this more mature solution."[167] Campbell's "more mature solution" does offer a way past the worn already–not yet proposal that is founded on a linear view of time, and it is entirely refreshing to find a Pauline scholar who reflects on the temporal assumptions that Paul has (and that interpreters bring to Paul's texts). Yet without more exegetical engagement with Paul himself on the

---

161. Campbell, *Pauline Dogmatics*, 583.
162. Campbell, *Pauline Dogmatics*, 158.
163. Campbell, *Pauline Dogmatics*, 158.
164. Campbell drops a hint that he thinks there will be a "perfect time" (*Pauline Dogmatics*, 158), and he speaks briefly about "the perfection of time" (163). Campbell's several references to the perfection of time are based not on exegesis of Paul but on Barth (158). (Admittedly, this observation begs the question of whether Barth's understanding is based on a reading of Paul.)
165. Campbell, *Pauline Dogmatics*, 159.
166. Campbell, *Pauline Dogmatics*, 159.
167. Campbell, *Pauline Dogmatics*, 164.

matter of time, one is left to wonder whether or not the apostle would welcome his devoted interpreter's correction.

Time in the Apocalyptic Paul Hypothesis

What is at stake in the apocalyptic interpretation of Paul is the understanding of how dire the situation of the present age is. From this interpretation's perspective, the salvation historical approach's emphasis on a progressive, unfolding plan of God diminishes the problem that God chose to fix. It further diminishes the extent of God's grace: God chooses, at the cost of God's own Son, to invade the horrific present age to liberate humanity and creation from evil powers. The apocalyptic interpretation of Paul offers what Beverly Gaventa has described as a "widescreen" description of the dilemma that God intervenes to fix.[168] In conjunction with that analysis of the dilemma, it emphasizes the immensity of God's gracious effort to defeat inimical powers. The problem is too tragic and the solution too remarkable to be fit into an idea of progressive salvation. The new world God offers is entirely discontinuous with the present horrendously polluted one.[169]

Time in the apocalyptic reading of Paul can hold within it two competing realities: the present evil age and the new creation. Though the competition between these realities is typically portrayed as one of opposing powers, there is an often-unacknowledged temporal dimension to these two realities. The present age is finite, since it will end when Christ returns; the new creation is a kind of temporality that is eternal. The apocalyptic interpretation conceives of both kinds of temporalities—one finite and the other eternal—existing at once, though only believers in Christ experience and know this.[170] Believers understand that eternity has invaded time as they know

168. Gaventa, "Cosmic Power of Sin."
169. As already pointed out, however, both Käsemann and Beker do maintain the idea of progressive salvation while also being apocalyptic interpreters of Paul.
170. Schweitzer, as pointed out above, is the outlier here: while the old age continues, those in Christ live as "already supernatural beings" (*Mysticism*, 110). Cf. Barth, who writes that those in Christ are in "the invisible New Age" (*Romans*, 497).

it. Further, believers are capable of living in both temporalities at once; they live in already–not yet.

Giorgio Agamben

Agamben's *The Time That Remains* has been an important part of the conversation about Paul's understanding of time and so warrants some attention before we move into my particular perspective. Since in structuring his description of Paul's view of time Agamben distinguishes what he calls "messianic time" from "the Jewish apocalyptic tradition and rabbinic tradition,"[171] it is fitting to discuss him here.

The apocalyptic, as opposed to the apostolic (Paul's) understanding, "contemplates the end."[172] Paul, however, does not contemplate the time of the end but rather lives the time of the end—time that now contracts itself and begins to end. Paul lives messianic time. Messianic time is the time of the now[173] that lasts until the parousia.[174] "Messianic time is that part of secular time which undergoes an entirely transformative contraction. . . . [It divides] the division between two times, [and] introduces a remainder (*resto*) into it that exceeds the division."[175] Working with Gustave Guillaume's linguistic and philosophical idea of "operational time," Agamben suggests that, for Paul, messianic time is the time we need to make time end, the time that is left to us.

The now, messianic time, which is operational time, "introduces a disconnection and delay into represented time."[176] But this is not a kind of time that supplements time or creates deferment. Messianic time, rather, "is the very opening through which we may seize hold of time, achieving our representation of time, making it end."[177] The significance of the Messiah for time, then, is that time may now

---

171. Agamben, *Time That Remains*, 61.
172. Agamben, *Time That Remains*, 62.
173. Agamben, *Time That Remains*, 53, 61.
174. Agamben, *Time That Remains*, 63.
175. Agamben, *Time That Remains*, 64.
176. Agamben, *Time That Remains*, 100.
177. Agamben, *Time That Remains*, 100.

end, and we may live in the only real time—the now. Messianic or operational time "holds within itself another time"[178]—the time that it takes time to end.[179]

For Agamben, Paul's time (messianic time) is the time between the resurrection of Jesus and the parousia, when the Messiah will be fully present and time "implodes into the other eon, into eternity."[180] Messianic time is, then, distinguished from what will be—"the *eschaton*, when time moves into eternity."[181] In messianic time there is "the paradoxical tension between an *already* and a *not yet* that defines the Pauline conception of salvation."[182] At the parousia this tension will end and so there will be "the end of time."[183]

In line with apocalyptic (and salvation historical) readers of Paul, then, Agamben thinks that the future has come into the present. Since the Messiah, there is no "clear division between the two *'olamim.*"[184] Moreover, like both apocalyptic and salvation historical interpreters, Agamben thinks that the kind of time believers are currently living will end at the parousia. Furthermore, like salvation historical thinkers, and a great proportion of apocalyptic interpreters, time for Agamben is fundamentally linear. His diagram, which represents three temporal events (A is creation; B is the messianic event, which is Jesus's resurrection; and C is "the *eschaton*, when time moves into eternity"[185]), is a line with the letters A, B, and C at progressive points on the line.

Summary of Apocalyptic and Salvation Historical Views of Time

Briefly, let us note the temporal claims common to salvation historical and apocalyptic interpreters, and to Agamben. A broad strokes summary indicates that salvation historical and apocalyptic readers,

178. Agamben, *Time That Remains*, 71.
179. Agamben, *Time That Remains*, 68.
180. Agamben, *Time That Remains*, 63.
181. Agamben, *Time That Remains*, 63 (italics original).
182. Agamben, *Time That Remains*, 69 (italics original).
183. Agamben, *Time That Remains*, 69.
184. Agamben, *Time That Remains*, 63.
185. Agamben, *Time That Remains*, 63 (italics original).

as well as Agamben, share the conviction that currently two ages exist at once and that believers live in both simultaneously.

Moreover, salvation historical and apocalyptic scholars, along with Agamben, understand Paul to think that the time that all humans currently live is finite; it will end. At the parousia, eternity will be established as the only temporality. This will affect all humanity. Currently there are two overlapping ages. Believers alone live in both at once. This already–not yet type of time will end once there is no longer a "not yet"—that is, when eternity is all there is. Further, both salvation historical and apocalyptic interpreters understand Paul to think that time and eternity are fundamentally distinct temporalities and that, when they engage, the structure of time is affected. In particular, when eternity engages with time, the present becomes capable of holding within itself at least a portion of the future.

3

Time in Christ—Not in the
Overlap of the Ages

The opinions on Paul's view of time described in the two previous chapters share a fundamental conviction that the apostle conceived of believers as living in the overlap of the old age and the new age. Further, the assumption common to Pauline interpreters of various stripes is that this overlap is due to Paul's Jewish heritage—a heritage that included a two-age framework.[1] The two-age framework is supposed to have shaped Jews' understanding of temporality as follows: in the present age, God's rule is challenged; this state of affairs is untenable and will be replaced at God's initiative when the new age manifests God's unencumbered reign. Paul, it is claimed, worked with and modified that scenario in light of Christ's resurrection—resurrection being an event that was not supposed to occur until

1. Increasingly, Pauline scholars are challenged by interaction with scholars of Jewish apocalyptic to recognize that they have an overly simplistic view of Jewish apocalyptic ideas regarding two ages. For instance, Matthew Goff, a scholar of Second Temple Jewish literature, writes, "It is not at all clear . . . that Jewish apocalypticism should be defined as having a 'two ages' doctrine" ("Heavenly Mysteries," 135). Loren Stuckenbruck demonstrates that some Jewish apocalyptic texts did not divide time or reality into this age ruled by evil powers and the age to come when these powers are defeated. Jews "could understand themselves as living in a time between God's proleptic establishment of control over evil and the effective defeat of it at the end" ("Posturing 'Apocalyptic' in Pauline Theology," 256).

the coming of the new age. The apostle solved the conundrum of Christ's resurrection being unaccompanied by resurrection of the faithful by envisioning the ages as nonsequential and consequently overlapping. The foundational assumption that a two-age scenario organized Paul's thinking is shared both by scholars who see Paul as convinced that God acts progressively[2] and by those who think the apostle thought apocalyptically.[3]

The problem with this fundamental interpretative assumption is, however, that Paul does not speak of the new age.[4] The significant detail that Paul does not speak of the new age is sometimes noted but then dismissed, either by claiming that Paul alludes to the idea[5] or by claiming that he uses other terms that convey the same thing. Martinus de Boer articulates the scholarly consensus when he states that new creation, kingdom of God, and eternal life are "surely other ways of speaking about the age to come."[6]

2. The salvation historical interpreter Dunn writes that Paul thinks "the ages overlap" (*Theology of Paul*, 464). He goes on: "The beginning of the age to come is pulled back into the present age, . . . but the present age has not yet ended, and will persist until the Parousia" (464). Recognizing that the two-ages idea is found in both apocalyptic and rabbinic works, N. T. Wright states that "one of the standard Jewish ways of addressing the problem of the creator and the cosmos was to speak in terms of two epochs of world history: the present age and the age to come. . . . Paul's specific contribution to this overarching narrative is to insist that the 'coming age' has already been inaugurated (though not yet completed) through Jesus" (*Paul and the Faithfulness of God*, 476–77). Wright claims that Gal. 1:4 is a "clear statement of the 'two ages' belief, together with an equally clear statement of the particular Pauline claim that these ages now *overlap*" (477 [italics original]).

3. The apocalyptic interpreter Martinus C. de Boer describes Paul as thinking that "believers live neither in the old age nor in the new: they live at the juncture of the ages where the forces of the new age . . . are in an ongoing struggle with the forces of the old age" (*Galatians*, 34).

4. Ephesians is the outlier here, but, even if we were to include its evidence, though its authorship is disputed, the reference in Eph. 1:21 to this age and the age to come is complicated by the two other references to "age" in this letter. Ephesians 2:7 speaks of the coming ages (plural) and 3:9 of the "ages" in which the ἡ οἰκονομία ("plan" or "stewardship") of the mystery was hidden in God. Ephesians does not, then, present a straightforward two-age temporality. Recently, the rather obvious but typically ignored fact that Paul does not speak of the new age has been noted and explored also by Jamie Davies in "Why Paul Doesn't Mention the 'Age to Come'" and *Apocalyptic Paul*. The publication of Davies's book coincided with the submission of my manuscript for this book. This has very unfortunately prohibited me from giving his book the attention it deserves.

5. Leander Keck writes that Paul "never states the [two-ages] idea fully: yet his allusions to it show how deeply ingrained it is in his thought" (*Christ's First Theologian*, 83). Cf. Furnish, *Theology and Ethics in Paul*, 115.

6. De Boer, "Paul and Jewish Apocalyptic Eschatology," 187n17. See also his *Galatians*, 17. Andrew Lincoln thinks that Paul equates kingdom of God with age to come (*Paradise Now and Not Yet*, 170).

The terms "new creation," "kingdom," and "eternal life" are, for Paul, undoubtedly new age concepts in the sense that they signify the redemptive presence and activity of God, which effect transformation of the present evil age. In this regard, the fact that Paul does not use the term "new age" is unproblematic. However, the lack of reference to "new age" does make problematic the assumption that an explicitly two-age temporal structure framed Paul's interpretation of Christ's resurrection. Since Paul speaks of the present age, if he were wedded to an inherited two-age framework, why would he avoid using the other term from that framework—the "new age" or "the age to come." Nevertheless, the standard view, particularly among apocalyptic interpreters of Paul, is that the apostle adapted the Jewish two-age temporal architecture, achieving a "Christological adaptation of Jewish apocalyptic eschatology."[7]

The effect of this widespread opinion is that Paul is understood as fitting Christ into his inherited framework. This viewpoint effectively sees Paul prioritizing that framework—essentially incorporating Christ into a structure that, though modified, continues to shape the apostle's understanding of Christ: Christ's resurrection inaugurates (rather than brings in fully) the new age. Paul, it is proposed, thought that believers live partially in the new age and partially in the old by virtue of their faith in Christ.

The perhaps unintended consequence of this view is that Paul is seen to regard the new age as God's salvific goal, with Christ as the means by which that goal is achieved. Now, as a consequence of Christ's resurrection, the goal of the new age is here in part, though it must contend with the ongoing old age. However, when Christ returns and believers are raised, all will be as it should be: the old age will finally be obliterated and the new age achieved in its fullness.

To the contrary, my reading of the evidence sees that Paul regarded not the new age but life in and with Christ as God's goal for humanity. Paul connects certain concepts with that life (those that have been proposed as his language for "new age") but makes clear

7. De Boer, *Galatians*, 34.

that *new creation, kingdom, and eternal life are the consequences and conditions of life with Christ*. Paul's overriding focus is on Christ; when he associates new age concepts with Christ, Christ remains the focus. This calls into question the opinion that the apostle fits Christ's resurrection into his inherited two-age framework, and so also the basis for the ubiquitous overlap of ages (already–not yet) hypothesis.

New Creation

Though the interpretative tradition's liberal use of the phrase "new creation" might lead one to think it was Paul's definition of God's salvific goal, in fact the phrase occurs only twice. We note also that it is anarthrous, which should caution an easy identification of new creation with "the new age." My reading of Paul's sparse use of "new creation" is that Christ, not καινὴ κτίσις (new creation), is the focus.

Galatians 6:14–15

In Galatians 6:14–15, Paul juxtaposes "new creation" with the "world." Whatever "world" signifies, at the least it denotes an aspect of, if not the equivalent of, the present evil age. Paul claims that the world, which includes distinctions between circumcision and uncircumcision, is crucified to him and he to it. The world remains, but not for Paul himself (and himself as a paradigm for others). Liberation from the world comes through the cross of Christ.[8] Christ's crucifixion creates the possibility of καινὴ κτίσις.

Paul's claim of "cosmic crucifixion"[9] in 6:14 stands in the face of his many interpreters who maintain that he thinks in terms of the overlap of the ages. As Andrew Boakye rightly puts it, "To Paul (representative of all believers here) the old world is no more."[10]

8. De Boer rightly opines that the construction with the masculine relative pronoun most likely refers not to Christ but to the cross (*Galatians*, 401).
9. I owe this phrase to Hubbard, *New Creation*, 131.
10. Boakye, *Death and Life*, 202. Cf. Frank Matera: "Paul has died to the present age, and the present age no longer has a claim upon him" (*Galatians*, 226).

Interpretation that equates "the world" here with "the present evil age," while maintaining that Paul thought in terms of the overlap of the ages, misses this.[11]

The single occurrence of new creation in Galatians, particularly in comparison to the letter's many references to corporate and individual union with Christ,[12] indicates that Paul does not find the concept of new creation the most descriptive of his experience and understanding. Not only is Christ's crucifixion the *foundation* of new creation,[13] but Paul strongly emphasizes union with Christ—not new creation—as the result of Christ's crucifixion.

2 Corinthians 5:17

In 2 Corinthians 5:17, Paul writes that being "in Christ" is "new creation." Paul couples his claim that "if anyone is in Christ, new creation" with the statement "the old things have gone away, behold, new things have come" (2 Cor. 5:17, my translation). This remarkable statement contrasts not two ages but old things and Christ (in whom is new creation and, so, new things). It is unlikely that τὰ ἀρχαῖα ("old things") signifies the present age.[14] Further, Paul does not repeat the phrase καινὴ κτίσις but instead uses the anarthrous adjective καινά to describe what has replaced τὰ ἀρχαῖα. Presumably "new things" refers to what Paul describes in the surrounding verses: the significance of Christ's death and resurrection. The result

11. De Boer walks a fine line: cosmos here is "the world of the law" (*Galatians*, 401). Paul has suffered the loss of that world (402). This can be heard as signifying world as worldview rather than an apocalyptic world/age. Yet shortly after this de Boer implicitly equates the world that was crucified to Paul with the present evil age (402). "The new creation to which Paul refers is thus the opposite of 'the present evil age.' . . . The coming of the new creation . . . signifies the invasion of 'the present evil age'" (402).

12. Teresa Morgan lists the following occurrences of "in Christ": Gal. 1:22; 2:4, 17; 3:14, 26, 28; 5:6, 10 (*Being "in Christ" in the Letters of Paul*, 303). In addition, passages such as 2:20; 4:6, 19; 5:24; 6:14, along with Paul's statement that God's Son was revealed in him (1:16), indicate the centrality of the idea of union with Christ in Galatians.

13. Dunn opines that new creation is not new age "precisely because the former starts with the cross" (*Theology of Paul*, 412).

14. Elsewhere Paul does not claim that the present age has ended, whereas he says that "the old things" have. (In Gal. 1:4 Paul asserts that Christ has liberated believers out of the present evil age, not that that age has been extinguished; Gal. 6:14 states that believers are dead to the world—the world itself is not destroyed.)

of Christ dying and being raised is that people might no longer live for themselves but for Christ (5:15); through Christ, God reconciles the world to Godself (5:19); God made Christ to be sin in order that believers might become God's righteousness in Christ (5:21). That is, "new things" have to do with the life that comes from Christ and the resulting life for and in Christ. The position of καινά in parallel to καινὴ κτίσις shapes the meaning of new creation: the work of Christ entailed in the phrase "new things" determines the meaning of new creation. This interpretation is made obvious by Paul's presentation of new creation as *in Christ*.

The new age concept of καινὴ κτίσις is defined and embraced by Christ. New creation is sourced in and defined by the person of the exalted Christ—a being who includes others in himself—in essence an alternative environment that shapes the new humanity and that the new humanity inhabits. To be clear, new creation signals more than an anthropological concept—a new humanity that exists in the present evil age.[15] It is a new humanity that exists *in Christ*.

Kingdom

Paul uses the kingdom of God as warrant for his reframing of the ethical focus of his Roman audience.[16] What people eat or imbibe is not what matters (Rom. 14:17). Rather, righteousness and peace and joy in the Holy Spirit are what God's reign is about.[17] Ernst Käsemann rightly notes regarding this verse that the kingdom is present because Christ is Lord (though with his characteristic concern to emphasize what he sees as Paul's eschatological reserve, Käsemann adds that the kingdom will be consummated at the telos).[18] Paul underscores Christ's lordship in the preceding verses. In Romans 14:5–11, the

15. *Pace* Hubbard, *New Creation*.

16. It is not necessary for the purposes of this study to discuss issues involved in Paul's mention of the kingdom as both present and future. The standard reading is that Rom. 14:17 and 1 Cor. 4:20 refer to the kingdom as present, while the kingdom is future in 1 Cor. 6:9–10; 15:24, 50; and Gal. 5:21.

17. For a helpful proposal of the concrete issues concerning eating and drinking reflected in this passage, see Shogren, "Is the Kingdom of God about Eating and Drinking or Isn't It?"

18. Käsemann, *Romans*, 377.

word κύριος ("lord") appears repeatedly, along with the strong statement that Christ has lordship over the dead and the living (14:9). The corollary of Christ's present lordship is the presence of the kingdom. Yet it is Christ and his lordship that are plainly of uppermost importance to Paul. The kingdom is the result of Christ's lordship, and Paul focuses on that lordship rather than on the kingdom.

Paul claims to know the nature of the kingdom and whether people are acting in accordance with it. He asserts that the kingdom of God is (manifest) in power (1 Cor. 4:20).[19] That Paul refers to God's reign here is most likely because he is countering the belief of some Corinthians that they are already reigning (4:8). Paul contrasts the expectations and conditions of these Corinthians with those of his team who are "fools for the sake of Christ" (4:10). He asks the Corinthians to imitate him (4:16), whose ways are in Christ (4:17). The kingdom that Paul knows demands sacrifice, and its power is God's—a power that Paul earlier reminded his hearers they witnessed while he was weak, fearful, and trembling (2:3–5). The character of the kingdom reflects not the age of bliss hoped for in Jewish thought but the character of Christ: the power of God in weakness and sacrifice.[20]

Paul uses hope for inheritance of the kingdom of God as a spur for the Corinthians to act in accordance with the righteousness they have been given. In 1 Corinthians 6:11, the apostle states that the Corinthians have been made righteous in the name of Christ. He warns that the ἄδικοι ("unrighteous, wrongdoers") will not inherit God's kingdom (6:9). It is those who have been made righteous who will inherit the kingdom. It is not necessary for purposes of this investigation to discuss whether ἄδικοι refers to those who are within the church, yet act unrighteously, or to those outside the church.[21]

---

19. Karl Paul Donfried suggests that here "power" refers to the deeds of power displayed in Paul's mission ("Kingdom of God in Paul").

20. Cf. Gordon D. Fee: "Paul . . . lived in the kinds of weaknesses that characterized his Lord" (*Corinthians*, 192).

21. First Corinthians 6:11 would suggest that ἄδικοι refers to those outside the church—Paul writes that they *were* people who did unrighteous things and have been washed and sanctified and made righteous.

What is relevant is to notice that inheritance of the kingdom of God depends on being made righteous in the name of Jesus Christ and in God's spirit (6:11). The repetition of the word "inherit" communicates that the kingdom is something the Corinthians can straightforwardly expect if they act according to the righteousness they have received. Jesus Christ and God's spirit are foundational to the righteousness that allows believers to inherit the kingdom. Paul presents inheritance of the kingdom as entirely dependent on the transformation to righteousness that comes in the name of Christ and in the spirit. The kingdom does not transform; it is Christ and the spirit who transform humanity, with the kingdom as the result.

Paul speaks of the telos when Christ hands over the kingdom to God—a kingdom that presumably consists of those who are raised and whose transformation confirms that every rule and authority and power hostile to resurrection life is destroyed. The kingdom, however, is not the focus, nor is it presented as the goal. The focus is Christ, as Paul writes in 1 Corinthians 15:22: "All will be made alive in Christ [not in the kingdom]." The goal is God being all in all (15:28), with Christ, who subjects himself to God, as part of that "all-ness."

Paul emphasizes ("I say this") that only what is imperishable can inherit the (imperishable) kingdom of God,[22] here affirming what he has just said: believers will bear the image of the man from heaven (1 Cor. 15:49). The man from heaven is "the last Adam, a life-making spirit" (15:45)[23]—that is, Jesus Christ. Bodies are made spiritual and capable of life in an imperishable kingdom because of Christ, and, moreover, the nature of their life in the kingdom is to bear Christ's image (15:49). Imperishability is the consequence of Christ, the life-giving spirit, and allows for correspondence to Christ, the man of heaven. This hope defines the nature of the kingdom.[24]

---

22. The parallelism in this verse, controlled by the word "inherit," suggests that Paul means that the kingdom itself is imperishable.

23. Hart's translation (New Testament).

24. Richard B. Hays decides that, since the best manuscripts have "let us bear the image of the man from heaven," Paul is here exhorting "his readers to look to the coming one, Jesus Christ, as the source and hope of transformation" (First Corinthians, 274).

In Galatians 5:21, Paul again speaks of inheriting God's kingdom. Those who inherit it are those who walk by the spirit and so do not gratify the desires of the flesh (5:16). By belonging to Christ Jesus, it is possible not to gratify the desires of the flesh, for through that belonging the flesh with its desires and passions is crucified (5:24). The way to inherit the kingdom, then, is by belonging to Christ Jesus.

When he was with the Thessalonians, Paul preached the gospel of God (1 Thess. 2:8, 9), which included the news that God's Son was raised from the dead and would come from heaven to save believers from the coming wrath (1:10). It also included exhortation to walk in a manner worthy of God (2:12). In this letter, which follows up on his evangelistic visit, Paul clarifies that God is the one who calls those who accept the good news into God's kingdom and glory (2:12). God's kingdom entails God's glory. That is, in God's kingdom is the presence of God (God's glory).[25] The focus here is not on the kingdom but on God: God's reign manifests God's glory. Elsewhere in the letter, Paul makes evident his belief that God's Son is currently with God and is the one who will, by saving believers from the coming wrath, make possible their entry into God's kingdom (1:10; 5:9). That is, Christ is an intrinsic part of God's kingdom, and he is also critical to entry into God's kingdom and God's glory. Christ's coming, though not described as such, is surely understood by Paul as the event that will manifest God's kingdom and glory. And the ultimate goal of that coming is that believers will be with the Lord always (4:17; 5:10). The reign of God makes possible life with Christ in God's glory.

Noticing that Paul's references to "new creation" and "kingdom of God" focus not on these new age concepts but rather on Christ and, furthermore, that these concepts are shaped by Paul's understanding of Christ should raise doubts about the claim that Paul organized his understanding of Christ's death, resurrection, and exaltation within a two-age framework, resulting in a conception

25. Weima's comment that God's kingdom and glory are aligned does not go far enough (1–2 Thessalonians, 158).

of the overlapping of the ages for believers. The evidence, rather, strongly suggests that Paul conceived of the present aeon and the exalted Christ as two mutually exclusive realities.

With his crucifixion, resurrection, and exaltation, Christ, through the spirit, offers union with his exalted self. The life of the exalted Christ, as we shall see in chapter 5, includes his incarnation. Prior to his resurrection and exaltation, the incarnated Christ engages with the present aeon. Subsequent to his resurrection and exaltation, however, Christ does not. As we will see, Paul understands Christ's faithfulness, suffering, and dying (his incarnation) to exist simultaneously with his resurrection and exaltation. This creates a reality—*the* reality—that reveals the poverty, impotence, and finitude of the present age and allows for life sustained and shaped by Christ alone. The crucified, risen, and exalted Christ does not engage with the present age but lives liberated from it. Presumably this is the necessary basis of Christ's ability to liberate humanity from the present evil age (Gal. 1:4).

Consequently, Paul portrays believers as living entirely in Christ. Those united with Christ are so entirely united with him that Paul uses the analogy of becoming one body as in marriage: "Anyone united to the Lord becomes one spirit with him" (1 Cor. 6:17). In 2 Corinthians 5:17, Paul states that "if anyone is in Christ, new creation; the old has gone away, behold new things have come" (my translation). Paul positions Christ and those united with Christ in a reality liberated and apart from the present age.[26] Consequently, believers can live as of the day (1 Thess. 5:5, 8) and in the day (Rom. 13:13) and "as if" the passing away of this world had occurred (1 Cor. 7:29–31). Paul exhorts the Corinthian deniers to recognize that they will be raised because of their solidarity with Christ's resurrection (1 Cor. 15; see also chap. 6 below).

Paul does not describe believers as partially in Christ and partially in the present evil age. They are entirely in Christ. (It may need to be pointed out that union with Christ is not the same as conformity

26. Above, we saw reasons to doubt that "the old" in 2 Cor. 5:17 references the present age. Paul is not claiming a relationship between Christ and the present age, even one of juxtaposition.

to Christ. Believers become like Christ through an ongoing process that can only take place by recognizing their union [Phil. 3:8–11]. That is, Paul does not present union with Christ as incomplete, though conformity with Christ may be [Gal. 4:19].) Importantly, it is Christ himself and not the new age that Paul conceives of as God's redemptive goal. Christ dominates the apostle's thinking—a being whose resurrection and exaltation Paul regards as offering a space and a time separate from that of the present evil age.

Eternal Life Is Christ and Believers' Time

Paul's references to ζωὴ αἰώνιος (typically translated as "eternal life"), though few and concentrated almost exclusively in Romans,[27] designate the temporality of God's solution to the problem of the present evil age. The phrase describes a kind of life, one that is qualified by the adjective αἰώνιος. As Ilaria Ramelli and David Bentley Hart correctly posit, the adjective αἰώνιος references the new age.[28] This phrase speaks of life having to do with an age—what Jamie P. Davies aptly calls "*aionial*" life.[29]

With aeon as the adjective's semantic root, the phrase emphasizes temporality. The noun "life" is itself a temporal category, if not a metonym for time.[30] Ζωὴ αἰώνιος is God's gift "in Christ Jesus" (Rom. 6:23); ζωὴ αἰώνιος is "in Christ" because it is Christ's temporality—the kind of time God and the exalted Christ live. This understanding is confirmed by Paul's use of the phrase in Romans 2:7, where it is positioned as equivalent to immortality—a kind of

27. The phrase occurs four time in Romans and once in Galatians.
28. Ramelli notes that αἰώνιος "bears the meaning 'eternal' only when it refers to God" (*Christian Doctrine of* Apokatastasis, 28). She opines that in Paul ζωὴ αἰώνιος is most often "connected with life in the next world" (31). Hart's translation echoes Ramelli's observations; he translates ζωὴ αἰώνιος as "life of the Age" (*New Testament*, esp. 537–43). Cf. N. T. Wright, who throughout his New Testament translation supplies "age to come" for ζωὴ αἰώνιος (*Kingdom New Testament*).
29. J. Davies, "Why Paul Doesn't Mention the 'Age to Come,'" 205.
30. Cf. Mauro Belcastro, who, in the course of arguing that people make their own time, writes, "I am my temporality" ("Advent of the Different," 487). Also Placher, who writes that life is "an obviously temporal category, for living things have properties that can exist only temporally" (*Narratives of a Vulnerable God*, 31).

time only divinity lives. Ζωὴ αἰώνιος is from the spirit (Gal. 6:8), which itself is available "in Christ Jesus" (3:14). "Aionial" life (ζωὴ αἰώνιος) is, then, from Christ and of Christ. It is Christ's kind of life, Christ's kind of time.

We might call this kind of time "life-time," for ζωὴ αἰώνιος is the kind of time that is apart from death and sin (Rom. 5:21). It is only by being freed from sin (which effectively means liberation from the old aeon) that the telos of ζωὴ αἰώνιος is available (6:22). Jesus Christ is the conduit for this alternative temporality (5:21).

Union with Christ allows believers to live to God since Christ himself does (Rom. 6:10–11). This is a kind of life that is at once a kind of time. Since Christ's resurrection, the power of death no longer lords it over him (6:9). Christ lives life-time—time fashioned by its unstoppable ongoingness. Union with Christ offers the same kind of time to believers. By living Christ's time, the death of believers' bodies is a moment of metamorphosis (more on this later). The time of believers is not shaped by an ending but by the fact that their mortal bodies will be transformed so as to allow for a fuller sharing in Christ by having bodies like his glorious body (Phil. 3:21). The time people live once they are united with Christ is life-time—time freed from death's power to stop time. This temporality is entirely different from the time of the present evil age, which I term "death-time."[31] In distinction from the time of this age, the temporality of those united with Christ is Christ's type of time—endless.[32]

Summary

Paul is not much interested in new age concepts except as they help him to convey the magnitude of God's transformation of existence

---

31. The fact that Paul does not mention gehenna or hell suggests that he does not think there is a kind of time that continues after physical death for those apart from Christ. (The lack of reference to hell might also be understood to indicate that Paul meant what he said in Rom. 5:18 that Christ's act of righteousness leads to righteousness of life for all. That is, at the telos no one is excluded from "aionial" life.)

32. What it means for Christ's temporality when Christ submits himself to God at the eschaton (1 Cor. 15:28), Paul does not say. Presumably, however, God's endless time will be the temporality of all that is in God.

by means of Christ. Paul's attention is on Christ and the wonders attending to union with him enabled by the spirit. The apostle's conception of the temporality lived by the faithful is shaped not by a two-age framework but by Christ.[33]

It must further be emphasized that it does not benefit our understanding of Paul to assume that he regards life with Christ as equivalent to living in the new age. For instance, when de Boer writes that "Paul's Christological adaptation of Jewish apocalyptic eschatology thus contains the well-known tension between an 'already' . . . and 'a still more,'"[34] his expression can readily lead to an identification of Christ with the new age.[35] There is, however, nothing in Paul that warrants this. Moreover, it is problematic to ignore the problem of how the concept of union with God's Messiah in any way accords with Jewish expectation for the age to come. This glaring problem has not been faced head-on by those who hold both that the apostle functioned with a modified two-age Jewish apocalyptic framework and that he conceived of participation in Christ. A handful of scholars do address this matter, but they have failed to convince.[36]

33. See my article "Christ Doesn't Fit."

34. De Boer, *Galatians*, 34.

35. Cf. Furnish, who is likewise convinced that Paul operates with the framework of the present age and the age to come and who claims that "the two ages 'meet,' as it were, in him through whom God is even in the present reconciling the world unto himself." Furnish continues: "The man 'in Christ' is 'a new creation.'" This implies that new creation is equivalent to the new age and that being "in Christ" is being in the new age (*Theology and Ethics*, 126).

36. According to Albert Schweitzer, Jewish eschatology conceived "of the preordained union of those who are elect to the Messianic Kingdom with one another and with the Messiah" (*Mysticism*, 101). Matthew V. Novenson rightly observes that it "has been well documented since, [that] substantiating this theory from the sources presents serious problems" (*Christ among the Messiahs*, 122).

N. T. Wright appeals to the idea of kingship in ancient Israel, that "the king and the people are bound together" (*Climax of the Covenant*, 46). Moreover, the way Paul made sense of Christ's resurrection in light of his Pharisaic expectations contributed to Paul's participation-in-Christ concept. Paul the Pharisee believed that resurrection would happen to all of Israel at the end. When he came to believe that it had happened to Jesus, "it meant at once that *Israel's God had done for Jesus what it had been supposed he would do for Israel*. . . . He was, in effect, Israel in Person. And it was precisely *as Messiah* that he therefore represented his people" (*Paul and the Faithfulness of God*, 827–28 [italics original]). Wright's assertion is, however, based on only a small slice of Jewish scripture (Samuel–Kings), a problem to which he himself alludes: "While these texts are not sufficient in and of themselves to suggest that such language was familiar in the first century, it does a least suggest a matrix of ideas out of which a fresh incorporative usage could grow, namely, that of the king representing the people" (*Climax of the Covenant*, 47).

The fact must be acknowledged that the apostle speaks not about the old age and the new but rather about the present evil age and Christ. We do not find evidence that Paul regarded Christ as a stand-in for the expected new age of Jewish apocalyptic. Paul understands Christ as an actual *being* in whom people may live. Unlike the new age, the exalted Christ loves, intercedes, will come again, and so on. Christ, for Paul, is presently active and is expected to participate in God-directed events at Christ's parousia. This bears little resemblance to the Jewish apocalyptic idea of the new age. Paul asserts not that believers live in a new age but that they are joined to Jesus Messiah.

Taking seriously these facts means both that our understanding of Paul's predominant union-with-Christ concept should be liberated from a two-age framework and that we should resist assuming that Paul placed Christ in the spot previously held by the new age. Rather, we must understand union with Christ as its own idea and certainly not another way of talking about the new age. This should not lead us to think, however, that Paul disregarded the matter of time by focusing on life with the exalted Christ rather than life in the new age. Quite the opposite is the case, as we shall see.

4

Christis Lives Time

———

Union with Christ is union with Christ's time. Believers have access to the exalted Christ's own temporality by virtue of their life in Christ. I have introduced the proposal that Paul understood there to be two types of time: death-time and life-time. It must be emphasized that death-time and life-time are not alternative appellations for the old and new ages. Rather, by speaking of death-time and life-time, I recast Paul's temporal thought outside the two-age framework, a framework that, as I have demonstrated, does not rest on adequate evidence.

What Is Time?

In the introduction, I offered some thoughts on how we commonly think about time, and I described some of the more influential theological and philosophical theories of time (and eternity). Here I articulate how I am using the concept of time in regard to investigating Paul's understanding of the temporality of those in union with the ascended Christ. The apostle, of course, does not ruminate on the nature of time. I must then necessarily start from the outside, as it were, with my own understanding of time. I present what I think is a commonplace understanding.

Time is essentially related to change; we cannot recognize change without time, nor time without change. This understanding was articulated long ago by Aristotle. He famously states at the beginning of *Physics* that "time cannot be disconnected from change."[1] Aristotle took this to be a commonsense understanding of time.

In addition to understanding time as essentially related to change, I understand it as intrinsically related to motion. This too is an ancient idea.[2] Motion is necessary for change, and change is necessary for the recognition of motion. Aristotle, of course, demurred from identifying time and motion: "Hence time is not movement, but only movement in so far as it admits of enumeration. A proof of this: we discriminate the more or the less by number, but more or less movement by time. Time then is a kind of number."[3] I, however, understand time to be more than counted motion. Time and motion are intrinsically related.[4]

The essential relatedness of time and motion account for the reality and manifestation of action, event, and change. Change happens because of actions, which produce events. Action, event, and change cannot happen without motion. Or to say the same thing another way: action, event, and change cannot happen without time. Whether motion is evident materially or in human thought alone, for time to be manifest there must be movement from one action, event, and change to another.

Temporal motion is manifest in pastness, presentness, and futurity. The tenses allow for action, event, and change. Even those who, like McTaggart, argue against the reality of time recognize the

---

1. Aristotle, *Physics* 4.11, 218b.
2. For examples of ancient philosophers who thought that time and motion were essentially connected, see Clark, "Theory of Time in Plotinus."
3. Aristotle, *Physics* 4.11.
4. Aristotle's reason for not identifying time and motion is that, whereas time is everywhere, motion is limited to the thing that is moving and its location (*Physics* 4.10). I see no reason that motion needs to be limited to things. Motion can occur in our minds, for instance; and it is possible to imagine motion in empty space. Time may be everywhere, as Aristotle conjectured, but so may be motion.

intrinsic connection between time, event, and change.[5] McTaggart's philosophical tour de force, which intends to awaken people to the erroneousness of commonplace perception, misses the wonder of the human ability both to synchronize past and future with the present and to distinguish between them. Indeed, as McTaggart notes, an event is future and will be present and past,[6] but this does not require, as he argues, that we understand the tenses (and so time) to be unreal. It rather says something about the motion of time and human capacity to comprehend that motion.

Time with its tenses reveals that an action, and so an event, has occurred. Without time, action or change is not possible. Action/event brings or seeks to bring change in various kinds of circumstances (whether internal or external, personal or social), and such change can only be effected in tenses. That is, change is only reckoned, made visible, or made possible if there is tensed time. Time is inextricable from action, event, and change. Tenses allow us to recognize and conceptually organize change—the movement from what was to what is to what will be.

One manifestation of the constant of time's being tied to action, event, and change is that humans can experience (perhaps typically do experience) the tenses of past, present, and future simultaneously, rather than sequentially. As quoted above, Augustine articulates this experience: "There are three times, a present of past things, a present of present things, and a present of future things. Some such different times do exist in the mind, but nowhere else that I can see. The present of past things is the memory; the present of present things is direct perception; and the present of future things is expectation."[7]

Wisdom teachers who advocate living in the present acknowledge this common experience and how challenging it is to do anything

5. McTaggart contends against time's existence by seeking to demonstrate that even the relations of past, present, and future (his A series) do not indicate change. Every event, like every moment, is past, present, and future. McTaggart concludes that nothing really is in time, for nothing really changes ("Time"). Despite my disagreement with McTaggart, I draw him in here because of our agreement in identifying change and time.

6. McTaggart, *Nature of Existence*, 20 (para. 329).

7. Augustine, *Confessions* 11.20.

in the present other than think about the past and plan for the future. Nevertheless, despite the past and future intruding on the present in personal experience, the sane person recognizes just that—that these are events from the past or events hoped for in the future.

Another manifestation of time's constant is that, outside of our personal experience, most humans organize our place in events sequentially. When we think about ourselves with a degree of objectivity, we keep the tenses separate: there is a past to our personal lives, our family's life, our culture's life, and so on; just so, there is a present and a future. This historical/chronological thinking about time conceives of the tenses as separate, sequential, and real.

In either manifestation, temporal motion is inextricably connected to action, event, and change. And the tenses are the way time is both constructed and conceived. Time with its motion requires tenses and is conceived of on the basis of the tenses. I submit that Paul worked with this commonplace understanding of time.

In addition, I understand time as intrinsically connected to life. Without life, there is no time. Life, understood as the fact and reality of existence entailing growth, loss, and change, is necessarily temporal. Without time, life with its events and change is not comprehensible. Without life, time has nothing to work with. Life and time are essential partners. I put forward that Paul would agree that to speak of life is to speak of time, and vice versa.

The Exalted Christ, Like God, Is a Temporal Being

Paul describes the exalted Christ living with God. The apostle says that Christ is at God's right hand (Rom. 8:34; also Col. 3:1), that God has highly exalted Christ (Phil. 2:9), and that Christ is currently in heaven (Phil. 3:20; 1 Thess. 1:10).[8] Since the ascended Christ

---

8. Though our question does not concern Paul's understanding of the location of God and Christ, it should be noted that Paul's conception that Christ and God are in heaven does not mean that he thinks they live in a location apart from humanity. The apostle regularly speaks of God, Christ, and their spirit as present in the midst of human life.

lives with God, presumably Paul conceived of Christ living God's temporality.

Though Paul describes God as having eternal power (Rom. 1:20), nowhere does the apostle say that God lives in, or is, eternity. Unlike Isaiah, Paul does not say that God "inhabits eternity" (Isa. 57:15). Nor does Paul state, as does Augustine, "Domine, cum tua sit aeternitas"[9] (You, God, *are* eternity).[10] It is important to recognize what Paul does *not* say in order to guard against simply assuming that he shared the classical Christian understanding of God and eternity; that understanding being that God lives eternity, which is non-time, non-change—a now containing all moments at once. Augustine, for instance, defined eternity as a "never-ending present."[11] For the great theologian, to live eternity means that all past time and all future time is at once.[12] This is, in effect, non-time. Ephraim Radner rightly describes patristic exegesis as understanding God's reality to be "non-temporal."[13]

Though Paul often expresses his desire for God to be blessed for ever and ever,[14] exhibiting his conviction about God's endless duration, the nature of God's duration is not eternal timelessness and non-change. Rather, Paul's letters indicate that he understood the eternal God to live a temporal existence in which there is past, present, and future, though for God these tenses are nonsequential. God knows all events or moments, whether they are past or future. Paul's statement that God passed over formerly committed sins (Rom. 3:25) indicates such an understanding of God's temporality: though the sins are in the past, God can pass over them. Likewise, Paul's statement in Romans 1:2 that God announced the gospel in advance to

9. Augustine, *Confessions* 11.1.1 (ed. O'Donnell).

10. Translated by Jenson, *Systematic Theology*, 29 (italics original).

11. Augustine, *Confessions* 11.13.

12. Augustine, *Confessions* 11.13.

13. Radner, *Time and the Word*, 57.

14. Paul uses the phrases εἰς τοὺς αἰῶνας, εἰς τὸν αἰῶνα, or εἰς τοὺς αἰῶνας τῶν αἰώνων. Apart from 2 Cor. 9:9, these phrases occur in doxologies. As a human glorifying (Rom. 11:36; 16:27; Gal. 1:5; Phil. 4:20) or blessing (Rom. 1:25; 9:5; 2 Cor. 11:31) God or Christ, Paul prays that such glory and blessing would continue forever. The apostle endorses endless (forever) human devotion to God. In the other occurrence of the phrase (2 Cor. 9:9), Paul quotes Ps. 111:3: "His righteousness endures forever."

his prophets in the holy writings indicates that the apostle did not conceive of God living tenses sequentially as do humans.[15]

Paul's notion of God's capacity to know all time at once does not, however, entail that Paul understood God to live a static existence—at least in relation to God's creation.[16] Does this mean that the apostle's understanding of the eternal God is akin to Oscar Cullmann's understanding of eternity as infinite duration?[17] The answer must be "no." In regard to Paul, what Cullmann's understanding misses is that the apostle thinks there is more than a quantitative distinction between the temporalities of God and humanity. The apostle understands there to be a primarily qualitative distinction: God lives a type of time that is life-time, not only because it does not end but, intrinsically related to its infinity, because there is in God's time only life. Life in life (life-time) has a completely different quality than life in death (death-time). I will describe this difference in the context of discussing Paul's two types of time.

There are, of course, other contemporary options for understanding God's eternity.[18] In my view, none comes as close to Paul as does Barth in *Church Dogmatics*. I mention Barth not in order to detail the similarities and differences between his and Paul's understanding of time—a book of its own, which I am far from qualified to write. Rather, I mention Barth to note that this great biblical theologian, who was deeply influenced by Paul, sees that God's eternity is temporal.[19] Barth's famous manifesto that "the theological concept of eternity must be set free from the Babylonian captivity

15. See my "Promise and Purpose," 13–14.

16. It must be noted that here we are speaking of what we can know about how Paul conceived of God's temporality only in relation to creation, not in Godself. As the apostle's citing of Job 41:3 in Rom. 11:34 indicates, Paul claims no information about the being of God *in se*. Paul considers God's temporality only *ad extra*, in regard to God's relation to God's creation.

17. Cullmann writes, "In the New Testament field it is not time and eternity that stand opposed, but limited time and unlimited, endless time" (*Christ and Time*, 46).

18. See Hunsinger for a brief summary, for instance, of the processional view of eternity in which "eternity, like time, is a flowing now, a *nunc fluens*, that not only moves along with time but also requires time for its own self-actualization" ("*Mysterium Trinitatis*," 188).

19. Of course, Barth's *Church Dogmatics* moves beyond the dramatic presentation of the absolute distinction between time and eternity that frames his famous Romans commentary.

of an abstract opposite to the concept of time"[20] results in his claim that God "is supremely temporal."[21]

Barth's manifesto and its enactment have their wise critics, in particular Robert Jenson, who accuses Barth of circumlocution.[22] Jenson states that in Barth we continue to find the "grin of the timeless cat."[23] Nevertheless, there is much that is Pauline in Barth's understanding of the eternal God's temporality. Whereas Cullmann proves a poor reader of Paul by missing the qualitative distinction between God's time and ours, Barth emphasizes the qualitative distinctiveness, strongly echoing Paul's thought. George Hunsinger writes about Barth on God's time: "In himself as pure eternity, God really has 'time,' that is, his own special mode of temporality."[24] This could just as easily be said of Paul's understanding of God's (and Christ's) time.

Both Barth and Paul understand God's life and God's time to be inextricable. Barth regards the biblical God as the living God: "God's being is *life*";[25] "life [is] the fundamental element in the divine being."[26] Likewise, Paul sees the time of God as ongoing and creative life—life more powerful than any forces of non-life. As we will see, Paul understands God to be active, event-creating, and change-creating. We might compare this to Barth's understanding of God's eternity: "Eternity is really beginning, really middle, and really end because it is really the living God. There really is in it, then, direction, and a direction which is irreversible."[27]

There are, however, two important differences to mention between Paul and Barth regarding God's time. Whereas Barth focuses on God's temporality, both between God and those living in created

20. Barth, *Church Dogmatics* II/1, 611.
21. Barth, *Church Dogmatics* III/2, 437.
22. Jenson, *Systematic Theology*, 35.
23. Jenson, *God after God*, 154. Cf. R. T. Mullins, who writes of the "Barthian Blunder," which rejects divine timelessness while affirming a kind of divine eternality that is indistinguishable from divine timelessness (*End of the Timeless God*, xvii).
24. Hunsinger, "*Mysterium Trinitatis*," 201.
25. Barth, *Church Dogmatics* II/1, 263 (italics original).
26. Barth, *Church Dogmatics* II/1, 322.
27. Barth, *Church Dogmatics* II/1, 639.

time and within Godself, Paul's focus is entirely on the former. Paul's conception of God's temporality is based on how God's time impacts creation. While Paul might say that the events God initiates in God's creation are consistent with God's life *in se*, Paul does not ruminate on God's inner life, as does Barth. Paul witnesses only to God's activity in creation's life and consequently to the manifestation of God's temporality in human time.

Furthermore, Barth's description of God's life and time in trinitarian terms[28] lacks a Pauline tone.[29] Though Paul has a trinitarian understanding, as is evident in his profoundly and fundamentally relational presentation of God the Father, Christ the Son, and the spirit of God and Christ,[30] and while the apostle mentions God, Christ, and the spirit when describing God's actions (that is, manifestations of God's temporality), the apostle does not explain God's temporality on the basis of the Trinity. This is so for the simple reason that Paul does not attempt to see into the life of God *in se*. While perhaps, if asked, the apostle would agree with one of his greatest interpreters that the time of the incarnated Christ reveals the nature of God's interior temporal life, this is not something I read Paul contemplating.

On the basis of the understanding of time described above, Paul thinks that God lives time. Paul understands God's temporality as eventful; in God's temporality things change—at least between God and God's creation. The most significant change Paul describes is creation's salvation by means of God's action of sending Christ. Along with this, the consequent events of the crucifixion and resurrection produce change in the relationship of God to creation and creation to God. These divine actions and events result in reconciliation (Rom. 5:10) and justification (5:16, 18). God sending Jesus Christ, God raising Jesus Christ, God highly exalting Christ,

28. See Hunsinger, "*Mysterium Trinitatis*"; also Langdon, *God the Eternal Contemporary*, 21.
29. *Pace* J. Davies, who finds that the "trinitarian formulation of the question of time and eternity" in Barth does resonate with Paul (*Apocalyptic Paul*, 129).
30. See especially W. Hill, *Paul and the Trinity*.

and God sending Christ's spirit into believers' hearts (Gal. 4:6) are temporal events both for humanity and for God. They are actions and events that produce change in the relationship between God and God's creation.

God's Tenses

Paul speaks in tenses about God's activity. For instance, Paul writes that God condemned (κατέκρινεν) sin in the flesh through the sending of God's Son (Rom. 8:3). Paul writes that God sent (ἐξαπέστειλεν) God's Son (Gal. 4:4).[31] God raised Christ (ἤγειρεν; 1 Cor. 15:15). These past tenses signal divinely initiated events from the perspective of human time, yet I propose that Paul also thinks they are a true representation of God's history with creation (though, again, tenses in God's life are not confining).

That Paul thinks that God has a history with creation may be evident in his curious mention of "the fullness of time" (Gal. 4:4), as if God were watching the χρόνος for the right moment to send God's Son. The phrase conveys something other than that God and time are separate, with God watching time from a detached atemporality. The fullness of time allows for a cosmic shift for humanity from slavery to τὰ στοιχεῖα τοῦ κόσμου ("the elemental spirits of the world") to the possibility of adoption as God's children (4:3–5), a shift comparable to the temporal change from being minors to being reckoned capable of inheriting (4:1–2). God is the generator of this cosmic shift. God is also intimately connected with it. God sends God's own spirit into the hearts of God's adopted, crying "Abba! Father!" (4:6).

In the present, God tests hearts and is a witness to Paul's exemplary behavior (1 Thess. 2:4, 10). In the future, God will bring to completion the good work that God began (Phil. 1:6). God's evident activity in human time indicates a divine eventful temporality, an active temporality that produces change—at least between God and God's creation. Being God, however, God lives eventful,

---

31. Cf. Col. 2:15: on the cross God exposed (ἐδειγμάτισεν) the principalities and powers.

changeful temporality without the blinkers and boundaries of tenses as humanity experiences tenses. Paul understands God to live tenses, although not in the way that humans do, for God does not know incompleteness, as tenses in chronological time imply.[32] Paul does not conceive of God's temporality as in any way limited by its tenses. For God, the past, present, and future are one, but nevertheless they are still past, present, and future rather than a singular Now.[33] God's tenses do not function chronologically. God's past, present, and future are not sequential or discrete. The past and future are always in the present for God. It is as if God looks at God's past, present, and future from a vantage point that allows God to see all of God's time (in addition to human time) at once. This perspective does not, however, collapse God's tenses into a tenseless Now. The fact that Paul believes that the living God acts to change the circumstances between God and God's creation indicates such.

The Temporality of Christ and of Believers Is God's Time

The apostle thinks that Christ's exalted life and God's life are consonant. This consonance is evident in Paul's conviction that God acts through the exalted Christ. For instance, the apostle writes that, through Jesus, God will bring with Jesus those who have fallen asleep (1 Thess. 4:14) and that the will of God is in Christ Jesus (5:18). The consonance between God's and Christ's life includes their temporality. God's time is the ascended Christ's time, and vice versa.

We will proceed on the basis that the exalted Christ lives God's time and that union with Christ entails union with Christ's temporality. Obviously, Paul does not think either he or other believers can, like God and Christ, see the past and future simultaneously with

---

32. Paul J. Griffiths remarks that tenses imply lack, and since God can lack nothing, God cannot live tenses (*Decreation*, 72–76).

33. Cf. Barth, who writes that when we take into account the triune God, we see that "there is a before and an after. . . . without dissolving the once-for-allness" (*Church Dogmatics* II/1, 615). As mentioned earlier, I do not see the Trinity as the reason Paul's thought contains the seemingly contrary ideas that God lives tenses and also knows all events and moments at once. Paul does not give or imply a reason for his holding both ideas; he simply functions with them.

the present. Paul clearly lives his life within the limits of sequential tenses and thinks his fellow believers do as well. Yet Paul considers that for believers the human experience of time is enveloped by another temporality—what I call "life-time." The fact that humans who are united with Christ live time sequentially and that God and Christ do not is a small distinction relative to the most profound temporal similarity lived by them and believers—all live life-time.

Paul's Two Types of Time

The fundamental feature of time as I have described it—that it is inextricably tied to action, event, and change—can, according to Paul, appear either finitely or infinitely. That is, time can either end or continue forever. The difference may on the surface appear to be a difference only of quantity, of duration: one time ends and another does not. However, for Paul, limited time and unlimited time have different qualities; in effect, the only real time is the one that does not end.

Time that ends has a different quality from time that does not. Time that ends is shaped by its end; time that does not end is shaped by the abundance of ongoingness, which for Paul is the abundance of life. This is not only everlasting duration but everlasting life. Seeking to resonate with Paul, I call the former type of time "death-time" and the latter "life-time." Paul's categories for the quantitative and qualitative distinctions between the two kinds of time are "death" and "life." Paul contrasts the rule of sin in death with the rule of grace through righteousness unto ζωὴ αἰώνιος, which he understands to be apart from death and so everlasting (Rom. 5:21). Sin's activity is in a temporality of death; there is another temporality that, being made possible by Christ (the one raised from death), is life from which death is excluded.

In Romans 5:17, the apostle contrasts not only two men (Adam, the one who trespassed, and Jesus Christ) but also two reigns: the reign of death and the reigning in life of those who receive the abundance of grace and the gift of righteousness. The temporal implication here is that there is time defined by death, and there is time defined by life. The difference in these temporalities goes beyond that of duration. In time defined by death, death is the ruler as a consequence of Adam's trespass. In the other time, believers reign in life by means of Jesus Christ. That is, not only does this latter type of time not end, but believers themselves reign along with life and the giver of that life, Jesus Christ. In one type of time, the end reigns; in the other, Jesus Christ, life, and believers reign. There is flatness and finitude to time over which death rules, in effect making this temporality an illusion; there is texture and abundance in the (real) time that the ascended Christ shares with those united with him.

In Romans 6:8–11, Paul claims that Christ's death means Christ will never die again, for death no longer rules him. The life Christ lives after the unrepeatable event of his death he lives to God. This life after his death means the exalted Christ lives an existence "which is forever beyond the reach of death."[34] The temporal significance of Romans 6:8–11 is that, in Christ's incarnated life, Christ lived a type of time in which death ruled, but the event of Christ's unique death opened up another type of time—one in which death is dead. Paul claims that this is also the case for those who have died with Christ. They can reckon themselves dead to sin and alive to God in Christ Jesus. That is, both Christ and those united with him live time without death—life-time.

Paul contrasts a way of living that bears fruit for death (Rom. 7:5) with one that serves in newness—that is, the spirit (7:6).[35] In addition to Romans 7:5–6 revealing something of Paul's conception of the collusion of flesh and the law, it also indicates a temporal framework. Activity occurs either in a temporality in which death (and so the end of time) is served[36] or in a temporality where people serve in newness—that is, the spirit. Understanding πνεύματος (7:6)

---

34. Cranfield, *Romans*, 1:314.

35. Cranfield rightly follows William Sanday and Arthur C. Headlam's opinion in their Romans commentary, explaining πνεύματος (spirit) as a genitive of apposition (Cranfield, *Romans*, 1:339).

36. N. T. Wright translates Rom. 7:5 as "when we were living a mortal human life" (*Kingdom New Testament*).

to refer to God's spirit, we may understand the phrase ἐν καινότητι πνεύματος in 7:6 to be referring to "newness of life" (6:4), since for Paul the spirit is life (8:10; cf. 8:2). The past (ὅτε [when]; 7:5) was a temporality organized by death. Now (νυνί; 7:6) believers live a temporality characterized by the spirit and so by life. Paul thinks that believers have experienced two types of time: one ruled by death, from which they have been liberated, and one of life, from which death has been expelled: death-time and life-time.

Paul says something similar in Romans 8:2, where he contrasts the law of the spirit of life in Christ Jesus with the law of sin and death. The temporal implication of the distinctions between the two laws is that obedience to one occurs in a type of time that is shaped by the fact that it ends—by death. Obedience to the law of the spirit of life takes place in Christ Jesus and so in a type of time from which death is excluded. Though, as Paul will go on to say, the bodies of those in Christ Jesus are mortal (8:11), the time of their mortality is life-time—time in which death's organizing power is no more. Those in Christ Jesus will physically die, but they live.

Consequently, believers walk/act in a type of time that is both quantitatively and qualitatively different from what they were in before they were "set free" (Rom. 8:2). Whereas they lived death-time, now because of God's action in Christ, they live life-time. This is the case even though their bodies are dead because of sin (8:10). This deadness is not fatal, since their bodies are given resurrection life through God's indwelling spirit (6:4; 8:11).

The two prime options for understanding Paul's emphasis in the phrase σῶμα νεκρόν (Rom. 8:10)—"mortal bodies" either signaling that bodies die or signaling "all in us that still remains subject to death"[37]—should both be heard. For Paul speaks both about resurrection (8:11) and about putting to death the body's deeds (8:13). That is, the apostle speaks about mortal bodies becoming incorruptible and about mortal bodies being purified of sin (and so of death's influence) prior to becoming spiritual bodies. In any

---

37. Calvin, *Romans and Thessalonians*, 166.

event, both future resurrection and present actions that defeat the remains of sin can take place only in time that is structured not by death but by life.

Paul's declaration in Galatians 5:24 that those who belong to Christ Jesus have crucified the flesh with its desires is another indication that the apostle thinks that being in Christ means living life-time: time structured by life and only life. To belong to Christ Jesus is to belong to the one who "set us free from the present evil age" (1:4)—that is, to belong to the one who lives apart from the present evil age. The temporal significance of such belonging is living the time of the exalted Christ—time not organized by death. The ethical and perhaps ontological consequence of living Christ's time by virtue of belonging to him is that those who do so have crucified the flesh. Defeat of the flesh can take place only in a type of time from which death—that anti-God entity that empowers sin in the flesh (Rom. 8:2–9)—has been excluded. Paul, then, conceived of two types of time: one that is dominated by death and another that is only life, for death has no power in it. Those united with Christ live his temporality—a type of time from which death is excluded.

Living life-time with mortal bodies is not an indication of living in the overlap of the ages or in an already–not yet existence. Paul identifies sin as the reason believers' bodies die, but he claims that nevertheless their bodies are united with Christ and God's spirit (Rom. 8:9–11). The exalted Christ lives in believers, which means that though their bodies are dead, they will live (8:10–11). Those in Christ are granted the liberty of working with and living with the spirit and Christ, which means having power over the deeds of the body (presumably deeds directed by sin). Their lives, even with mortal bodies, are structured by life. They live in a type of time from which death's power has been exorcised. They live not in a mixture or overlap of two ages but in the one time of the risen and exalted Jesus Christ. This makes it possible for them, by means of the spirit, to kill the deeds of the body (8:13).

The two types of time I have explored are lived in interaction with human chronological time. Human chronological time is the venue for all humans. However, according to Paul, chronological time is environed by either death-time or life-time. The larger temporal environment of either death-time or life-time profoundly shapes existence in human chronological time. We turn now to investigating more fully Paul's conception of the nature of the exalted Christ's time: life-time.

5

The Nature of the Exalted
Christ's Time

Paul speaks of Christ's past, present, and future. There is fluidity to Christ's tenses; we will see that Christ's incarnated past coexists with the exalted Christ's present. Christ's time does not lock the tenses into sequence, nor does it lock them into dependence on each other. The past, present, and future coexist at once. Union with Christ makes possible access to Christ's present and to a significant portion both of Christ's past and of Christ's future.

Christ's Past

Christ's Prehuman Life

Paul rarely and briefly refers to the past of Christ's prehuman life, which includes Christ's instrumentality in creating all things (1 Cor. 8:6).[1] Christ's prehuman life also involves his presence in earlier moments of human time. Christ was the rock that followed behind Moses and the Israelites (10:4). Paul's reference to Christ's

---

1. Philippians 2:6 most likely also refers to Christ's life with God prior to his incarnation.

presence at creation and events in Israel's history obliquely suggests that union with Christ entails some sort of communion with these events.

Christ's Incarnated Past

The majority of Paul's references to Christ's past concern Christ's incarnated life. We shall see that Paul conceives of union with Christ as allowing for access to and even union with these events. When speaking of Christ's human life, Paul writes, among other things, that

> Christ was born from David's seed (Rom. 1:3);
> Christ became for us wisdom from God (1 Cor. 1:30);
> Christ freed us for freedom (Gal. 5:1);
> Christ was made sin for us (2 Cor. 5:21);
> Christ became poor though being rich (2 Cor. 8:9);
> Christ gave himself for our sins (Gal. 1:4);
> Christ died/was crucified (Rom. 5:6, 8; 1 Cor. 5:7; 8:11; 15:3;
>   2 Cor. 5:15; Gal. 2:21; 1 Thess. 4:14; 5:10); and
> Christ rose or was raised (2 Cor. 5:15; Gal. 1:1; 1 Thess. 4:14).

Christ's Incarnated Past Affects Subsequent Generations

The past in Christ's human life functions, as does the past in other human lives, by affecting what comes after. Paul believes that Christ's incarnated life achieved results, such as the reception by Paul and the gentiles of the promise of the spirit (Gal. 3:14)—that is, Christ's human past affects the present of subsequent generations.

Christ's Incarnated Past Is Present in the Present of Humans

Christ's past functions beyond the human experience of an event in the past, affecting future events and people. *Christ's past is present and available in the human present.* When Paul writes that the cup of blessing is participation (κοινωνία) with Christ's blood, and the bread is likewise participation in the body of Christ (1 Cor. 10:16), this understanding is evident. Paul affirms elsewhere that Christ came in the likeness of sinful flesh (Rom. 8:3) and that he was in human form (Phil. 2:7); he was a human composed of body and blood. Yet despite the exalted Christ no longer being flesh and blood, Paul conceives of Christ's blood and body as being available to be shared. Christ's blood and body can be participated in by those living after his incarnation. Christ's temporality allows for his past to be in his present and so in the present tense of those united with him.

Christ's Suffering and Death

To the Corinthians Paul writes that "the sufferings of Christ are abundant for us" (2 Cor. 1:5). Relatedly, Paul believes that he and his companions are always carrying the death of Jesus in their bodies (4:10). To the Philippians, Paul describes his deepest desire as knowing Christ and the power of his resurrection and the fellowship of his sufferings, being conformed to his death (Phil. 3:10): Paul's desire is to share actually in Christ's sufferings and to take on the form of Christ's death. The apostle's hope/expectation is, in effect, to transcend the boundaries of human temporality, having direct access to past events—not because he is a time traveler but because Christ's past is present. Christ's sufferings and death, though events in humanity's (and Christ's) past, are also present to and for Paul.[2]

Paul underscores this conviction about the presence of Christ's past in his statement that Christ loved him and gave himself for him (Gal. 2:20). Though Christ and Paul did not meet before Christ's crucifixion,[3] Paul conceives of Christ's self-offering as directed to

---

2. Colossians corroborates this: Christ's death in his body of flesh has now (νυνί) reconciled the Colossians (Col. 1:22; cf. Rom. 5:11). Christ's death, though in the past of human time, is present now. It is not only that an event happened in the past but that people living after the event have access to it.

3. Stanley E. Porter's attempt to reinstate an older theory that Paul met Jesus, based primarily on particular readings of Acts 9:1–9, 1 Cor. 9:1, and 2 Cor. 5:16, does not convince (*When Paul Met Jesus*).

him personally. Christ's past can be present in subsequent human presents.

Paul frames the present sufferings of believers as suffering with Christ (Rom. 8:17).[4] The suffering with Christ that the children of God know could refer either to the suffering Christ experienced in his incarnated state or to Christ suffering still in his life with God as exalted Son. It has been interpreted both ways. Joseph A. Fitzmyer takes the reference to be to Christ's historical death;[5] C. E. B. Cranfield, on the other hand, states that because the verb is in the present tense it must refer to the suffering that necessarily accompanies faithfulness to Christ "in a world which does not yet know Him as Lord."[6] Cranfield also ponders whether Paul might think "that the exalted Christ participates in His brethren's sufferings."[7]

There are two related differences between these interpretations. One difference is temporal: Paul is thinking either of an event in the past or of current suffering. Another difference is that of focus: Paul is focusing either on Christ's sufferings or on believers'; Paul is saying either that Christ suffers with believers or that believers suffer with Christ. The context indicates that Paul is thinking about Christ's sufferings in his incarnated past, for the apostle describes the children, with the help of the spirit of sonship, crying the same words that Jesus used in his incarnated life: "Abba! Father!" (Gal. 4:6). This strongly suggests that Paul's focus is on Christ in his incarnated life. Moreover, Paul presents suffering as the prerequisite for being glorified—a sequence which happened in Christ's earthly and then ascended life. On the other hand, it is hard to imagine that Paul thought that Christ's suffering in his exalted life leads to glorification. In his exalted state (Phil. 2:9), Christ is already glorified. (This does not mean that Paul does not conceive of Christ suffering

---

4. Käsemann's claim that Rom. 8:18 is a sharp break of thought does not warrant his conclusion that εἴπερ in 8:17 introduces a condition rather than stating a fact. One senses that Käsemann's concern to affirm eschatological tension in Paul dictates his interpretation: he hears Paul in Rom. 8:17 warning against enthusiastic certainty (*Romans*, 229). Cranfield rightly states that εἴπερ states "a fact which confirms what has just been said" (*Romans*, 1:407).

5. Fitzmyer, *Romans*, 502.

6. Cranfield, *Romans*, 1:408.

7. Cranfield, *Romans*, 1:408.

while at the same time being glorified.) These observations tip the interpretative scale toward a reading that hears Paul as focusing on Christ's sufferings, and these being in his incarnated life. The sufferings the children share, then, are the sufferings of Christ's incarnated past. We have here another example of the apostle conceiving of Christ's past in the human present.

In 1 Corinthians, we find further indication that Christ's incarnated past is also the exalted Christ's present. Paul says he preaches Christ crucified (1 Cor. 1:23), the power and wisdom of God (1:24). That Christ crucified can be the power and wisdom of God to humans living after the event of Christ's crucifixion indicates that, for Paul, Christ's crucifixion remains active in Christ's temporality.[8] In Galatians, Paul speaks of himself as being co-crucified with Christ (Gal. 2:19). Paul conceives of the event of Christ's crucifixion as present to those united with Christ. The past is in Christ's present.

In Romans, Paul states that believers are baptized into Christ's death; in fact, believers were buried with Christ by means of their baptism into his death (Rom. 6:2–4). Union with Christ means direct access to moments in Christ's incarnated past: Christ's death and burial. This is the case not because believers travel to Christ's past but because Christ's past is present and can be known in human present tenses. The apostle writes that believers are organically united (σύμφυτοι) in the likeness of Christ's death (6:5).[9] "Likeness" signals that believers share in the benefits but not the work of Christ's death.[10] Those who are in Christ's death are, then, co-planted in a similar though nonidentical death. Christ's death is unique in that

---

8. Cf. Colossians, which exhorts its hearers to recognize that they died with Christ—ἀπεθάνετε σὺν Χριστῷ (Col. 2:20). Christ's death, while an event in Christ's and humanity's past, is present and "enter-able" in the present tenses of humans. It is *not just the consequences* of his death that may be entered but *Christ's death itself*. The particular manner of Christ's death—crucifixion—is highlighted. What is envisaged is not simply that believers reap the benefits of something Christ did in the past but that believers enter into the actual event.

9. Cranfield wisely stays away from hearing in the phrase "likeness of his death" a reference to the rite of baptism and suggests that here Paul echoes the thought of Phil. 3:10—conformity to Christ's death (*Romans*, 1:308).

10. Cf. Cranfield, *Romans*, 1:308.

he is the first human to die to sin "once for all (time)"[11] (6:10)—and so to be liberated from death (6:9). Yet while Christ's death is stupendously singular and unrepeatable—a point Paul does not want missed—it is not locked in the past, nor is it simply an event that has continuing effects.[12] Christ's death may be entered and shared subsequent to that event. Paul underscores this in the first part of Romans 6: the old person of believers has been co-crucified with Christ (6:6); believers have died with Christ (6:8).

Christ's Resurrection

Christ's resurrection, though an event in Christ's and humanity's past, is present for those living after that event. Christ's resurrection is present in believers' present. They can walk in newness of life just as (ὥσπερ) Christ was raised out of the dead (Rom. 6:4).[13] Though it is in believers' future that they will know liberation of their mortal bodies—that is, their *own* resurrection (1 Cor. 15:20–23; 1 Thess. 4:14)—in their temporal presents, believers share in *Christ's* resurrection. An event in Christ's and humanity's past is present in Christ's present tense.

Christ's Past Is Present in the Human Past

Paul may also think that Christ's death was effective for people living prior to its occurrence in human history. Paul writes that when we were enemies we were reconciled to God by the death of God's Son (Rom. 5:10). "Enemies" signals Paul's judgment that humanity is enslaved to sin. Given Paul's earlier description in Romans of all of humanity being in such a condition (1:18–20; 3:9–18, 23), this strongly suggests that Paul thought that Christ's death reconciled humanity in each generation—not just those who lived after Christ's death.[14] Romans 5:18 may reasonably be heard to say that Christ's

---

11. This is Leander Keck's translation of ἐφάπαξ (*Romans*, 164).

12. Fitzmyer speaks misleadingly of the "result" of Christ's death (*Romans*, 435).

13. The author of Colossians writes that believers are raised with Christ (Col. 3:1).

14. Cf. Augustine, who writes, "The Christian religion existed and was not missing among the ancients from the beginning of the human race, until Christ came 'in the flesh'" (*Retractationes* 1.12.3).

act of righteousness brings righteousness and life to all—in every historical period. Whether or not this refers to universal salvation is not the issue at hand. In regard to Christ's temporality, however, this suggests that Paul thought that an act in Christ's human past affected all of humanity, even those who lived before the incarnation. In effect, Christ's past spans all of human time.

Christ's Present

As perceived by those in him, the present of the exalted Christ is full of activity. Perhaps better put, Christ's activity in those united with him is a sign of Christ's present tense. Christ's present is active and interwoven with the lives of those joined to him. Christ lives in Paul (Gal. 2:20) and in believers more generally (Rom. 8:10). In various ways Paul indicates that Christ's present intersects with his own. In Christ, Paul was caught up into paradise (2 Cor. 12:2–4). Speaking of occurrences in his past that were, of course, in his present when they happened, Paul writes that, along with God, Jesus Christ made Paul an apostle (Gal. 1:1; cf. Rom. 1:5). Paul received his gospel through a revelation of Jesus Christ (Gal. 1:12). Christ (God's Son) was revealed in Paul (1:16). Christ loves Paul (2:20). Christ's truth is within Paul, and Christ speaks in Paul (2 Cor. 11:10; 13:3). The Lord[15] handed over precious information to Paul concerning the Lord's supper (1 Cor. 11:23). The Lord gives authority to Paul (2 Cor. 13:10); the Lord commends (10:18). The Lord will or will not permit Paul's travel plans (1 Cor. 16:7). Christ gives Paul commands (e.g., 9:14), though in the case of the unmarried, he does not (7:25). In 1 Corinthians 9:1 Paul writes that he has "seen Jesus our Lord," which could refer to a particular experience or to the visions and revelations of the Lord that Paul claims in 2 Corinthians 12:1. In any event, these references indicate an understanding that Christ is present in Paul's present.[16]

15. Understanding, along with Fee, that "the Lord" refers to Jesus Christ (*Corinthians*, 548). "Lord" is Paul's regular designation for Jesus (e.g., Rom. 10:9; 1 Cor. 12:3).
16. As mentioned, though Paul speaks of something in his past, these events happened in Paul's present tense.

Believers act in Christ's present. They labor in the Lord (1 Cor. 15:58). Their "amen" to the truth that all the promises of God find their "yes" in Christ is uttered through Christ (2 Cor. 1:20). Paul makes his appeal to the Corinthians through Christ (10:1). He and his companions speak in Christ in the sight of God (12:19). Through the gospel, Paul became the father of the Corinthians in Christ (4:15). Fruits of righteousness come through Jesus Christ (Phil. 1:11). Christ's current activity is evident in the presence of Christ's gospel (1 Cor. 9:12).[17]

Christ is active in the human present. Christ becomes betrothed to the Corinthians (2 Cor. 11:2). Christ provides for and cares for believers. Through Christ, comfort abounds (1:5). The love of Christ constrains believers (5:14). Paul writes that Christ enriched the Corinthians with all speech and knowledge and that Christ sustains believers until the end (1 Cor. 1:5, 8). The fellowship of God's Son (1:9) indicates that Christ shares his life with believers.

Believers are the body of Christ (1 Cor. 12:27). "Body" is more than a common ancient metaphor for unity. The concept of "body of Christ" points to the oneness of Christ and believers, a union which includes union with Christ's temporality. Believers live in Christ's present. Consequently, Paul and his companions manifest the life of Jesus (2 Cor. 4:10); they are baptized into Christ and have put on Christ (Gal. 3:27). Christ's present envelops human temporality, and humans united with Christ live their temporality in Christ's temporality.[18]

Union with Christ and Christ's Faith

Paul exhorts believers to consider themselves alive to God *in* Christ Jesus (Rom. 6:11). That is, Christ is the context in which believers can reckon their aliveness to God; Christ's present tense is believers' present tense. Nowhere is this clearer than in Galatians 2:20, where Paul writes that Christ lives in him.

---

17. Understanding the phrase "gospel of Christ" to indicate not the gospel about Christ but Christ's good tidings (see Hart, *New Testament*, 334).

18. Cf. Col 3:1–3, which claims that believers' lives are hidden with Christ, who is sitting at the right hand of God.

Christ's present includes Christ's faith. The exalted Christ remains the obedient Son. Christ's faith is his disposition toward God, which includes his faithfulness to those who belong to him.[19] Likewise, believers' faith, which is a sharing in Christ's faith, is their disposition toward God. Christ's present faith is that in which the faithful participate.

Christ's faith makes righteous those who believe (Gal. 2:16). If we take πίστεως 'Ιησοῦ Χριστοῦ as a subjective genitive (faith of Jesus Christ), then the first and third clauses refer to Christ's faith.[20] Christ's faith indicates not only his faith during his earthly life but his continuing and constant faith in his exalted life.[21] Christ's faith allows for the promise to be given to those who believe (3:22).

Christ's faith, through which and in which believers believe, takes place in Christ's present. Christ's continuing faith in his exalted existence is instrumental in believers being children of God. David Bentley Hart correctly renders Paul's meaning in the latter part of Galatians 3:26: "through the faithfulness within the Anointed One Jesus."[22]

Imitation of Christ

Paul's imitation-of-Christ motif (1 Cor. 4:16; 11:1) likewise works with the idea that Christ is not merely a historical model for good behavior. In the context of Paul's union-with-Christ concept, imitation is the reproduction of the living and present Christ. Believers can, then, have the same disposition as Christ (Phil. 2:5).

Christ's Future

Paul describes events in Christ's future: the day of the Lord, the parousia, and Christ's appearing. It appears that these are different ways

19. David J. Downs and Benjamin J. Lappenga's work explores almost exclusively the exalted Lord's faithfulness, with only a rare nod to Christ's faithfulness to God (*Faithfulness of the Risen Christ*).

20. See my "Peter in the Middle."

21. Cf. 1 Cor. 15:28, where Paul writes that at the end Christ will be subjected to God. This ultimate obedience is the ultimate act of faith.

22. Hart, *New Testament*, 374.

for the apostle to speak of the same event. In 1 Corinthians 1:7–8, right after speaking of τὴν ἀποκάλυψιν τοῦ κυρίου ἡμῶν Ἰησοῦ Χριστοῦ ("the revelation of our Lord Jesus Christ"), Paul refers to the day of Christ; he also writes that at Christ's parousia, Christ will be visible (1 Thess. 4:15–17).

When Christ comes from heaven, he will act in or achieve several extraordinarily beneficial and transformative events. Consequently, Paul expresses longing for Christ's coming—Marana-tha (1 Cor. 16:22)[23]—and declares that the Lord's Supper is to be eaten as a proclamation of the Lord's death "until he comes" (11:26). The apostle believes that the Lord's coming will have marvelous consequences for those united with Christ. It both "rescues us from the wrath that is coming" (1 Thess. 1:10; cf. Phil. 3:20, where the reference to a Savior implies rescue) and will result in Christ transforming the bodies of believers so that they are like his glorious body (Phil. 3:21).

Given the wonders that the eschatological events will achieve for believers, and for creation (Rom. 8:19–23), it is not surprising that we should miss that the apostle thinks that Christ's parousia is primarily about Christ. Paul draws attention to this in the phrase ἐν τῇ αὐτοῦ παρουσίᾳ ("in *his* coming"; 1 Thess. 2:19). The parousia is an event in Christ's life, in Christ's future. It is Christ's day (Phil. 2:16; 1 Thess. 5:2; cf. 1 Cor. 1:8, where the day is spoken of as "the day of our Lord Jesus Christ"). While the day is also God's day, since it is at God's direction and because of God's purposes that the Lord Jesus Christ saves us (1 Thess. 5:9), Paul emphasizes that it is "the day of the Lord" (1 Cor. 5:5; see also Phil. 1:6). It is a day in which Christ will act.

Paul refers to the event of the revelation of Christ and the day of the Lord as the τέλος (1 Cor. 1:7–8). The "end" is "the day of the Lord Jesus" (2 Cor. 1:13–14). We should not add the words "of time" to "end."[24] Paul should be heard to be saying only what he

---

23. The Aramaic phrase can mean either "the Lord has come" or "our Lord, come." In the context and given Paul's agenda with the Corinthians, it most likely means the latter.

24. It is a scholarly commonplace to speak of the "end of time" (see, e.g., Beker, *Triumph*, 357). It is especially important to be careful about this when we take into account that the Jewish expectation for a day of the Lord typically signals the cleansing of creation, not the end of time.

does say: the day of the Lord Jesus is a moment in Christ's future that is the goal or end of Christ's work for God on our behalf.

Paul's references to Christ's parousia clearly indicate the apostle's conviction that the exalted Christ has more to do—he will be revealed at the telos and on that day his actions will alter creation for the better. Paul describes several actions and stages that occur at Christ's coming. When Christ comes, he will descend (καταβήσεται; 1 Thess. 4:16) from heaven. As Gaventa recognizes, Paul poetically describes a transcendent scene;[25] Christ, in the clouds in the air, welcomes the resurrected to be with him always. In 1 Corinthians, likewise, Paul envisions Christ's activity at his coming to allow for the making alive of those who are Christ's (1 Cor. 15:23). To the Corinthians Paul also writes that God will raise them, along with him and others, to be with Jesus (2 Cor. 4:14). The time (καιρός; 1 Cor. 4:5) of the Lord's coming will "bring to light the things now hidden in darkness and will disclose the purposes of the heart" (1 Cor. 4:5; cf. 1 Cor. 3:13). In Romans 2:16 (understanding "the day" to refer to the day of Christ), the apostle declares that God will judge people's secrets through Christ Jesus.

In 2 Corinthians, Paul writes that Jesus will occupy a judgment seat before which "all of us must appear" (5:10). Here we encounter the challenge of understanding the chronology of Christ's judgment, for Paul offers disparate opinions on when believers are judged. In 2 Corinthians 5, Christ's judgment seems to occur upon a person's death, whereas in 1 Corinthians 4:5, it awaits Christ's parousia. Further, the undramatic description of being with the Lord after death in 2 Corinthians 5:8–9, which makes no mention of the reception of spiritual or resurrection bodies, contrasts with the breathtaking vision of the Lord descending from heaven and believers meeting him in the air and so being with him forever. (This apparent discrepancy has, of course, been explained as the result of Paul's developing eschatological ideas.)[26]

---

25. Gaventa, *First and Second Thessalonians*, 66.
26. Schnelle puts it that by the time of writing 2 Corinthians, Paul's acute expectation of the eschaton has "relaxed" (*Apostle Paul*, 251).

Subsequent to his parousia, Christ will reign until he places every enemy under his feet, including the last one—death, which is presently being destroyed (1 Cor. 15:25–26).[27] When all things are subjected to Christ, then the Son himself will be subjected to God (understanding, as argued below, that the phrase "the one who put all things in subjection under him" refers to God [15:28]). This is the final event Paul describes in Christ's future: his being subjected to God so that God may be all in all.[28]

Christ's Day Is Revelatory of Christ's Present in Which Believers Live

While Paul thinks that Christ has more to do, much of that activity will not change Christ's existence. On the basis of my definition of time as motion manifest in action and event and productive of change, since the majority of Christ's eschatological actions do not produce change for him, they are not indicative of temporal movement.

Unlike Christ's incarnation, crucifixion, resurrection, and exaltation, Christ's actions at his day/parousia, except for his ultimate subjection to God, do not signal temporal change from before to after. Christ's exalted life with a glorious body (Phil. 3:21) and his utter filial faithful obedience are *revealed* at the eschaton.[29]

Christ's day/parousia and his judgment do not change his existence, apart from opening it up. What is still to come for Christ is that his present tense will be revealed.[30] When Christ shares the full glory of his exalted life with those who belong to him, it will be a revealing of what is now hidden in plain sight to believers. It will not be something new in itself, but a new quality of experience

27. "Destroy" is in the present indicative in the Greek.
28. This may be the "perfect" or "complete" to which Paul refers in 1 Cor. 13:10: ὅταν δὲ ἔλθῃ τὸ τέλειον.
29. Christ is perennially obedient to the Father. See, e.g., 1 Cor. 3:23 and 8:6, which distinguish between God the Father as the goal of all and Christ as the conduit of all.
30. My observation may resonate with Barth's opinion that "nothing different takes place" (*Church Dogmatics* IV/3, 293) in the three comings of the resurrection, of the Holy Spirit, and of the parousia. Thanks to Jamie Davies for pointing out this Barth reference.

of what is. In effect, the eschaton fits within the time Christ presently lives. Apart from the singular reference to Christ's handing over his reign and being subjected to God (1 Cor. 15:24, 28), the future events in which Christ takes part do not create change in Christ's life[31]—except insofar as he shares with others the fullness of his current exalted life. The exalted Christ has a future tense in a qualified sense. *What Christ has not yet enacted is lifting the veil on his present tense.*

As noted, in only three letters does Paul describe Christ coming from heaven (1 Corinthians, Philippians, and 1 Thessalonians). Elsewhere, Paul speaks of Christ's day. The other eschatological actions Paul envisions for Christ are his handing to God his reign over the inimical powers and then being subjected to God. These actions are all revelatory. Christ's parousia and his day reveal the glorious nature of the exalted Christ's life, and his handing over of his reign and his subjection unveil the profundity of Christ's obedience to God. While these actions are future, they reveal Christ's present. *Christ's future actions reveal his present.* These actions are Christ's future tense in the sense that he has not done them. Given, however, that when he does do them, little will change for Christ, they indicate a rather limited range for Christ's future tense.

The eschatological events in which Christ acts confirm and manifest the present nature of Christ's life. His resurrection destroyed death for him, as Paul states in Romans 6:9: "We know that Christ, being raised from the dead, will never die again; death no longer has dominion over him." Paul's affirmation that Christ has been raised from the dead (1 Cor. 15:20) says the same thing. Subsequent to his crucifixion, resurrection, and exaltation to life in heaven with God, Christ's enemies—every rule and authority and power (15:24)—have no power over him. This is made evident at the telos (15:24).[32]

---

31. The one caveat here must be that Christ's subjection to God at the eschaton, so that God is all in all, will mean (though Paul doesn't write about this) that Christ's present will no longer include Christ's suffering.

32. Cf. Col. 2:15: Christ's crucifixion disarmed and triumphed over the principalities and powers.

Christ's handing over of his reign is still to come. Yet when understood as a feature of his subjection to God (1 Cor. 15:28), it is an act that does not change Christ's present state. (Presumably, the one change will be that suffering will no longer be part of Christ's life as a result of God's "all-ness." This is, however, not something that Paul ponders out loud.) The event of Christ being subjected to God manifests Christ's present existence. Christ's life—whether his earthly or exalted life—is lived in obedience as God's Son. The apostle sums this up when he writes that Christ is God's (1 Cor. 3:23). The subjection of Christ the Son to God at the end makes visible what currently is. Paul understands the future events in which Christ acts as events that reveal and make tangible to humanity and creation the life Christ lives in Christ's present tense. They are, then, events in the future of humanity and creation that bring Christ's present tense into the open and in which Christ's current existence is made available to others.

Paul's vision is not of Christ having a future that is now partially present in the human present. Rather, the apostle thinks that *believers'* future will be changed when they have complete access to Christ's present—their bodies will become incorruptible. None of the eschatological events Paul describes change the circumstance of Christ's life. The Christ-centered events in the future are future for believers, but for Christ, they are a publication of his present. The exalted Christ's future tense is, then, a qualified future. The most we might say is that Christ has a limited future tense—some actions are still to be taken, yet these actions will be a disclosure of Christ's present tense. The eschatological events Paul depicts are, in essence, an unveiling of Christ's present tense. Paul's words in 1 Corinthians 1:7–8 make my point most directly; the day of our Lord Jesus Christ is equivalent to the revealing of our Lord Jesus Christ: Christ's day is when Christ is revealed.

How This Affects Those United with Him

Admittedly, while these eschatological events reveal Christ's present tense, they are future in human chronological time. Nevertheless, and importantly, in life-time—the environment in which believers experience chronological time—these events do not produce change between Christ and those united with him. Believers continue to belong to Christ at and through the eschatological events in which he takes part. The fact that believers do not yet have glorious bodies like Christ's is not because they are only partially united with him, nor is it because their salvation is incomplete. Mortality/corruptibility experiences Christ's risen and exalted life (life-time) in a particular manner. That manner does not, however, signify that life-time is limited by death. Paul describes the present power of life and its victory over death in several astonishing statements: "I am convinced that neither death, nor life . . . will be able to separate us from the love of God in Christ Jesus our Lord" (Rom. 8:38–39); and, "If we live, we live to the Lord, and if we die, we die to the Lord; so then, whether we live or whether we die, we are the Lord's" (14:8; see also 1 Thess. 5:10).

Importantly, the day of the Lord does not interfere with believers' union with Christ. Paul speaks about believers being proudly aware of each other on the day of the Lord Jesus (2 Cor. 1:14). He expresses this sentiment shortly after describing the profundity of believers' fellowship with Christ's suffering and consolation and of Paul and his fellow workers' unity with the Corinthians' sufferings for the sake of their consolation (1:3–7). The degree of unity between believers and Christ is immeasurable. It is not broken on Christ's day. That Paul can say that "now is the day of salvation" (6:2) points to the apostle's rock-hard certainty that those united with Christ will remain united on Christ's day. The day of salvation will always be "now," including and especially on the day of our Lord Jesus. It is those who currently belong to Christ who are raised at his coming (1 Cor. 15:23).

That Paul thinks that now those united with Christ can and should walk as in the day (Rom. 13:12–13) indicates that at the event of the day they will continue to live in it. Christ's day does not change believers' connection to Christ. Paul's statement that believers are of and belong to the day (1 Thess. 5:5, 8) illuminates his understanding that believers remain in the day at the event of the day.

Union with Christ at his day does not mean that believers escape judgment of their works (1 Cor. 3:13). Nevertheless, as long as their works are done in Christ, they will be saved (3:10–15). Those whose work is built on the foundation of Christ (3:11, 14) have their lives judged on the day. They will be judged while at once being integrally connected to their foundation—Christ. Paul even assures salvation on the day of the Lord Jesus to the man who crossed sexual boundaries, as long as Satan destroys the flesh (5:5). Presumably, Paul thinks that being Christ's (3:23) ensures salvation.[33] Belonging to Christ entails continued unity with him, including at Christ's day and at believers' judgment. Believers are completely and continually in union with Christ. This does not change at Christ's day.

---

33. I mention below the distinction between present justification and union with Christ, and assured future salvation from God's wrath.

6

The Future in the Exalted Christ's Time

Christ's future, I have argued, largely entails an unveiling of his present tense. Two significant passages illustrate this claim: 1 Corinthians 15 and Romans 8. I have chosen these passages for the obvious reason that they are typically understood to be about the future for both believers *and* Christ.

Revelation of Christ's Present Tense in 1 Corinthians 15

In 1 Corinthians 15:20–57, Paul's most extensive description of a Christ-centered eschatological event, the apostle indicates his conviction that at Christ's parousia, Christ's present reality is unveiled.

Subject of Verbs in 1 Corinthians 15:20–28

The mysteries of 1 Corinthians 15:20–28 abound, including questions about the subject of several of its verbs and the temporal meaning of most of the verbs. These questions are directly relevant to our inquiry into Paul's conception of Christ's future, given that this passage describes what happens at Christ's parousia.

Verbs without designated subjects occur in 1 Corinthians 15:24–28. The options for their subject are, in most cases, either Christ or God.¹ As is to be expected, solid arguments have been made for both.² Without going into inordinate detail, I propose that Christ is the subject of the verbs in 15:24–26, 27a, and 28a. Since the subject of παραδιδῷ ("he hands over"; 15:24a) is obviously Christ, the subject of the next verb, καταργήσῃ ("destroy"; 15:24b), should also be understood as Christ. This rationale affects how we interpret Paul's other references to subjection of the powers. In 15:27c, Paul takes pains to correct a potential misunderstanding: that the subjected powers include God. That Paul feels constrained to write δῆλον ὅτι ἐκτὸς τοῦ ὑποτάξαντος αὐτῷ τὰ πάντα ("it is evident that this does not include the one who put all things in subjection under him") indicates that Christ is the agent in the action of destroying and subjecting the powers in the previous verbs. Paul is saying, in effect, that Christ is the one doing the destroying and subjecting of all powers, with God (the one who subordinated all things) excepted. That is, Christ does not subject the one who enabled him to have power over the powers. The pronoun αὐτῷ ("him") in 15:27c refers to Christ. Paul's caveat in 15:27c makes plain that he sees Christ as the agent in the previous references to subjecting the powers: as mentioned, καταργήσῃ (15:24), and also θῇ ("put"; 15:25), ὑπέταξεν ("subjected"; 15:27a), and ὑποτέτακται ("subject"; 15:27b). Christ is also the subject of ὑποταγῇ ("subjected"; 15:28).

Christ hands over the kingdom to God (1 Cor. 15:24) when he has destroyed all rule and all authority and power. Using and changing Psalm 110:1, Paul claims that Christ rules until he has placed all the enemies under his (own) feet (1 Cor. 15:25).³ If Christ is the

---

1. Εἴπῃ in 15:27b has been understood to have as its subject God or Christ. I read the subject to be the Scripture Paul cites: "it says."

2. For a sampling of important and distinctive views, see Lambrecht, "Paul's Christological Use of Scripture," esp. 508–11.

3. Lambrecht calls Paul's use of αὐτοῦ here "loose Hellenistic grammar" ("Paul's Christological Use of Scripture," 509). Relying on M. Zerwick, Lambrecht notes that αὐτοῦ is an

agent in verses 24 and 25, then in verse 26 Christ should be under-stood as the force behind the ongoing destruction of death (note the present passive indicative; καταργεῖται).[4] In 15:27a Paul again uses (and changes) scriptural language,[5] underscoring the idea that all things are subjected under Christ's feet. In the next verse, Paul repeats the thought about all things being subjected to him(self), that is, Christ (15:28).

Temporal Sense of the Verbs in 1 Corinthians 15:22–28

While the action in this passage, which ostensibly concerns the future, is framed by the future indicative verbs ζῳοποιηθήσονται ("will be made alive"; 1 Cor. 15:22) and ὑποταγήσεται ("will be sub-jected"; 15:28b), none of the verbs between that frame appear as future indicatives. This makes relating the grammar to the content notoriously difficult. Since we are concerned with Paul's under-standing of Christ's future, this difficulty is ours.

There are no verbs in 15:23. In 15:24 we find a present subjunctive (παραδιδῷ) and an aorist subjunctive (καταργήσῃ), introduced by the temporal adverb ὅταν ("when"), where we would expect straightfor-ward futures. Interpreters will attempt to alleviate the challenge by declaring καταργήσῃ (15:24) a "futurum exactum."[6] In 15:25, there is an infinitive (βασιλεύειν, "reign") and the aorist active subjunc-tive of the LXX citation (θῇ). First Corinthians 15:26 uses a present indicative (καταργεῖται). In 15:27 Paul reproduces the grammar of the LXX (ὑπέταξεν, aorist active indicative), though he transposes it

example of "the Hellenistic neglect of the reflexive pronoun, especially in the possessive geni-tive," adding that "in view of 15:27c–28, it is very unlikely that αὐτοῦ in 15:25b (and 15:27a) refers to God" (522n47).

4. Martinus C. de Boer correctly interprets the present tense here to mean not only that the destruction of death is certain but that, because of Christ's resurrection, "its destruction, and those of the other powers, has in fact begun" (*Defeat of Death*, 122).

5. Here Paul uses language from Ps. 8:6. It is unclear whether Paul alludes to Ps. 8 and, earlier, to Ps. 110 in expectation that his hearers might catch the significance of the changes he makes, such as the change of the first person of Ps. 110:1 to a third-person θῇ and the addition of αὐτοῦ (1 Cor. 15:25), and of the second person in Ps. 8:6 to a third person (1 Cor. 15:27). The fact that Paul draws attention to his reference to Ps. 8:6 by using εἴπῃ suggests that at the very least he recruits Scripture as an authoritative voice supporting his own claims.

6. See Lambrecht, "Structure and Line," 146.

into the third person and uses an aorist subjunctive (εἴπῃ, "it says") to introduce his paraphrastic comment on the Scripture in which he uses a perfect passive indicative (ὑποτέτακται). Paul uses another aorist subjunctive in 15:28a (ὑποταγῇ) when speaking about Christ's subjection of all things. Finally, as mentioned, a straightforward future indicative that depicts Christ's subjection to God (15:28b) echoes the future in 15:22.

All that detail to say that, while Paul frames the events in 15:23–28a with unambiguous future tenses, he avoids using straightforward futures when describing these events. It cannot be that Paul's verbal choices are determined by the Scriptures he uses, since he is so evidently free about changing Scripture's words to suit his purposes. And it is head-scratching that he does not stick to clear future tenses if, as discussed below, de Boer is right that Paul is trying to correct the Corinthians' soteriological understanding of these Scriptures.[7] The fact that (unlike in 15:51–57) Paul does not privilege future indicatives is noteworthy. His odd choice not only of tense but also of mood begs consideration.

The mixture of verbal moods in this passage or, better put, the fact that the sequence of events is not presented exclusively in the indicative mood[8] may ask readers to focus less on temporal reference than on what grammarians call verbal aspect. Grammarians generally agree that only the indicative mood in Hellenistic Greek unequivocally refers to temporal placement. Given the confusing mixture of moods and tenses, Paul's concern appears to be to present the order of parousia events from a certain perspective. The paucity of indicatives suggests that Paul is not so much interested in describing Christ's coming in a step-by-step fashion as in drawing attention to the whole of the event.[9] We might say that Paul is

7. We find the present, aorist, and perfect but no future tense in these verses. De Boer himself writes, "Paul's use of tenses exhibits an almost unbearable tension, particularly in 15:27–28 where the subordination of all things to Christ can be spoken of as both a past and a future reality" (*Defeat of Death*, 123).

8. Only three of the seven verbs (or eight, if we count the infinitive) in 15:23–28a are in the indicative.

9. Constantine R. Campbell helpfully distinguishes between two types of verbal aspect; one is imperfective, which views the action as unfolding, and the other perfective, which views the

viewing the parousia here not chiefly from the perspective of human chronological time but from Christ's time.

That is not to say that Paul is uninterested in the sequence of parousia events, as his temporal conjunctions indicate. However, Paul has his eyes on both chronological time and Christ's time, with the latter of chief importance to him here. The events at the parousia are sequential from the perspective of human time—something Paul emphasizes at the end of the chapter, with his liberal use of future indicatives in 1 Corinthians 15:51–57. Presumably since (as we shall see) Paul's concern at this point is to emphasize to the Corinthian deniers that Christ's resurrection means that they too will live bodily immortality, the apostle saw it as rhetorically advantageous to dramatize this. By presenting a sequence of events surrounding resurrection transformation, Paul shines a light on his conviction that believers will be raised with spiritual bodies. Importantly, however, he locates these events in Christ's time. (As mentioned, while the parousia events are future for humans, that is not entirely the case for Christ.) The strange paucity of future indicatives in 15:22–28 appears to be Paul's way of signaling that here he has his gaze primarily fixed on Christ's time.

What Paul Wants the "Deniers" to Know

According to de Boer, the Corinthian "deniers" of the resurrection base their conviction on traditions that used Psalm 110:1 and Psalm 8:6. The deniers understood Christ's resurrection to mean that he was currently exalted over the principalities and powers.[10] The mistake Paul seeks to correct is not this Christological understanding

---

action as a whole. Campbell uses the standard example of different ways of viewing a parade. From the ground, the parade is seen unfolding (imperfective aspect) while from a helicopter the action is seen as a whole (perfective aspect) (*Advances in the Study of Greek*, 107). On the basis of the tenses in this passage, it is difficult to claim which aspect Paul adopts, since the passage is dominated neither by present and imperfect tenses, which would argue for an imperfective aspect, nor by the aorist, which would indicate a perfective aspect. Moreover, as mentioned, the fact that Paul does not stick with the indicative mood strongly suggests that he is not primarily interested in detailing temporal sequence. The apostle's focus appears to be on describing a sequence of events in the context of the end of these events—a perfective aspect.

10. De Boer, *Defeat of Death*, 118.

(with which Paul agrees)[11] but the soteriological one that some Corinthians took from it. Some at Corinth think that since all the powers, even death, are already under Christ's feet, they too are exalted.[12]
Paul, de Boer argues, disagrees with the Corinthians not over their
Christology but over the soteriological significance of Christ's current reign over the powers. That reign does not mean that believers also are exalted and reign (see 1 Cor. 4:8). Such soteriological
exaltation awaits the completion of Christ's destruction of death.
De Boer claims that Paul problematizes death for the Corinthians,
who, in light of Christ's reign, have not considered it a problem.[13]
Of course, de Boer's explanation for why Paul goes to such
lengths to expound his understanding of the believers' resurrection
at Christ's parousia is one among many.[14] I single it out because in
one way I entirely agree with him and in another I do not. Along with
others, I read Paul as convinced that the risen Christ is triumphant
over all anti-God powers. Christ's resurrection is Christ's triumph.[15]
However, unlike de Boer, I do not think that Paul is concerned with
instructing the deniers that they themselves do not share that triumph. Quite the opposite: Paul wants the deniers of the resurrection

11. De Boer distinguishes himself from Käsemann and Beker, who think that Christ has not
yet defeated death (de Boer, *Defeat of Death*, 187). De Boer writes that "Paul is as triumphalist
as the Corinthians" in regard to believing that already Christ has subordinated the powers,
including death (123).

12. De Boer opines that "in denying the resurrection of the dead, the Corinthian gnos-
tics could sacramentally and pneumatically claim Christ's exaltation as their own" (*Defeat of
Death*, 123).

13. De Boer, *Defeat of Death*, 124.

14. Broadly speaking, the two main options are that Paul wants to correct an over-realized
eschatology (e.g., Thiselton, "Realized Eschatology at Corinth"; Tuckett, "Corinthians Who
Say") or that the apostle wants to teach the deniers to think eschatologically (e.g., Hays, "Conversion of the Imagination").

15. Lambrecht: "From the resurrection onwards Christ is reigning and the purpose of [his]
kingship is the subjection of all enemies" ("Paul's Christological Use of Scripture," 507). C. E.
Hill observes that 1 Cor. 15:24 and 26 "cannot be seen as the beginning point of the reign"
("Paul's Understanding of Christ's Kingdom," 315). Hill continues: "Paul understands the
kingdom of Christ in 1 Cor 15:24–28 to be Christ's present, cosmic lordship which he exercises
from heaven. It does not await the Parousia for its inauguration, it . . . began with the resurrection of an acquisition of life-giving prerogatives by the Last Adam, and the accession of God's
throne in heaven by the greater son of David" (317). Novenson comments that he finds Hill's
view "compelling in light of the striking differences between 1 Cor 15:20–28 and Rev 20:1–6"
(Novenson, *Christ among the Messiahs*, 144n30).

to see that their bodies will be changed precisely because death and sin now have no power over them.[16]

From what we can tell of Paul's understanding of the views of the deniers,[17] they rejected the idea that Christ's resurrection meant that they too would be raised (1 Cor. 15:12–13). They likely resisted the thought of their resurrection because they did not want or hope for a continuation of bodily life—in whatever form those bodies might be. Resurrection—the raising of bodies—was a vastly different hope than that of achieving bodiless immortality, which many Greco-Roman philosophies held out. If the Corinthian deniers hoped for anything beyond this life, it was most likely a disembodied continuation of life.[18] Paul's extended description of heavenly/imperishable/spiritual bodies (15:35–49) may be understood as a response to the deniers' resistance to the idea of bodily resurrection. Having imbibed from Greco-Roman culture the conviction that the body is a grave, Paul's original audience would have been offended by the thought of an embodied immortality.

Paul's conviction, however, is that Christ's resurrection from the dead resulted in his living in a spiritual body. In fact, as Paul emphasizes at the beginning of 1 Corinthians 15, Christ confirmed his spirit-body—it appeared to Cephas, the twelve, more than five hundred, and to Paul (15:5–8). The resurrection of Christ is a bodily resurrection; put another way, resurrection is necessarily resurrection of the body. To repeat, this is a different understanding of the nature

16. There are various proposals about why the deniers resisted the idea of their own resurrection. See Tuckett, "Corinthians Who Say," for a review of the more influential ones. In my view, one of the most compelling is that of A. J. M. Wedderburn, who proposes that, as Greeks, they understood their reception of spiritual experiences as the bestowal of "divine gifts of life and wisdom" (*Baptism and Resurrection*, 395). They expected to be freed from the body, and their extraordinary experiences suggested to them that they had already achieved entrance to "a new age and new world" (395). They did not desire or think they needed bodily resurrection.

17. Some scholars propose that Paul misunderstood the position of the Corinthian deniers. See, e.g., Kümmel and Lietzmann, *An die Korinther I–II*, 193; Bultmann, *Theology of the New Testament*, 1:169.

18. Argued influentially by Gerhard Sellin, who grounds his argument in an investigation of Hellenistic wisdom traditions, including Philo, which distinguish between two classes of people: the spiritual and the non-spiritual. The spiritual are the more advanced in wisdom and understand that the body is an obstacle to the spirit and will necessarily be discarded (*Der Streit um die Auferstehung der Toten*, 30–31).

of life after death than that of the immortality of the soul. According to Paul, the mortal body must be clothed with immortality (15:53; cf. 2 Cor. 5:1–4); that is, he held a concept that seemed irretrievably paradoxical to many in the Greco-Roman world: bodily immortality.

The Corinthian deniers appear to have welcomed the idea that Christ dealt with their sins (1 Cor. 15:17), meaning that "this life" (15:19) would not hinder them from achieving disembodied immortality.[19] Paul clarifies what is at stake in such a view: in light of Christ's (bodily) resurrection, to reject hope for a similar resurrection is to lose out on sharing Christ's glorious embodied life. Paul reframes the deniers' view: they are hoping for this life only when they limit their conception of Christ's resurrection to dealing with their sins so that their souls can live in immortality. If the Corinthian deniers do not see this, they have no hope for anything beyond this life since whatever life there is after death is only available bodily. Indeed, if those who have died in Christ are not united with Christ's bodily resurrection, they have perished (15:18).

No Longer Subject to Death

The fact that those who belong to Christ do not yet have incorruptible bodies does not signify to Paul that believers are still subject to death. Paul considers it critical that the Corinthians understand that their ongoing salvation (σῴζεσθε, "being saved"; 1 Cor. 15:2) grants them not just freedom from sin in this life (15:17), which some at Corinth likely equated with having all that humans might want (4:8), but also the certainty of imperishable bodies. Paul's emphasis that belief in Christ's resurrection is at once belief in their own underlines his conviction about the importance of recognizing that, in Christ, God does not offer escape from bodies but escape from *corruptible* bodies. Another way to put this is that Paul thinks that to consider

---

19. In this context, the reference in 4:8 to already reigning may mean that, by virtue of their spiritual experiences, the "deniers" understand themselves to be already living immortality. On the basis of other verses, Bultmann opines that "the gnosticizing party in Corinth" spiritualized the resurrection and so believed that the resurrection had already occurred (*Theology of the New Testament*, 1:169).

bodies as dispensable is to misunderstand the salvation offered by Christ's cross and resurrection. Christ does not provide disembodied immortality but immortality embodied. Paul wants the Corinthians to see that bodily corruptibility is a problem that God through Christ has solved. This is so because death has lost its power—now.

Paul is not concerned to problematize death, as de Boer proposes, but rather to problematize Christ's resurrection. The apostle wants the deniers to see the scope of the significance of Christ's resurrection. It has not just defeated the power of sin, which the Corinthians appear to value (1 Cor. 15:17). Paul wants them to understand that Christ's resurrection has made death so ineffective that dying is merely entry into life in incorruptible bodies (15:35–38, 42–44). When Christ manifests his risen state at the parousia, his triumph over sin and death—in which believers share—will be visible. Believers' bodies will be changed to be like Christ's. Their union with Christ will be manifest in a spectacular fashion.

Paul is not teaching eschatological caution or clarifying a time table for when death will finally be vanquished. Rather, he is concerned that the deniers recognize the full range of wonders afforded to those who belong to Christ. They are not only freed from sin, filled with God's spirit, and so able to live this life with a sense of liberty; they are also destined to share Christ's risen existence in spiritual bodies like Christ's. That is, their union with Christ is much more expansive than they recognize.

Paul seeks to convince the deniers not only of the solidarity between Christ's resurrection and theirs[20] but also that death (like sin) has no role to play in the lives of those in union with Christ— not even as that which will liberate them from embodied existence (if this is what the deniers hoped for). This is the case because of Christ's resurrection.[21] Those in union with Christ will receive imperishable bodies with which to enjoy God's reign (1 Cor. 15:50–53).

---

20. So Holleman, *Resurrection and Parousia*.

21. In distinction from the role Paul gives sin and death in Rom. 5:12, where he describes the situation Christ came to rectify, in 1 Cor. 15, Paul portrays the situation after Christ's resurrection, in which death (and sin) have no power.

The apostle wants the Corinthians to know that denial of bodily incorruptibility diminishes the significance of Christ's resurrection. Paul is concerned not with death but with the significance of union with Christ. He wants those who are in Christ (1 Cor. 1:2, 4–5) to know more than they do at their current stage of maturity (3:1). Paul desires that the deniers recognize that the wisdom of God, righteousness, sanctification, and redemption (1:30) that they have received includes sharing Christ's risen life, which means that they, like Christ, will have spiritual bodies. Paul is concerned that some Corinthians have not apprehended the horizon-shattering importance of Christ's resurrection; Christ's resurrection offers more than forgiveness of sins and a sense of power in this life. It means also that bodies are destined for embodied immortality like Christ lives. Death now has no power for those in Christ because they live in the present tense of the risen and exalted Christ.

Paul's Concern Is Not with the Timing of Believers' Resurrection

Paul is intent not on curbing the deniers' enthusiasm but on reframing and enlarging it. As those who belong to Christ, they, like Christ and through Christ (1 Cor. 15:45), will have spiritual bodies. Paul is not focused on clarifying that this wondrous event is yet to come; if he were, surely the verbs in these verses would be uniformly future indicative.[22] Paul is not correcting the deniers by "insisting on the futurity of the resurrection, taking seriously the reality and seriousness of death."[23] Rather, he is stressing that nothing more has to happen in order for those in Christ to receive bodies that will not die. Importantly, when Paul sequences the events attending Christ's coming, he places the resurrection of those who belong to Christ[24] before the statement about Christ's destroying (καταργεῖται) the last enemy, death. In other words, *the obliteration of death is presented*

22. As mentioned, grammarians recognize that the indicative mood is the one mood in ancient Greek certain to convey temporal reference. So C. Campbell, *Advances in the Study of Greek*, esp. 105–33.
23. Tuckett, "Corinthians Who Say," 274.
24. See parallelism between 1 Cor. 15:21 and 15:22; being made alive is to be resurrected.

neither as necessary in order for those in Christ to be raised nor as the result of their resurrection. Christ's continuous activity of destroying death takes place somewhat independently of believers' resurrection.

De Boer's proposal that Paul distinguishes between Christology and soteriology—Paul believes that Christ has subordinated death in his resurrection, yet believers must wait until their resurrection for this to be true for them—presumes that Paul is concerned about timing. Paul wants the deniers to know that they do not yet have what Christ has now. In essence, Paul wants them to know that the nature of their salvation is that they share only partially in Christ: "The soteriological application of Christ's exaltation over the powers can only be construed in terms of promise."[25] Paul, de Boer claims, exhorts the deniers that they must accept that there is a temporal gap between how Christ lives and how they will eventually live.

Paul's chief and primary concern, however, is *not* with timing.[26] The apostle is intent on underlining the solidarity between believers and Christ: Christ's resurrection means their resurrection. Paul speaks about their resurrection at Christ's parousia for the purpose of emphasizing that their belonging to Christ means that nothing Christ has is withheld from them. Because Christ is raised, so will believers be (1 Cor. 15:12–19).[27] The fact that believers are not yet raised bodily is not a sign that there is something lacking in their unity with Christ. Paul's point is to underscore the entirety of their unity with Christ—an entirety which means that they will certainly have bodies like Christ's imperishable one. Since they live in the one who has an imperishable body, when this will happen is inconsequential. It is the case and will be manifest at Christ's parousia.

---

25. De Boer, *Defeat of Death*, 123.
26. This does not mean that he is uninterested in a sequence of events at the parousia.
27. Cf. Holleman, whose study emphasizes that unity with Christ is the ground of believers' eschatological resurrection—that is, "the eschatological resurrection is a participation in Jesus' resurrection" (*Resurrection and Parousia*, 173). See also C. E. Hill: "Union or solidarity between Christ and his people . . . is essential to Paul's insistence upon a bodily resurrection of believers" ("Paul's Understanding of Christ's Kingdom," 303).

This aligns with Paul's words earlier in the letter: believers are so completely united to Christ that the reason not to sleep with a prostitute is because the one who is united to the Lord becomes one spirit with him (1 Cor. 6:17). Elsewhere, Paul claims that believers now share Christ's resurrection life (Rom. 6:4; cf. Col. 3:1) and belong to and can act as in the day (the day of Christ; Rom. 13:13; 1 Thess. 5:5, 8). Living in the day does not indicate that a future event for Christ has partially come into the present but rather that Christ's present is currently available to those united with him. That those united with Christ may at present live as in the day (Rom. 13; 2 Cor. 6:2; 1 Thess. 5) confirms my proposition that in 1 Corinthians 15 the parousia is the unveiling of Christ's present reality.

Paul decidedly does not limit union with Christ. The basis of Paul's soteriology and ethics is, rather, that believers are completely joined to Christ. (This is to be distinguished from conformity to Christ.) Admittedly, those joined to Christ do not yet have glorious bodies like Christ's. This is, however, of no moment to Paul, for that will come (1 Cor. 15:16–19). Believers can know that they are now free of the power of death (e.g., 2 Cor. 4:10–5:5). Their physical deaths are simply doors to a fuller experience of resurrection life. To repeat: the power of death is not an obstacle to believers receiving the fullness of their salvation (imperishable bodies). Being in Christ is being in the one who has conquered death. Mortal believers live in Christ's present reality.

The Destruction of Death Has Occurred

Believers do not await salvation from death at Christ's parousia. They await, as Paul puts it in Romans, the redemption of their bodies (Rom. 8:23)[28] or, as in Philippians, the transformation of humble bodies into the form of Christ's body of glory (Phil. 3:21). When speaking of the human situation after Christ's resurrection, Paul does not present the power of death as the cause of present corruptibility or as an obstacle to future incorruptibility. Death's

---

28. Although Rom. 8 does not mention Christ's parousia in connection with this redemption.

destruction is not identified as an obstacle or an event necessary in order for either the "dead in Christ" or those who are alive at "the coming of the Lord" (1 Thess. 4:15–16) to be always with the Lord (obviously in an incorruptible state). The resurrection of believers is sure not because of a future event (Christ's return) but because of Christ's resurrection, in which death was triumphed over.

Death's entrance into the world through sin (Rom. 5:12) is a problem that is solved through Christ's entrance into the world. Justification, which comes through Christ (5:1), is in effect the defeat of sin. And where sin is defeated, so is death. Some interpreters, however, distinguish the effect of Christ's cross, which has dealt with sin, from the effect of Christ's resurrection, which is supposedly still to be appropriated by believers when death is finally defeated.[29] Joseph Longarino[30] takes up J. Christiaan Beker's problematizing of Christian mortality: given Paul's conviction of the interrelatedness of sin and death, if Christ's cross and resurrection defeated sin, why are believers mortal?[31] What these scholars miss is that Paul does not think believers' death is a problem. Rather than being troubled by the physical death of believers, Paul discounts it,[32] as evidenced by his remarkable statements about the insignificance of physical death in Romans 8:38 and 14:7–8 and 1 Thessalonians 5:10. Notice also 1 Corinthians 3:21–23: "For all things are yours, whether Paul or Apollos or Cephas or the world or life or death or the present or the future—all belong to you, and you belong to Christ, and Christ belongs to God."

Paul is not much exercised about the fact that believers currently have mortal bodies. Rather, as he states in Romans, he is certain that

29. E.g., Käsemann, "Primitive Christian Apocalyptic," 132–33.

30. Longarino proposes that Paul thinks that subsequent to Christ's resurrection, God uses death for God's purposes—to shape people more fully into Christ's image. "In the hands of God, death becomes a tool to fashion communion between God and humanity, on the one hand, and among humans, on the other" (*Pauline Theology and the Problem of Death*, 161).

31. Beker, *Paul the Apostle*, 221.

32. He does acknowledge that for those who are not believers physical death is problematic—they grieve without hope (1 Thess. 4:13)—and recognizes that believers will grieve.

It is as conceivable that the Thessalonians did not know how to make sense of physical death because Paul did not think it would happen prior to Christ's parousia (the standard interpretation) as to imagine that Paul had not thought it important enough to mention on his evangelistic visit.

since the spirit of the one who raised Christ from the dead lives in their mortal bodies, those bodies will be given resurrection life (Rom. 8:9–11). The accomplished defeat of death at Christ's resurrection is assumed throughout Paul's writing. In the two occurrences where Paul explicitly mentions death's defeat (1 Cor. 15:26, 54–55), that defeat is already accomplished by Christ's resurrection.[33]

We should also underscore that, except in 1 Corinthians 15, Paul does not mention the destruction of death when speaking of believers' resurrection or of believers' receiving glorious bodies (e.g., Rom. 8:23; Phil. 3:21; 1 Thess. 4:14–17). Moreover, as mentioned, the sequence of events in 1 Corinthians 15:22–26 does not indicate that Paul thinks the defeat of death is the essential preamble to believers' resurrection. Death is the last enemy being destroyed, and it is a defeated one with no power over Christ or over those who are in Christ. Believers can be raised because of the defeat of death accomplished at Christ's resurrection. Those living in Christ are not hostage to death, and their physical deaths allow entry to a greater experience of union with Christ.[34]

In 1 Corinthians 15:22–28, the parousia event is seen as a whole; the focus is less on a series of events and more—much more—on Christ. At the eschaton the glorious revelation of Christ's presence embraces and enables the resurrection of those who belong to him. The future event of Christ's coming makes manifest Christ's present exalted reality. Christ's present reality is that all inimical powers, including death, are in submission.[35] Death is being destroyed, and so the present age, from which believers are liberated, is passing away (1 Cor. 7:31).

The telos when Christ hands to God his current rule over the powers (1 Cor. 15:24) and then is subjected to God (15:28) does not

---

33. De Boer rightly understands Paul in 1 Cor. 15:26–27 to be claiming that death is already subordinated to the lordship of Christ because Christ has been raised (*Defeat of Death*).

34. It is hard to know whether Paul thought that the moment of death would give immediate access to the glories of life with Christ (Phil. 1:23) or whether transformation to incorruptible life awaits Christ's return (1 Cor. 15:23; 1 Thess. 4:13–17).

35. Gordon D. Fee writes concerning 1 Cor. 15:26, "In a sense, the final enemy to be subdued, is already being destroyed through the resurrection of Christ" (*Corinthians*, 757).

change circumstances for Christ. Christ has been raised from the dead (15:20) and now rules all the powers, even death. Neither the event of Christ handing his rule to God nor his subjection to God change Christ's situation. Christ's future actions reveal his present tense.

1 Corinthians 15:51–57

Though Christ is mentioned only once in 1 Corinthians 15:51–57, Christ's risen and exalted state is the ground for Paul's claims. The basis upon which believers know that they too will be changed from mortality to immortality is that Christ has been. This is now a principle that can be declared—as Paul does in 15:53: a principle that illuminates the reality of the defeat of death (15:54–55). That is, 15:53–56 describes what has been achieved in Christ's resurrection.[36] This is confirmed by Paul's statement that God is the one who gives (see the present active participle) to believers the (same) victory over death by means of Christ (15:57).

In 1 Corinthians 15:51–55, Paul dramatizes an event that is future for believers. However, this transformative event is grounded in what has already occurred through Christ's resurrection. Christ's time envelops human chronological time. That Paul speaks of Christ's resurrection as the firstfruits (15:20) underscores his conviction that Christ's resurrection will necessarily be reproduced in all who belong to Christ. The immortality of the faithful is the necessary (δεῖ;

---

36. Contra Hollander and Holleman, who read this as referring to "the end of time when death will be 'swallowed up in victory' (v. 54)" ("Relationship of Death, Sin, and Law," 273). Note not only that neither here nor elsewhere does Paul refer to "the end of time" but also that the Isaiah and Hosea citations (15:54b–55) function to declare what has happened (κατεπόθη— aorist indicative). As Gordon Fee writes, "These two passages are in fact fulfilled in Christ" (*Corinthians*, 803). There is, of course, expectation for those who belong to Christ to be transformed into imperishable and immortal existence (15:54a). Yet the certainty of that expectation (ὅταν; 15:54a) and its grounding in the present reality of life in the one who defeated death mean that effectively believers currently live in victory over death.

Though not on the basis of these verses, Athanasius puts it this way: "He surrendered His body to death. . . . This He did out of sheer love for us, so that in His death all might die, and the law of death thereby be abolished [and] . . . voided of its power for men" (*On the Incarnation*, 34). He continues, "All men were clothed with incorruption in the promise of the resurrection" (35).

15:53) outcome of what is. Unlike in 15:20–28, here Paul trains his focus on the eschatological event from the perspective of human chronological time, as evidenced by the numerous future indicatives. From the vantage point of human time, when this great event occurs then will come to pass (τότε γενήσεται; 15:54) the word that was written. However, as I discuss throughout, Paul's clear conviction is that Christ, in whom believers live, has already swallowed death in victory: "Christ, being raised from the dead, will never die again; death no longer has dominion over him" (Rom. 6:9).

As in 1 Corinthians 15:20–28, Paul has his eyes on both human chronological time and Christ's time, though unlike those earlier verses, here his interest is chiefly on sequential time—perhaps in order to drive home to the deniers his conviction about the necessity of believing in bodily resurrection. Nonetheless, Christ's time as the surrounding and defining time remains in view. It is because of Christ's victory over death that those joined to Christ can and must expect their own immortality.

It might also be noted that my reading of 1 Corinthians 15:53–57 as referring primarily to the situation subsequent to Christ's resurrection, rather than to what will happen "at the last trumpet," makes sense of Paul's mention of sin and the law in 15:56. As elsewhere, here Paul bundles death, sin, and the law (see Rom. 5–8). In 1 Corinthians 15:56, Paul nods to the claims he makes in Romans where he states that those united with Christ are capable of reckoning themselves dead to sin (Rom. 6:11) because they are united with Christ's death and life (6:4). Sin's continued existence can, according to Paul, be avoided subsequent to union with Christ crucified, risen, and exalted. Likewise, Paul asserts that believers have died to the law (7:4). There is no hint of reserve in these statements. Through Christ's death and resurrection, believers are dead to sin and to the law. This conviction is embedded in 1 Corinthians 15:56. Gordon D. Fee understands Paul well on 15:56: "Both sin and the law have already been overcome in the cross."[37]

37. Fee, *Corinthians*, 807.

Summary

In 1 Corinthians 15, Paul speaks of a future event for the faithful that is certain because they live presently in the victory of Christ's resurrection—they live in Christ's time. Believers' future transformation is absolutely and unequivocally guaranteed because of Christ's resurrection. That transformation is not yet, but its certainty transforms that "not yet" into present victory. Those united with Christ are, like Christ, free of the power of death. Though they do not yet experience incorruptibility, their certain transformation from corruptibility to incorruptibility means that they, like the one to whom they are joined, live victorious over death.

The eschatological events in which Christ acts confirm and manifest the present nature of Christ's life. His resurrection has, for him, destroyed death, as Paul states in Romans 6:9: "We know that Christ, being raised from the dead, will never die again; death no longer has dominion over him." Paul's affirmation that Christ has been raised from the dead (1 Cor. 15:20) says the same thing. Subsequent to Christ's crucifixion, resurrection, and exaltation, his enemies—every rule and authority and power (15:24)—have no power over him. This is made evident to creation at the telos (15:24). (Colossians 2:15 corroborates this: Christ's crucifixion disarmed and triumphed over the principalities and powers.)

Christ's handing over of his reign is still to come. Yet when understood as a feature of his subjection to God (1 Cor. 15:28), it is an act that does not change Christ's present. Christ's present existence is one of obedience to God. Christ's life—whether his earthly life or his exalted one—is lived in obedience as God's Son. This is entailed in Paul's theme of Christ's faithfulness. Teresa Morgan rightly includes Christ's faithfulness to God in her analysis of Paul's use of "faith": "Christ is both faithful to God and worthy of God's trust [and] trustworthy by human beings and trusted by them."[38] The apostle sums this up when he writes that Christ is God's (3:23). The subjection of Christ the Son to God at the end is a manifestation of what currently is.

---

38. Morgan, *Roman Faith and Christian Faith*, 274.

Paul understands that the future events in which Christ acts reveal and make tangible to humanity and creation the life Christ lives in Christ's present tense. They are, then, events in the future of humanity and creation that bring Christ's present tense into the open, and in which the space of Christ's current existence is made available to others. Paul's vision is not of Christ having a future that is now partially present in humanity's present. Rather, the apostle thinks that believers' future will be changed when Christ's present is revealed.

Revelation of Christ's Present Tense in Romans 8

Both 1 Corinthians 15 and Romans 8 exhibit anticipation of the revelation of Christ's present tense. In Romans 8, however, rather than describing an eschatological appearance from heaven that confirms and reveals Christ's present glory, Paul eschews such a scene and instead grounds coming glory in Christ's present life.

The revelation of the coming glory is perceived from τοῦ νῦν καιροῦ (Rom. 8:18). The "now time" is not the remaining present evil age, as standard interpretation assumes.[39] Leander Keck, for instance, says that the phrase "is a surrogate for what still remains of 'the present age.'"[40] However, as in Romans 3:21; 5:9, 11; and 7:6, the "now time" should be understood as the time of God's action in Christ. Coming right after Romans 8:17, which speaks of being co-heirs with Christ and of the necessity of co-suffering in order to be co-glorified, "now time" refers to time in union with Christ. That Christ's suffering and glorification are and will be shared makes plain that the "now time" is the time of Christ. Co-suffering that leads to co-glorification (8:17) takes place through unity with Christ, and so in Christ's time.

---

39. E.g., Blackwell, "*Greek Life of Adam and Eve* and Romans 8:14–39," 111. Käsemann has a more nuanced interpretation: the "now time" is not just the earthly present or the evil age or the age of salvation. "It involves the moment of destiny which precedes the revelation of future glory" (*Romans*, 232).

40. Keck, *Romans*, 209. C. E. B. Cranfield, on the other hand, acknowledges, with qualifications, the opinion of John Chrysostom that the glory already exists, though it remains to be revealed (*Romans*, 1:409).

Being in Christ is to be in the νῦν καιρός: the now time that is life-time. Anticipation of the glory that is to be revealed to those in Christ and the revealing of the children of God to creation (Rom. 8:18–19) is not expectation for another temporality or age. It is expectation that occurs—and can only occur—because believers live in the "now time," which is the time of Christ.[41] The glory to be revealed is the glory of conformity to God's Son, which entails being righteous (8:29–30).[42] Believers are righteous through the faith of Jesus (3:26), and so, since Jesus lives in glory, Paul can speak of them as already glorified: by virtue of being called and justified, believers currently are glorified (8:30). Standard commentary on "the glory of the children of God" (8:21) understands Paul to be referring to future glory.[43] This is usually stated without argument and without relating this verse to Paul's statements about believers' current adoption, their being led by the spirit of God (8:14), being children of God (8:16), and as those who are justified and so glorified (8:30).

I read Paul to be saying, rather, that what believers do not yet have is perfected freedom, which Paul describes in Romans 8:23 as the liberation of their bodies. However, since they are justified and the children of God, they now have glory (8:30), albeit not palpably or visibly.[44] Verse 21 reads, then, that creation itself will be set free

41. Cf. Barth, who describes the present time as "the ocean of concrete, observable reality, in which the submarine island of the 'Now' of divine revelation is altogether submerged but remains, nevertheless intact. . . . This 'Now' (iii.21), this 'Moment' beyond all time . . . which is not point in the midst of other points, Jesus Christ crucified and risen" (*Romans*, 304).

42. Mathias Nygaard rightly notes that for Paul "justification is not an end in itself but a step towards the goal of sharing in glory" ("Romans 8," 169).

43. E.g., Dunn, *Romans 1–8*, 472; Fitzmyer, *Romans*, 509.

44. Cranfield writes that Paul indeed thought the glory to be revealed is "in some sense already ours . . . but it is important not to stress this in such a way as to obscure the vastness of the difference between our present condition and that which is to be ours" (*Romans*, 1:409–10).

Michael Wolter, though framing his comment in the "interplay of the 'already now' and the 'not yet,'" elegantly states: "The 'glory' of those who believe . . . is self-evidently an eschatic reality that already exists, and in fact exactly like their 'justification' or the fact that God 'called' them or that God had made them 'heirs' (8:17) or that they are 'children of light' (1 Thess 5:5). What is still yet to come is the transformation of those who believe into this reality (according to Rom 8:24–25, what is 'seen'). The 'glory of God' in the present is therefore experientially perceptible only in the mode of hope. As such, however, it is perceptible" (*Paul*, 188).

from slavery to corruption into the kind of freedom that is fitting to the glory of the children of God—glory that (as evidenced by Paul's vision) is present to the eyes of faith. It is to be noted that Paul does not describe God's children as in bondage to corruption, as is creation. While believers' freedom awaits perfecting in the liberation of their bodies, this will be consistent with their present glory. They await not liberation from slavery but revelation (8:18–19). That is, *creation's current situation is drastically different from what it will be, whereas the circumstance of the children of God is not.*[45] Paul makes this plain at the end of Romans 8. Now and always believers have all that matters—"the love of God in Christ Jesus our Lord" (8:39). Neither death nor things that are to come (8:38) can interfere with this most foundational and transformational reality. The glory that the children of God will have revealed to them is both the liberation of creation and the redemption of their bodies (8:19–23). The redemption of their bodies will give God's children the freedom that their current glory lacks; as 8:30 makes plain, however, it will not *introduce* them to glory.

The great distinction between Romans 8 and 1 Corinthians 15 is that in Romans 8 there is no mention of a cataclysmic event.[46] Unlike 1 Corinthians 15, in Romans 8 the hope of life for mortal bodies is not connected to Christ's parousia, or the "end." Redemption of corruptible bodies is conceived of as an outworking of what is. Being co-heirs with Christ (8:17), which in context includes living his resurrection life (8:11), is not dependent on the eschaton.[47] Believers *are* children of God as the spirit co-witnesses with their spirit (8:16). They *are* heirs of God and fellow heirs of Christ. What is required

45. Cf. Fitzmyer, who writes that believers "live in the power of [Christ's] risen, glorious life; they are thus freed proleptically from the powers of sin, death, and corruption" (*Romans*, 509).

46. Contra Käsemann, who claims that what Paul has in view here is the parousia (*Romans*, 232).

47. As mentioned elsewhere, Paul conceives of salvation at the eschaton as salvation from God's eschatological wrath. In Rom. 13:11, Paul claims that believers know the *kairos*, which is the hour to awaken to the time in which they are living (to awaken out of sleep) and see that "salvation is nearer to us now than when we became believers." Salvation refers to deliverance from the wrath of God at the eschaton as Rom. 5:9 makes plain (cf. 13:5). For believers, the eschaton is a day of salvation when their glory will be revealed alongside Christ's.

is suffering with Christ. That is, Christ's present life, which as we have seen includes his suffering, is where believers live. And Christ's present life, which is one of glory, is what believers know and will know. The reason believers live both in suffering and in glory is because Christ does. It is on account of living in the νῦν καιρός (Christ's time) that believers anticipate that glory will be revealed to them (8:18) and that they can perceive creation eagerly waiting the revealing of the children of God (8:19). In 8:18 Paul reiterates what he said in the previous verse: the glory that will be revealed to those united with Christ, which necessitates co-suffering, is what believers are experiencing in the "now time."

My locating of present suffering in Christ and in the time of Christ is, of course, a very different reading than that which sources suffering in the old age.[48] I also distinguish myself somewhat from Morna D. Hooker's suggestion that Adamic sufferings are "pulled over"[49] into life with Christ because of Paul's experience in which he is able to treat his sufferings "as though they were in Christ."[50] Hooker queries whether this might be because for Paul "Christ is fully one with man in all his experiences."[51] I agree with Hooker that believers may understand their suffering "in terms of life in Christ,"[52] however, as I discuss below, it is important to recognize that Paul thinks suffering with Christ is suffering with *Christ's* sufferings, which are transformed by Christ's resurrection. While presumably Paul understands the exalted Christ's sufferings as a sharing in the suffering of creation (including humanity enslaved to the present age), they are not, as they were prior to his exaltation, caused by this age. Christ's resurrection and exaltation completely obliterated any power that this age had over him during his incarnated suffering. The exalted Christ's ongoing suffering (which takes place in Christ's present tense) is not for the purpose of defeating the powers of this

48. *Pace* Eastman, "Christian Experience and Paul's Logic of Solidarity," esp. pp. 247 and 248.
49. Hooker, "Interchange in Christ," 23.
50. Hooker, "Interchange in Christ," 24.
51. Hooker, "Interchange in Christ," 24.
52. Hooker, "Interchange in Christ," 24.

age, for the resurrection has done that. Consequently, believers' suffering is not, as Hooker would have it, Adamic suffering that has been baptized into Christ,[53] if by that she means it is caused by the power of sin to which Adam was subject. Paul states that, through Christ, believers have prevailed completely (ὑπερνικῶμεν; Rom. 8:37) and that they endure their tribulations entirely within Christ's love (8:37–39).

Believers suffer, as does the exalted Christ in whom they live, not because they remain partially subject to the present age but because from a situation of liberty they groan along with the unliberated. Believers share *Christ's* suffering; like Christ, their suffering is embraced by, even defined by, resurrection and exaltation. And so Paul describes those in Christ suffering in the presence of the spirit and with hope and in the knowledge of glory (Rom. 5:2–3). This is a distinction with a difference, for when believers' suffering is understood to be caused by the powers of this age, it leads to or reinforces the false idea that they are partially in thrall to this age. If, however, we see that Paul understood that it is the exalted Christ's suffering that believers share, then their tribulations are seen to be evidence of life in Christ alone, and suffering can be understood to be enveloped and transformed by resurrection life.[54]

It is noteworthy that Paul does not say that creation itself is aware of its waiting with eager longing (Rom. 8:19) and groaning together until now. On the other hand, "we know" that all of creation has been groaning together in the pains of childbirth until now (8:22). "Now" here echoes the phrase νῦν καιροῦ; the time in which believers live allows for insight into creation's long-standing trauma and knowledge that this "now time" promises release and birth. If we understand τοῦ νῦν καιροῦ and τοῦ νῦν to refer to Christ's time, we will read Paul as saying that the perspective of Christ's time affords knowledge that the subjection of creation was done in

---

53. Hooker, "Interchange in Christ," 24.

54. This idea shares a kinship with that of Simone Weil, who writes, "The extreme greatness of Christianity lies in the fact that it does not seek a supernatural remedy for suffering but a supernatural use for it" (*Gravity and Grace*, 81).

hope (8:20). The children of God identify with this hope, for they themselves eagerly wait for their bodies to be redeemed (8:23). The adopted children of God (8:15) fully anticipate that their adoption will be manifest in redeemed bodies. They see that they and creation are integrally connected; their hope and creation's are one and the same—freedom from corruption (8:21)—though, as mentioned, God's children are not in bondage to corruption. This hope is available in the νῦν καιρός—in the time of Christ.

Paul speaks of believers being adopted and yet waiting for adoption (Rom. 8:15–17, 23). The redemption of believers' bodies is a flowering of the life believers have; it is not transference from one reality to another. The adoption of believers will be published, and they will experience it more completely. Adoption manifest in redeemed bodies will display in a more wondrous way present existence in life-time. The redemption of believers' bodies will not locate them in another temporality; it will confirm their adopted status.

The coming glory that will be revealed is the glory that now is and in which union with Christ is lived. That Paul does not connect the revelation to believers with a parousia-like scene suggests that by the time he writes Romans, Paul sees more clearly Christ's present glory, even in the midst of the groaning of creation and of believers. In what is probably his last letter, the apostle perceives more fully that in the "now time" (Christ's time), glory is not only coming but is. Consequently, he may have decided that mention of a cataclysmic event would be a distraction. The coming revelation of glory is consonant with what is—Christ's present in which believers live.

7

Union with Christ and Time

I have grounded my reading in the claim that Paul conceives of believers living not in an age but in the being of Christ. The faithful live joined to Christ, and consequently their temporality is Christ's. Though they continue to live chronological time, that time is embedded in and transformed by another temporality—Christ's time. Likewise, the chronological time of "those who are perishing" is surrounded and shaped by death-time. The recognition that Paul's union-with-Christ concept has temporal implications has been inadequately touched on in previous scholarly explorations. In what follows, I briefly analyze some of the more important discussions of this central Pauline concept as they relate to the matter of time.

Paul's union-with-Christ theme has been interpreted in various tones from the ethereal to the down-to-earth. This ranges from Adolf Deissmann's famous claim that Paul conceived of it like being in the air we breathe,[1] to Teresa Morgan's more prosaic contention that being "in Christ" means being under Christ's authority and

1. "Just as the air of life, which we breathe is 'in' us and fills us, and yet we at the same time live in this air and breathe it, so it is also with the Christ-intimacy of the Apostle Paul: Christ in him, he in Christ" (Deissmann, *Paul*, 140). See also in *Die neutestamentliche Formel "in Christo Jesu"*: "Christus ist das Element, innerhalb dessen der Christ lebt und alle Äusserungen des eigentümlich christlichen Lebens zur Erscheinung kommen" (81–82).

protection.[2] The history of this research is easily accessible and need not be rehearsed in detail here.[3] Scholarly interest has often focused on what the preposition ἐν ("in") signifies in one of the key union-with-Christ phrases—ἐν Χριστῷ ("in Christ").[4] More recently, the significance of Χριστός in those phrases has been addressed.[5]

In regard to the meaning of ἐν, the main discussion is whether it should be understood modally or locatively; and, if the latter, whether this entails an ontological dimension. For instance, though he does not base his claim on a grammatical claim about ἐν, William Wrede understands Paul to think that the church is those "in Christ" and consequently "the new humanity itself."[6]

As far as I know, while the modal and spatial dimensions of being "in Christ" have received significant attention, the temporal implication of union with Christ has not been addressed directly. However, although rarely drawing more than a passing interpretative glance, and sometimes not even that, there are indeed temporal implications. Moreover, the common claims about union with Christ—for instance, about the future coming into the present, or about believers participating in the events of Christ's death and resurrection—are made without pondering how Paul might have thought that this could be. That is, the kind of temporality that would allow for such strange happenings is not considered. What most interests me regarding temporality is more than the obvious fact that people live in union with Christ during their chronological time. I am interested in the *kind* of time in which this life joined to Christ occurs.

2. Morgan, *Being "in Christ" in the Letters of Paul*.
3. See especially C. Campbell, *Paul and Union with Christ*, 31–58; Hewitt, *Messiah and Scripture*, 7–41; Wolter, *Paul*, 221–52. For some comments on the reception history of interpretation of "in Christ," especially from a theological standpoint, see Thate, Vanhoozer, and Campbell, eds., *"In Christ" in Paul*, 3–36.
4. The concept of union with Christ is expressed with more than "in Christ." C. Campbell patiently explores various Pauline phrases that contribute to the idea that believers are united with Christ (*Paul and Union with Christ*).
5. See especially Hewitt, *Messiah and Scripture*.
6. Wrede, *Paul*, 119 (italics original). Cf. Wrede's claim that for Paul redemption "signifies . . . *a change in the nature of humanity*" (112 [italics original]); and Andrew Chester, who understands Paul to think that "those in Christ are now (proleptically) being transformed into this resurrection form of glory" (*Messiah and Exaltation*, 88).

Various Interpretations of Union with Christ and Time

James D. G. Dunn investigates the various Pauline phrases that contribute to the apostle's union-with-Christ theme, concluding that "Paul and his converts must have sensed Christ as a living presence which pervaded their assemblies and their daily lives."[7] The sense of "being bound up with Christ focused on two soteriological moments"—one is Christ's death and resurrection and the other is "that event's impact on individual lives."[8] Further, participation in Christ involves "a cosmic salvation process."[9] That is, a new creation that starts with Christ's cross is in the process of coming to be. The unexplored temporal aspects of participating in Christ's living presence are that there are *events* that have changed and will change individual lives and reality itself. Events necessarily indicate temporality, as does the idea of process.

W. D. Davies, equating being "in Israel" with being "in Christ," writes that "the real member of the Old Israel is he who has appropriated to himself the history of his people: he has himself been in bondage in Egypt, has himself been delivered therefrom."[10] Likewise, for Paul "the Christian individual re-enacts in his own experience the life of Christ. . . . Just as the true Jew is he who has made the history of his nation his own history, so the Christian is he who has made the history of Christ his own."[11] *Robert Tannehill* claims that, for Paul, Christ's death and resurrection "do not just produce benefits for the believer, but also are events in which the believer himself partakes. . . . [The believer] continues to participate in Christ's death and resurrection in his daily life."[12] *Michael Gorman* sees Christ's exaltation as also part of the context in which believers live: "The narrative of the crucified and exalted Christ is the normative life-narrative within which the community's own life-narrative takes place and by which it is shaped."[13] *Michel*

7. Dunn, *Theology of Paul*, 408.
8. Dunn, *Theology of Paul*, 410.
9. Dunn, *Theology of Paul*, 411.
10. Davies, *Paul and Rabbinic Judaism*, 104.
11. Davies, *Paul and Rabbinic Judaism*, 107.
12. Tannehill, *Dying and Rising with Christ*, 1.
13. Gorman, *Cruciformity*, 44 (italics original).

Bouttier suggests that "in Christ'" signifies, for Paul, being taken up into Christ's entire story: "Etre en Christ ce n'est point un *état*, c'est littéralement être entraîné dans son histoire, passée, présente et future!"[14] Union with Christ is more than involvement in the past events of Christ's death and resurrection. It also entails communion with Christ's present at the right hand of God and with Christ's eschatological events.[15]

Constantine R. Campbell defines four aspects to Paul's union-with-Christ theme: union, participation, identification, and incorporation. He steers away from using the term "union" as the sole term since he says that "it is *static*, referring to a state of affairs or mode of existence," which, unlike the aspect of participation, does not adequately "convey more dynamic notions such as the dynamic, active partaking in the *events* of Christ's narrative."[16] Campbell is somewhat vague in regard to the nature of believers' participation in the events of Christ's narrative, saying that "the significance of these events pertain to us as it pertains to him."[17]

Thinking about Christ's history and the events of his life (both incarnated and exalted) necessarily involves thinking about time. *Udo Schnelle* recognizes this. While he understands the primary meaning of "in Christ" as locative, "indicating a sphere of being,"[18] his interpretation acknowledges not only a spatial aspect but also a temporal one. Schnelle describes life in Christ as "lived between the beginning of salvation and its consummation" and terms this temporality "the new time between the times."[19] Schnelle does little to explore this new time apart from claiming that the perception of believers in regard to time is changed.[20] He writes, "Baptized believers live in the consciousness of contemporaneity with these events [Christ's resurrection and return], which factually are past and still

14. "To be in Christ is not a *state*, it is literally to be drawn into his history, past, present and future!" (Bouttier, *En Christ*, 97 [italics original]).
15. Bouttier, *En Christ*, 133.
16. Campbell, *Paul and Union with Christ*, 413 (italics original).
17. Campbell, *Paul and Union with Christ*, 408.
18. Schnelle, *Apostle Paul*, 481.
19. Schnelle, *Apostle Paul*, 482.
20. Schnelle, *Apostle Paul*, 482.

to come."[21] This begs the questions, What kind of time might make past events present to human beings, and what kind of time might make eschatological events contemporary?

Albert Schweitzer understands Paul to think that union with Christ is "an actual physical union between Christ and the Elect."[22] There is a "reciprocity of relations" in Paul's claims about Christ suffering for the faithful and they for Christ and for one another. This reciprocity "is founded on the fact that the existences in question are physically interdependent in the same corporeity, and the one can pass over into the other."[23] The corporeity that believers share with each other and with Christ "is in a special way susceptible to the action of powers of death and resurrection, and in consequence capable of acquiring the resurrection state of existence before the general resurrection of the dead takes place."[24] Schweitzer's remarkable interpretation assumes activity and interchange between Christ and believers, which is to say that it assumes a temporality as well as a corporeality. The temporality involved in Schweitzer's interpretation is that the future (the resurrection of the dead) is actualized in the present in those who are united to Christ: "they are already creatures of the new world."[25]

E. P. Sanders agrees with Schweitzer's understanding that Paul thinks that participation in Christ is real and actual,[26] though Sanders is skeptical about Schweitzer's logic. Sanders's presentation of Paul's view in regard to union with Christ—that believers are "one Spirit" with Christ while they await the certainty of "future full salvation"[27]—has temporal implications. "At present" believers "participate in Christ's body"[28] while waiting for Christ's return. Though he does not explore the idea, presumably Sanders would think that union with Christ is not life in a static or atemporal

21. Schnelle, *Apostle Paul*, 594.
22. Schweitzer, *Mysticism*, 127.
23. Schweitzer, *Mysticism*, 127.
24. Schweitzer, *Mysticism*, 116.
25. Schweitzer, *Mysticism*, 116.
26. Sanders, *Paul and Palestinian Judaism*, 462.
27. Sanders, *Paul and Palestinian Judaism*, 463.
28. Sanders, *Paul and Palestinian Judaism*, 463.

existence since there is a future event in Christ's life—Christ's return.

Grant Macaskill's exploration of the theme of union with Christ in the New Testament claims that in regard to Paul, at important points the phrase "in Christ" has a locative sense: "it demarcates a sphere (or state) of existence that is eschatological and that has come to realization in, and through, the incarnational narrative of the crucified and risen Son."[29] Though Macaskill's language of "state" might convey the idea of a static existence, it is clear that he thinks that Paul understands being in Christ as dynamic and progressive. The spirit enables believers' existence to be transformed such that they are conformed to "the likeness of the crucified and risen Son."[30] Such transformation certainly takes place over human chronological time, but it is also suggestive of taking place in a particular kind of time—the one lived by Christ and the spirit.

Teresa Morgan argues that "in Christ" is not union language.[31] She contends that ἐν with the dative has an encheiristic meaning ("in the hands of"): "Saying that someone, or something, is in the hands of a person often means that he, she, or it is their responsibility."[32] Morgan argues that Paul uses this grammatical construction to indicate his conviction that the faithful are under Christ's "authority and protection" and "are a new creation living in a new age."[33] Morgan's view has temporal implications. To be under Christ's lordship is not to be under the powers of the present age. An age is a reality characterized by certain kinds of power and a certain kind of time. By extension, living under Christ's lordship is to live in a reality with not only a certain kind of power but also a certain kind of time—one distinct from that of the present evil age. Though Morgan writes

29. Macaskill, *Union with Christ*, 249.
30. Macaskill, *Union with Christ*, 249.
31. Morgan, *Being "in Christ" in the Letters of Paul*, 195.
32. Morgan, *Being "in Christ" in the Letters of Paul*, 17. Michael Wolter shares a similar view, although on a different basis and from a different perspective. Unlike Morgan, Wolter does not base his opinion on a grammatical investigation. Further, he focuses on the effect for the believer: being "in Christ" expresses "an existential belonging and dependence that cannot be imaged as closer and nearer" (*Paul*, 239). Morgan, on the other hand, emphasizes the authority and care of Christ.
33. Morgan, *Being "in Christ" in the Letters of Paul*, 243.

that life in Christ's hands is "not a temporal or temporary condition but part of eternal life already active in the present age,"[34] it appears she understands temporal merely to signify human chronological and moral life. The matter of what kind of temporality might allow part of eternal life to be active now is not addressed, but certainly her statement surfaces the issue.

N. T. *Wright* proposes that, for Paul, Jesus is Israel's Messiah, with whom believers are in solidarity by virtue of being "in Christ."[35] Those "in Christ" are to "be characterized by his 'faithfulness,' expressed in terms of his death and resurrection."[36] As vague as this statement is, it harbors a temporal implication: living in solidarity with the Messiah who died and was raised is believing not only in the truth of those temporal events but in the presence of those events—being in the new age while still being in the present one. Wright claims that to live "in Messiah" is to live in the overlap of the "age to come" and the "present age."[37]

A. J. M. *Wedderburn* explores the various meanings of ἐν and notes how strange it is in the phrase "in Christ" or "in the Lord," since these are not the kind of words usually connected to ἐν: Christ "is not a time or a place, an abstract noun or an instrument in the normal senses of these terms."[38] Wedderburn concludes that Paul understands Christ, like Abraham, to be a representative figure through whom God acts. God acts in Christ, and the faithful are caught up with him "in that divine initiative of grace."[39] Wedderburn's brief but important investigation raises the fact that ἐν can be understood temporally ("it is therefore hardly likely that anything in the ἐν construction as such is going to dictate whether these phrases are to be interpreted locally or temporally or in any other way")[40] and contemplates, though rejects, the idea that Christ is a time.

---

34. Morgan, *Being "in Christ" in the Letters of Paul*, 246.
35. N. T. Wright, *Paul and the Faithfulness of God*, 835.
36. N. T. Wright, *Paul and the Faithfulness of God*, 835.
37. N. T. Wright, *Paul and the Faithfulness of God*, 1101.
38. Wedderburn, "Some Observations," 88.
39. Wedderburn, "Some Observations," 91.
40. Wedderburn, "Some Observations," 87.

Joshua W. Jipp contends that Jesus, for Paul, is the Davidic Messiah whose narrative includes his crucifixion, resurrection, and exaltation. Christ's subjects (believers) share "in the identity and rule of Jesus the Messiah."[41] Christ unites his people to himself so that "they are incorporated into his cruciform pattern of love for the other," which happens by means of Christ's presence.[42] Jipp's claim that Paul thought of Jesus as present and uniting people to himself entails an unspoken understanding of a temporality for Christ. If Christ is active in uniting people to himself, he must live a kind of time; and his presence, which according to Jipp allows believers to share his rule, raises the question of whether Paul assumes that believers live in Christ's time.

The Temporality of Union with Christ

My concern is not to take a stand on a particular interpretation of the phrase "in Christ," or of Paul's union-with-Christ theme, but rather to point out that various interpretations entail largely unaddressed temporal implications. My view is that Paul regarded union with Christ to involve union with a kind of time. If it were the case that Paul had spoken of believers being in the new age, this would go without saying—to live in the new age would, among other things, be to live in the temporality of the new age. But Paul does not speak of believers living in the new age. The apostle identifies the faithful as those liberated from the present evil age and united with Christ. Union with Christ does not transport believers out of human chronological time, but it does transform the living of human chronological time. Union with Christ entails union with Christ's temporality while living chronological time.

It is important to underscore that the Christ in whom believers live is the exalted Christ. Paul envisions Christ to be living with God (Rom. 8:34). Christ's exalted life includes his incarnated life. Moreover, by means of the spirit, the exalted Christ is not restricted

41. Jipp, *Christ Is King*, 275.
42. Jipp, *Christ Is King*, 67.

to heaven, as Ernst Käsemann in particular stressed.[43] Through the spirit, Christ is present and active in human life. For Paul, however, Christ's presence and activity do not overshadow Christ's life in God's life. Rather, Christ's exalted life both supports Christ's spirit-mediated activity in human life and is the environment for believers' knowledge and experience of God in Christ. Consequently, the apostle encourages believers to recognize that in Christ they too can be alive to God (Rom. 6:8–11).

A further point to clarify is that while Paul thinks that Christ's spirit and God's spirit allow for union with Christ (Rom. 8:9),[44] that union is with *Christ*. That is, believers are united with Christ *through* the spirit but not with Christ *as* the spirit.[45]

Eschatology in the Context of Christ's Time

From the perspective of human chronological time, there awaits the full revelation of Christ's present tense, and so it is right to speak of future eschatology. Yet, since for Paul the temporal horizon of those united with Christ is Christ's time, not human time, Paul pushes believers to understand eschatology in the context of life-time. Those joined to Christ wait for the future in chronological time *enveloped by Christ's time*. Christ's time conditions the experience of the human future tense. There are more events still to come, but waiting takes place in Christ's exalted present: life-time.

This gives hope a particular quality for believers. Hope is not wishing for something that is not yet; it is a capacity—aligned with faith (1 Cor. 13:13; 1 Thess. 1:3)—to know what will be in light of what is. Hope knows that what is not seen is nevertheless there, and so it allows for patience (Rom. 8:25). Moreover, hope is a condition of existence: believers are saved in hope (8:24); creation was subjected in hope (8:20). Hope is not wishing beyond the present for

---

43. Käsemann, *Romans*, 222.
44. See the excellent article by Susan Eastman, "Oneself in Another."
45. Contra Deissmann's claim on the basis of 2 Cor. 3:17 ("The Lord is spirit") that the "in Christ" phrase refers to Christ as spirit (*Paul*, 138). Wolter correctly writes that to be "in Christ" is not "an aspect of Pauline pneumatology" (*Paul*, 237).

a better future; it is the product of full engagement in the present because God's love, mediated by the spirit, allows for this (5:1–5). Believers live *in* hope; hope is grounded in awareness of what is.

Until Christ's day, Paul expects growth in and demonstration of purity and righteousness among those united with Christ (Phil. 1:6, 10). This growth takes place both in human chronological time's expectation of Christ's day and in life-time—the possession of the realization of that growth. Consequently, Paul says he is convinced (πεποιθώς; 1:6) that the one who began a good work will complete it. Christ's day will involve making plain the quality of believers' lives (1 Cor. 3:13; 5:5; 2 Cor. 1:14; Phil. 2:16). Presumably, such becomes apparent because of the light that shines from the visible presence of Christ's ascended existence. That is, the judgment that accompanies Christ's day is an organic part of the revelation of Christ's present, for the visibility of his glorious life makes obvious all that is shameful. Likewise, what is blameless and righteous in believers' lives will be seen on the day of Christ (Phil. 1:6, 10).

What is to come includes liberation from mortality. The rising of the dead in Christ and the transformation of the living occur at Christ's day (1 Thess. 4:13–5:2). While this is transformative for those in Christ, for Christ himself it is the disclosure of his present existence. Occasionally Paul describes this event as Christ's parousia—his official visit.[46] This visit allows those who are joined to him to perceive Christ's present in a new way. The dead and the living in Christ will meet the Lord in the air and so always be with him (1 Thess. 4:14–17). They "will . . . bear the image of the man of heaven" (1 Cor. 15:49), for they will be imperishable. Those in union with Christ will, in other words, see and know fully the wonder of Christ's temporality—life-time, time without Death.[47]

The unveiling that believers await at Christ's day/parousia will not, however, change their temporality. Believers live now in life-time.

46. Jeffrey A. D. Weima rightly understands Paul's reference to parousia as echoing its common use to refer to an official visit of a king or dignitary (*1–2 Thessalonians*, 320).

47. I will capitalize "Death" from here on, not so much to indicate entire agreement with the apocalyptic reading as to follow its important recognition that for Paul, Death is a suprahuman, anti-god power.

Paul's ease with speaking of believers living resurrection life prior to Christ's day/parousia indicates that he understood them to live life without Death prior to their bodies being given incorruptibility. Believers clearly have mortal bodies (Rom. 8:11)[48] that are "dead because of sin" (8:10), but nevertheless they are not living in mortal time—death-time. Sin no longer has power over them.[49] Paul's declaration in Romans 8:1–2 that "there is therefore now no condemnation" is a statement that those in Christ Jesus are no longer under the reign of Sin. They are set free. This echoes the claim in Galatians 1:4 that believers are liberated from the present evil age (cf. Col. 1:13). The mortal bodies of believers live life-time.[50] The eschaton—when full access to the divine present is granted and mortal bodies are transformed—is less change than confirmation: it publicizes Christ's present in which Death and Sin are powerless.

The present wonder of life in Christ draws Paul's gaze much more than events that are future in human time. The marvel that Christ's present is available upon union with Christ and prior to its revelation at Christ's day/parousia is Paul's primary focus. Only three letters mention the parousia, and though most of them mention Christ's day, in each letter Paul primarily attends to aspects of what currently is—aspects that are conditioned by the present temporality of the exalted Christ in which believers live: life-time.

It is further to be noted that in the two letters in which, arguably, Paul most robustly and fulsomely preaches his message (Romans and Galatians), eschatological references are sparse. In Romans and Galatians, Paul trains his vision on the awe of current life in union with the exalted Christ. Further, in neither Romans nor Galatians does Paul indicate that believers' physical death is problematic or in need of explanation. Only three passages in Romans mention or

48. J. Christiaan Beker claims that the term τὰ θνητὰ σώματα ("the mortal bodies") signifies "an 'interim' reality" between being "the body of sin" and "the spiritual body"; it is a kind of body fit for life "between the times" (*Paul the Apostle*, 288). This freights the adjective θνητά with more than is reasonable. Paul is merely acknowledging that believers' bodies die.

49. As Morna D. Hooker puts it, "To be 'in Christ' . . . means to share in his death to sin and in his release from the power of sin" ("Interchange and Atonement," 34).

50. Even the dead are "in Christ" (1 Thess. 4:16); Death is excluded from their temporality. They are in life-time.

allude to the future resurrection of believers: Romans 6:4–11; 8:11; and 8:18–25. In this letter Paul does not discuss Christ's parousia; he speaks of "the day" in only two adjoining verses (13:12–13).[51] The reference to "the day" in Romans 13 functions to encourage present living in the light of the day, rather than to focus attention to the future. Galatians makes no mention either of eschatological events or of believers' future resurrection.[52] Paul's comment about reaping from the spirit eternal life (Gal. 6:7–9) is best read as expressing a thought comparable to Romans 8:9–11. Eternal life is the quality of life that flows from the spirit and is known now in union with Christ, just as it will be after physical death. In Galatians, what is awaited is the hope of righteousness (Gal. 5:5), which Paul is at pains to clarify is available now through the spirit (5:16–25). The law (that is, righteousness) can be fulfilled in the freedom of the spirit. In light of the lack of eschatological references in Galatians, the hope that is awaited is righteousness that can, by the spirit, be lived now. Presumably, this is the meaning of 5:6; it is faith working through love and not the law's demand for circumcision that fulfills the law (cf. 5:14).

Paul's gospel concerns the present presence of the exalted Christ's temporality—life-time. His gospel is not reliant on a completing event. Paul thinks that those united with the exalted Christ live Christ's temporality. Their time is freed from the limitations of Death's rule. Their physical deaths merely open them to the full wonder of that freedom (whether Paul envisioned that happening at the eschaton or upon each person's death).

Two Modes of Resurrection

Paul speaks of the resurrection of those united with Christ in two ways. One way is as an event and condition while living with mortal

---

51. The reference in Rom. 2:16 is to the day when God judges, and the object of God's judgment is the gentiles who do not have the law (2:14). As mentioned above, presumably this refers to non-believers in Christ. Here I am focusing on Paul's references to Christ's day and how that affects those united with Christ.
52. J. Louis Martyn's remarkable apocalyptic reading of Galatians rather submerges this fact (*Galatians*).

bodies (Rom. 6:4; 8:10; cf. Col. 3:1). This manifestation of resurrection is connected to Christ's own death and resurrection. In Romans, Paul writes that our burial with Christ by baptism results in our being enabled, like Christ, to walk in newness of life (Rom. 6:4). This entails the capacity to put to death the deeds of the body by means of the spirit, which results in life (8:13); that is, the declaration that "you will live" (8:13) includes resurrection life while in mortal bodies. Paul claims that if the spirit of the one who raised Jesus from the dead dwells in believers, then their mortal bodies will also be given life (8:11). Even while believers live with corruptible bodies, Christ shares his resurrection with those joined to him. Christ shares his resurrection before the eschatological revealing of Christ's present tense; those united with Christ live his temporality of life-time prior to the eschaton. *The destruction of Death happens for believers when they are united with the exalted Christ.*

Paul also, of course, speaks of resurrection as transformation of mortal bodies. Christ will share his resurrection in a manner that will result in believers' bodies being changed, as was Christ's body. Those who belong to Christ will be made alive (1 Cor. 15:22–23); the dead and the living will meet the Lord in the air and be with Christ always (1 Thess. 4:15–17). Believers' humble bodies will be conformed to Christ's glorious body (Phil. 3:21). *Resurrection will no longer be limited by mortality.* While sometimes Paul connects believers' transformation to the parousia, other times he speaks of transformation apart from that particular event. Without mention of a cataclysmic event, Paul claims that the bodies of the children of God will be redeemed (Rom. 8:23), that believers will be raised with Christ (1 Cor. 6:14, 2 Cor. 4:14).

Living Life-Time/Christ's Time

At the point of union with Christ, believers no longer live death-time but life-time; at the point of union, while living in mortal bodies, believers are already free of Death. In Christ's time, the death of believers' bodies is not fatal; their mortality becomes enveloped in and suffused by life. Those united with Christ are, like Christ, liberated from Death. Even before their bodily transformation, there is no death-time in the temporality of those united with Christ. The apostle is convinced that though the day is near and not here, those in Christ can act as if the day has arrived (Rom. 13:13). Paul thinks it possible that while living in mortal bodies, believers are of the day and belong to it (1 Thess. 5:5, 8). Because the time is contracted—ὁ καιρὸς συνεσταλμένος ἐστίν (1 Cor. 7:29)—believers can act as if the passing away of the shape of the world has already happened.[53] Paul encourages those in Christ to recognize that though in the present time they see enigmatically, they are looking at what they will "then" (τότε) be able to see face to face; this knowledge is a part (ἐκ μέρους) of the complete knowledge they will have (13:12). He is confident that those in Christ will see face to face and understand exactly (13:12). Though in 1 Corinthians 13 Paul is overtly speaking about the greatness of love, his claim that love never ends and that there is a "then" when sight will be unimpeded indicates that he thinks of love in a context beyond the reach of Death.

Paul speaks of the freedom of the glory of the children of God (Rom. 8:21). As argued above, read in the context of 8:14–30, Romans 8:21 indicates that the children of God—those who have received the spirit of sonship and so cry "Abba," and who know they are children of God (8:14–16)—exist *now* in glory. As Paul says in 8:30, the siblings of God's Son are ἐδόξασεν ("glorified"). Though a further experience awaits God's children—the redemption of their bodies (8:23), which confirms they have received the spirit of adoption (8:15)—they are at present God's children, living in glory.

Paul speaks with assurance and awe about his receiving τὴν ἐξανάστασιν τὴν ἐκ νεκρῶν ("the resurrection from the dead"; Phil. 3:11).[54]

---

53. I find helpful Giorgio Agamben's understanding that ὁ καιρὸς συνεσταλμένος means "the time that contracts itself and begins to end" (*Time That Remains*, 62). Agamben's proposal that Paul lives in messianic time, which is neither this age "nor the apocalyptic *eschaton*" (62 [italics original]), resonates somewhat with my proposal about the temporal significance of Paul's union-with-Christ concept. I do not, however, think that Agamben's messianic time as operational time correctly understands Paul, nor do I think that "an *already* and a *not yet* . . . defines the Pauline conception of salvation" (69 [italics original]).

54. See my "Timely Pastoral Response to Suffering," 82.

He is certain that there is now (ἔχομεν, "we have") in heaven a building from God which will replace believers' earthly dwelling (2 Cor. 5:1). The apostle claims that anyone in Christ is new creation, that everything is new (5:17), and that now is the day of salvation (6:2). In 2 Corinthians, Paul makes these claims in close proximity to his statement that current affliction is producing in believers an eternal weight of glory (4:17) and the capacity to look at things that are not seen—things that are eternal (4:18). Those united with Christ can understand that their affliction is productive of the glory that they see even though it is invisible.

The Cosmic Significance of the Unveiling of Christ's Present Tense at the Eschaton

The significance of the unveiling of Christ's present tense at the eschaton is not only that believers will be liberated from mortality but that all of creation will know freedom from decay. Paul says as much: creation waits eagerly for the revealing of the children of God (Rom. 8:19–23).[55] Because of the spirit, God's children know that creation groans just as they do for the redemption of their bodies (8:23). The groaning of the children of God is not a self-focused longing.[56] Believers' deep longing is a spirit-inspired understanding that, when their bodies are transformed, creation will be liberated from its bondage to corruption. The unveiling of Christ's present tense will mean the unveiling of the children of God (8:19), which will release creation itself into the freedom of the glory of the children of God (8:21).

The telos, which ends death-time, does not cause believers to be concerned for themselves—though, by means of God's spirit, they care about it for the sake of everyone and everything else. Believers

55. See Susan Eastman for a compelling argument that by "creation" Paul signifies all of humanity, including unbelievers and most especially Israel ("Whose Apocalypse?," 276).

56. Beker rightly sees that Paul is concerned not just for believers but for "unredeemed creation" (*Paul the Apostle*, 364), yet Beker's concern to direct attention to Paul's conviction that God cares not just for believers but for all creation misses Paul's certainty about the present defeat of Death for those in union with Christ. For believers, physical death is not fatal.

are already liberated from Death and so from death-time. They live life-time: resurrected life in mortal bodies, knowing their bodies will be changed. For those in union with Christ what is "not yet," to use common interpretative parlance, is the expansion to all of creation of *what they already know.*

Not "Already–Not Yet"

Paul did not think in terms of "already–not yet," if that moniker signals that believers remain enslaved to Death.[57] Paul believes that those united with Christ are, like Christ, now liberated from Death. Those who belong to Christ live life-time in mortal bodies; there is no death-time in the temporality of those united with Christ. For Paul, there is a categorical difference between the time that those united with Christ live and the time lived by those who are not: believers live time without Death and so without end, time in the abundance of life. Their mortality is relativized by the certainty that they will receive spiritual, imperishable bodies (1 Cor. 15:42–44; 2 Cor. 4:16–5:4). On the other hand, as Paul's participle makes clear, those who are "perishing" (2 Cor. 4:3) live the illusory time that is bounded by Death.

The difference between the already–not yet perspective and my own is my emphasis on the completeness and adequacy of Christ's present life for believers.[58] The already–not yet interpretation misreads Paul's understanding of the "not yet." What is still to come is the elimination of mortally wounded Death, not for the sake of believers but for the sake of all of creation—so that God can be all

---

57. De Boer, for instance, writes that Paul thinks that "when God sent forth his Son into the world . . . to liberate human beings from enslaving powers . . . , God began a unified apocalyptic drama of cosmic rectification that will reach its conclusion at Christ's Parousia. . . . Believers live neither in the old age nor in the new; they live at the juncture of the ages where the forces of the new age . . . are in an ongoing struggle with the forces of the old age (esp. sin [and] *death*)" (*Galatians*, 34 [italics mine]).

58. Contra Beker: "The longing for the redemption of the body . . . signifies that 'the mortal body' of the Christian, along with creation itself, is subject to the power of death" (*Triumph*, 364). "The existential reality of our 'mortal bodies' reminds us daily of the beckoning of the apocalyptic hour" (367).

in all. Further, unlike the standard interpretation, it is not that there is an "already" that is currently incomplete until what is "not yet" arrives. To the contrary, apart from Christ's handing over his reign to God, *what is now is complete, though it has not yet been revealed.* This is why believers can wait with patience for what they do not see (Rom. 8:25). From the vantage point of *human* time, already–not yet may be a fitting description, but Paul's focus is on *Christ's* time.

Those united with the one over whom Death has no power await the revelatory publication of what they already know—victory over Death. At that revelation, their bodies will be changed. Those joined to Christ are certain of completely sharing Christ's present life, including incorruptible bodies. This certainty is not contingent but rather grounded in Christ's present, the disclosure of which on Christ's day will reveal believers' own glory.

The final end of wounded Death is of consequence for those living the type of time that is shaped by it—death-time. Believers do not wait for this "not yet" for their own sakes. Living the time of the exalted Christ, they, like Christ, look for what is "not yet" for the sake of God's goal—being all in all. In fact, it seems that Paul understands Christ to be keeping Death in a defeated position (observe the present indicative καταργεῖται in 1 Cor. 15:26) until he hands to God his reign over the powers. Believers do not live in eschatological tension due to the overlap of two ages. Paul does not think that either those in Christ or those who are not live in any sort of overlap. There is no both/and but only either/or.

8

Life in Christ's Time

Suffering, Physical Death, and Sin

Standard readings of Paul, which rely on the assumption that the apostle worked with a modified two-age temporality, claim that the apostle understood the conditions of suffering, physical death, and sin as symptoms of the still-unvanquished present evil age. The apocalyptic interpretation, in particular, argues that since believers live in the overlap of the ages, they remain subject to the conditions of the old age until the eschaton.[1] My proposal raises the question, How does Paul understand suffering, physical death, and sin for those who share Christ's temporality?

Suffering

Paul declares his desire to suffer with Christ (Phil. 3:10) and the necessity of doing so (Rom. 8:17). Whether or not one understands, as do I, that Paul conceives of the exalted Christ as also the crucified and suffering Christ, it is incontrovertible that Paul understands

---

1. J. Christiaan Beker influentially argued for this position (*Paul the Apostle*, 364).

union with Christ to involve suffering. This is seen in the fact that Paul presents his own sufferings as consonant with being in Christ. Whether he is in chains writing to the Philippians or detailing his travails to the Corinthians (2 Cor. 11:23–29), Paul will base his apostolic authority on his sufferings.

The apostle does not source suffering in the present evil age; he does not claim that suffering is the result of that age seeping into Christ's exalted presence or that it is a consequence of oppositional encounter with this age.[2] Indeed, if it were the case that Paul regarded his sufferings as symptoms of the overlap of the present age it is astonishing that he should display such acceptance of them. And if he boasts in his suffering because he sees himself contesting the evil age, it is curious that he describes his travails not as slings and arrows from that age but as "the death of Jesus" (2 Cor. 4:10). Suffering is what Christ does, and what those united with him must also do.

It may be asked, since Christ's own sufferings were caused by the rulers of this age (1 Cor. 2:8) and were for the sake of defeating those powers,[3] does that not mean that sharing Christ's suffering is also caused by inimical powers and is for the purpose of defeating those powers? That is, as is often claimed, is not the suffering of those in Christ because they are in combat with the ongoing power and influence of the present evil age?[4] What is missed here, as mentioned, is Paul's certainty that Christ's resurrection changes Christ's sufferings. Whereas Christ was in the likeness of sinful flesh when he was crucified by the powers of the present age (Rom. 8:3), his resurrection defeated those powers: "Christ, being raised from the dead, will never die again; death no longer has dominion over him. The death he died, he died to sin" (6:9–10a). Those united

2. *Pace* Eastman, *Recovering Paul's Mother Tongue*, 109.
3. See Alexandra R. Brown's fine apocalyptic reading of this passage in *The Cross and Human Transformation*.
4. As will be discussed below, the apocalyptic scholarly circle's conviction about the overlap of the ages entails a claim that Paul thinks there is an ongoing cosmic war between God and anti-God powers. See especially Martyn, "From Paul to Flannery O'Connor," 282–83; and Eastman, who writes of the Galatians communities as "the site of cosmic warfare" (*Recovering Paul's Mother Tongue*, 51).

with Christ share this same victorious stance in relation to the powers of this age: "You also must consider yourselves dead to sin and
alive to God in Christ Jesus" (6:11). *Christ's ongoing suffering in
which believers share (8:17) is, then, not for the sake of defeating
the powers, for that has been accomplished.* Suffering with Christ
is for the sake of manifesting God's victory through Christ: "We
have this treasure in clay jars, *so that it may be made clear that this
extraordinary power belongs to God* and does not come from us.
We are afflicted in every way" (2 Cor. 4:7–8a). Suffering is not a
foreign invader into life in Christ or a consequence of the clash of
the ages; it is part of life in Christ.[5]

Paul does not explain either the mystery of Christ's ongoing suffering or the necessity of those united with Christ to suffer with
him.[6] This is to be noted as a caution to interpreters (including me)
who are ready to claim or assume that for Paul the present age is the
cause of believers' suffering.[7] What is clear is that Paul understands
that the suffering of believers is done in the presence of the spirit,
with hope, and in the knowledge of glory. Paul asserts that believers can rejoice in suffering (Rom. 5:3). Though in Romans 5:3 Paul
does not state that this suffering is "with Christ," the fact that the
sufferers are those who have been made righteous, have peace toward
God, stand in grace, hope in the glory of God, and know God's
love through the gift of the Holy Spirit (5:1–5) clearly indicates
that this is with-Christ suffering. Later in the letter Paul describes
the sufferings of the "now time" (8:18), which, as argued above, describes suffering with Christ (8:17). This suffering is endured while
having the firstfruits of the spirit (8:23), living in hope (8:24), and

5. Paul does describe the exalted Christ keeping Death in a defeated position (1 Cor. 15:26).
However, this activity, which is revealed at the eschaton, is not something the apostle asks of
believers.
6. This is the case also for one of his heirs (Col. 1:24).
7. E.g., Beker understands the mortal body as an "'interim' reality . . . subject both to the
rule of the Spirit and to the rule of death" (*Paul the Apostle*, 288). The body is the constant
amid the "discontinuity of the 'ages'" (288). Consequently, the body suffers even while being
in Christ (367). It is to be noted that when Beker uses the term "discontinuity," he is speaking
of the "radical discontinuity between the 'old man' . . . and 'the new creation'" that takes place
because believers live "between the times" (288). My earlier work assumed this (*At the Heart
of the Gospel*).

as glorified (8:30). Believers' dispositions of joy and hope in the face of suffering reveal what Paul proclaims: "Who will separate us from the love of Christ? Will hardship, or distress . . . ? No, in all these things we are more than conquerors through him who loved us. . . . [Nothing] will be able to separate us from the love of God in Christ Jesus our Lord" (8:35–39). Salvation from the powers of the present age is accomplished; the work left on the part of believers is the manifestation (not the accomplishment) of that salvation.[8] In light of Christ's resurrection, then, the function of the suffering of Christ, and of those united with him, is revelatory of the defeat of Sin and Death; it is not for the purpose of their defeat.

Paul's equanimity with suffering indicates his conviction that he lives the time of the exalted Christ whose present life includes his crucifixion. Unlike physical death, which not only is adiaphora but is the gateway to incorruptibility, and unlike sinning, which is to be avoided, Paul regards suffering as essential and integral to union with Christ. (Presumably Paul thinks that Christ's suffering will end once God is all in all, though the apostle does not offer his thoughts on this.)

Physical Death

In Christ, dying has a meaning entirely different from that in the present evil age. In the present age, death is caused by the powers of Sin and Death (Rom. 5:12). On the other hand, in Christ—over whom Death does not rule (6:9)—dying is a transformative event. It is hard to know whether Paul thought that the moment of death gives immediate access to the glories of life with Christ (Phil. 1:23), or whether he thought transformation to incorruptible life awaits Christ's return (1 Cor. 15:23; 1 Thess. 4:13–17). What is clear is

8. Beker claims that Paul thinks of believers' suffering as redemptive (*Paul the Apostle*, 302). There is, however, a distinction to be made between Christ's redemptive suffering that defeated the cause of suffering—Sin and Death—and suffering with the exalted Christ. The latter kind of suffering is in the context of victory, and its purpose is to share in Christ's glory (Rom. 8:17–18). The groaning and suffering that come from awareness of God's victory, and from enacting it through proclamation and love, manifest the salvation that has been accomplished.

that on the rare occasion when Paul writes about it, he indicates that dying is not a problem. I take his remarkable statements about death's insignificance (Rom. 8:38; 14:7–8; 1 Cor. 3:21–23; 1 Thess. 5:10) as indicators of how profoundly his conviction of being united with Christ affects his understanding of the meaning of dying. Rather than seeing it as an affront sourced in the present evil age, Paul has almost incomprehensible equanimity about physical death.[9] I suggest that this is because the apostle contextualizes it in his union with Christ, whose resurrection and exaltation reframe death. "Death no longer has dominion over" Christ (Rom. 6:9), and that is the case also for those in him.[10] For those in union with Christ, physical dying is not a sign of Death's power.

The reference to the defeating of Death in 1 Corinthians 15:26 is, of course, regularly taken as evidence that Paul saw believers' physical deaths as the result of Death's continuing power; that is, believers die because the present evil age still affects them. As detailed above, I see things differently. In the sequence of events Paul describes in 15:23–26, he presents believers' resurrection before mentioning the destruction of Death; further, the verb "to destroy" (15:26) is in the present tense, which, as de Boer rightly notes, indicates that Paul thinks that Death's "destruction, and those of the other powers, has in fact begun."[11] Only twice in his letters (15:26, 54–55) does Paul speak of Death's defeat, and in both cases the defeat is already accomplished through Christ's resurrection.[12] In 15:51–57,

9. As noted earlier, the Thessalonians' worry about the death of some of their members (1 Thess. 4:13) may not have been because Paul had neglected to address the issue because he thought Christ would return imminently but, rather, because the apostle had just not thought to mention it in his evangelistic visit. The apostle saw dying as inconsequential in light of the surety of believers' resurrection.

10. As noted earlier, Athanasius put it this way: "He surrendered His body to death. . . . This He did out of sheer love for us, so that in His death all might die, and the law of death thereby be abolished [and] . . . voided of its power for men" (*On the Incarnation*, 34). "All men were clothed with incorruption in the promise of the resurrection" (35).

11. De Boer, *Defeat of Death*, 122.

12. As noted above, when Paul speaks of the resurrection of believers elsewhere, he does not mention defeat of the power of Death (e.g., Rom. 8:23; Phil. 3:21; 1 Thess. 4:14–17). Paul apparently sees no obstacle to believers sharing incorruptible life when they die. That is, physical death in union with Christ is not a sign of the continuing power of the present evil age; it is entry into a new way of being united with Christ.

Paul explains that the reason believers' transformation from mortality to immortality can and must (δεῖ; 15:53) occur is because of the victory over Death (and Sin and the law) that has already happened in Christ. Believers live presently in the victory of Christ's resurrection (15:57). They, like Christ, are free of the power of Death.

Sin

Morna Hooker's characteristically trenchant definition of Sin serves well: "Sin is for Paul an alien power that corrupts the world and leads to death, because of the weakness of the flesh (Rom. 6–7)."[13] This definition largely accords with much of what apocalyptic interpreters of Paul understand as the apostle's conception of Sin: Paul regards Sin as a power that causes people to do sinful acts.[14] That is, for Paul, Sin is an enslaving entity that compels people to sin. I agree with Susan Eastman's lively description of Paul's conception of Sin. Sin is the result of "the primal transgression of Adam. . . . Henceforth sin rampages through human existence, holding humanity captive."[15]

I have also been helped by those who disagree with the apocalyptic view and emphasize that for Paul Sin resides in the human person, in particular in the passions of the body.[16] I understand Paul to think that the passions are part of bodies and not, as J. Louis

---

13. Hooker, "On Becoming the Righteousness of God," 369. Matthew Croasmun seeks to make the mythological conception of Sin intelligible to contemporary Westerners in his *The Emergence of Sin*.

14. Gabriele Boccaccini writes, "Paul exploits the Enochic view of evil by radicalizing its power. While in Enoch, people (Jews and Gentiles alike) are struggling against the influence of evil forces, Paul envisions a postwar scenario where 'all, both Jews and Greeks, are under the power of sin' (Rom. 3:9). Adam and Eve have lost the battle against the devil, and as a result, all their descendants have been 'enslaved to sin'" (introduction to *Paul and the Jew*, 12). Gaventa speaks of Sin as a "cosmic terrorist" ("Cosmic Power of Sin," 235). De Boer agrees with Käsemann that humanity is subject to Sin and Death (*Defeat of Death*, 161).

15. Eastman, *Paul and the Person*, 111.

16. See especially Stanley K. Stowers, who roots Paul's conviction about the coming transformation of bodies in the apostle's understanding that "the body of dust with its passions and appetitive desires" needs to be "replaced with a body made of πνεῦμα (e.g., 1 Cor 15:42–53)" ("Paul's Four Discourses about Sin," 127). See also Wasserman, *Apocalypse as Holy War*, 173–202.

Martyn proposes, sourced in an apocalyptic power—the Flesh.[17] Sin uses the flesh—that is, the passions of the body.[18] Nevertheless, the philosophical view of Paul's understanding of Sin is unpersuasive at the point at which it claims that we best read Paul's personification of Sin metaphorically.[19] I see the apostle as convinced that he lives in a cosmos inhabited by beings and powers greater than the human mind and capacities—powers capable of controlling humans. The clear fact of the apostle's conviction that humans are in need of God's deliverance puts the lie to the idea that he thought of the power of Sin metaphorically.[20] Greco-Roman moral psychology, which assumes that reason in concert with the "logos" can control the passions, is not Paul's moral psychology.

For Paul, Sin is a power that rules humanity in death-time. Romans 5:12 makes clear that Paul sees Death and Sin as co-dependents. Time that ends—death-time—is time dominated by Sin and Death. Sin uses humanity's passions, and in that regard the law proves useful to Sin. The law identifies what the passions desire (Rom. 7:7), causing people to do sinful actions and have sinful dispositions. It is heuristically useful to distinguish between Sin and sinning: the former refers to a suprahuman power capable of enslaving humanity, and the latter is humanity's response, sourced in their passions, which results in sinning.

Though we might wish he had, Paul does not ponder whether it would have been better for God to have obliterated the possibility of sinning for those united to Christ. And neither does the apostle

17. See his "Daily Life of the Church," 256. Teresa Morgan aptly writes that Martyn "exaggerates in calling spirit and flesh '. . . a pair of warriors, locked in combat'" (*Being "in Christ" in the Letters of Paul*, 167n25).

18. I find helpful Joseph Longarino's careful analysis of Paul's understanding of Sin, in particular his reading of Rom. 8:13: "Paul assumes that the flesh or body of a Christian per se is still the seat of ἁμαρτία" (*Pauline Theology and the Problem of Death*, 104). See also Wasserman, "Paul among the Philosophers."

19. Wasserman proposes that we should interpret Paul's personification of Sin as a literary device ("Paul among the Philosophers," 388, 402). She charges that apocalyptic interpretation is indefensible historically and denies "Paul the use of metaphor and personification" (402).

20. Joseph Longarino understands Paul to regard Sin as the passions that reside in the flesh. Longarino also sees that the apostle understands the intractable dominance of Sin in human life and so the need for divine intervention ("Apocalyptic and the Passions," 596).

contemplate why God allows death-time and Satan to survive. (I discuss Satan below.) Though we might desire a theodicy from Paul, we do not find one. Paul's focus, rather, is almost entirely on life-time and what that means for those who live it.

Union with Christ is freedom from Sin, but it does not obliter-ate the capacity for sinning.[21] Sin can be compared to a colonizing power, which distorts and disfigures the character and appetites of those it oppresses. In a post-colonial context, when the colonizing power is defeated, the previously enslaved find it challenging to fully claim their free identity. Their character and desires have been so shaped by the colonizer that it is a work in progress for them to see themselves as truly separate from the colonizer and free to act that way.[22] Likewise, for Paul, those liberated from Sin must learn to see that their identity and actions can be guided by Christ and the Spirit and not the enslaver from which they are now free.

It is important to note that Paul does not state that believers' ca-pacity to sin is the result of overlapping ages. When believers sin, it is *not* because they are partially in thrall to the power of Sin. Paul is unequivocal about the totality of Christ's victory over Sin, as state-ments like 2 Corinthians 5:21 make clear.[23] Romans 6:10 indicates that while Christ's death to Sin did not obliterate it (Christ died to Sin; he did not kill Sin), Christ himself died to it. Union with Christ allows for the same kind of life as Christ lives: life dead to Sin (Rom. 6:11). For those in Christ, sinning becomes avoidable.

Martyn's influential depiction of apocalyptic war between the Spirit and the Flesh inaugurated by God's invasion in Christ involves describing "the Flesh" as "actively seeking a military base of opera-tions" in communities of believers.[24] I read Paul differently. Paul does

21. Beker does not see this distinction, assuming that Paul thinks that "because sin has been overcome, the 'desires of the flesh' have also been eradicated by Christians (Gal 5:16, 24)" (*Paul the Apostle*, 218). On the other hand, Longarino rightly sees that for Paul the force of Sin "is no longer an insurmountable barrier to obedience to God" (*Pauline Theology and the Problem of Death*, 99).

22. See my "Reading Romans 7 in Conversation with Post-Colonial Theory."

23. As Schnelle writes, "As the sinless one (2 Cor. 5:21), [Christ] entered into the realm of sin and overcame it" (*Apostle Paul*, 437).

24. Martyn, "Daily Life of the Church," 259.

not see "the Flesh,"[25] or Sin, as the problem after people are united with Christ. *It is rather believers' perceptions of their relationship to Sin and its influence on the flesh that is the problem.* Because of God's victory over Sin, those in Christ can choose to set their mind not on flesh but on things of the Spirit (Rom. 8:3–6); they can learn not to use their freedom as an opportunity for the flesh (Gal. 5:13); they can reckon themselves dead to Sin (Rom. 6:11).

Paul, however, does not think that those united with Christ enter a totalitarian regime: God does not turn believers into prisoners of God's victory. The apostle claims that while the level of obedience that would be asked of a slave is asked of those in union with Christ, God does not enslave to the degree that human choice is taken away. Romans 6:16–23 is a good example of Paul describing those in Christ living with a mixture of their own and divine agency: humans both *present* themselves (6:16, 19) and become obedient (6:17); they *receive* liberation and consequently become slaves of righteousness (6:18, 22). At Romans 13:12–14 we see another example of Paul's belief in freedom of choice for those united with Christ: believers can make a choice to do works of darkness, but they can also make a choice to put on the armor of light, which is Christ Jesus.

Paul's regular exhortations not to sin indicate his conviction that believers are not prisoners of God's triumph. By the grace of God, through the Spirit and the wonder of being justified, those united with Christ can demonstrate that Sin has no power. However, they can also choose sinning, even though they are liberated from Sin. God allows believers moral agency. Just as they are capable of sinning, so they are capable in Christ of putting to death the deeds of the body (Rom. 8:13) and of reckoning Sin to be dead (6:11). The freedom in Christ to choose sinning or righteousness is not a sign that God's victory is incomplete. Rather, believers' very capacity to choose is because of God's victory over Sin at Christ's cross and resurrection.

In one passage Paul appears to think that the power of Sin also allows some freedom: people not identified as united with Christ

---

25. As mentioned above, I do not think that Paul regards "the flesh" as a power, though he does think that Sin is.

(gentiles and Jews) can, Paul says, obey the law (Rom. 2:12–16). This statement should, however, be read in the context of Paul building his case toward his claim that all (gentiles and Jews) are under Sin (3:9). By Romans 3, Paul's view becomes clear: unlike God's rule, which gives leeway for those under it to continue sinning, Sin does not allow those under it to choose righteousness.[26] Eastman states that within the situation of enslaved humanity Paul thinks of human actors as "both captive and complicit."[27] I would add that for Paul the complicity of those apart from Christ is not based in the freedom to choose against Sin but is the result of Sin's distortion of the will so that humans apart from Christ will necessarily comply with Sin. Consequently, "there is no one righteous" (3:10).

Believers, however, are entirely capable of keeping defeated Sin in its impotent, excluded position. Such activity on believers' part is not engagement in an ongoing battle for victory but enactment of their freedom and demonstration of Sin's powerlessness. Union with Christ allows for avoidance of sinning. Put another way, believers wrestle against sinning *not in spite of being in Christ but because of being in Christ*. The power of Sin is excluded from life-time and so those who live Christ's temporality are enabled to avoid sinning.

Warfare Imagery

On occasion, Paul uses warfare imagery to describe how believers can demonstrate God's victory and Sin's defeat. Interpreters will understand this imagery to mean that Paul sees believers as soldiers in an unfinished battle.[28] A stream of scholarship, usually aligned with the apocalyptic interpretation, takes Paul's warfare imagery as evidence that his gospel is shaped by what Peter Macky called the

---

26. Though I disagree with Douglas A. Campbell's contention that the first chapters of Romans are not Paul's thought, he rightly observes that Paul sees only "divine rescue" as the answer to those apart from Christ (*Deliverance of God*, 90).

27. Eastman, *Paul and the Person*, 111.

28. Martyn writes, "God has placed us in the front trenches of his apocalyptic war of redemption" ("From Paul to Flannery O'Connor," 297). Gaventa concludes that Paul thinks that "transformed human beings serve as God's agents, God's weapons" ("Rhetoric of Violence," 71).

"cosmic battle myth."[29] It is claimed that Paul shared with other Jews a concept of a battle between God and suprahuman forces of evil.[30] It is undoubtedly the case that Jewish texts portray God as a warrior in battle with hostile forces.[31] It is also clear that Paul portrays Christ's death and resurrection as God's contest with hostile powers. In 1 Corinthians 2:8 Paul states that the rulers of this age crucified the Lord of glory. G. B. Caird rightly states that "this passage must be interpreted in the light of 1 Corinthians xv. 24, where it is obvious that the principalities, authorities, and powers . . . are spiritual beings."[32] The question at hand is not whether God fights suprahuman powers but whether Paul thinks that the battle continues or that Christ's crucifixion, resurrection, and exaltation concluded that battle. The apocalyptic interpretation of Paul typically regards it as axiomatic that Paul shares with Jewish apocalyptic the idea that a cosmic battle continues between God and evil powers. J. Louis Martyn's interpretation of Paul famously argues that "the coming of Christ is the invasion of Christ. And as invasion, that event has unleashed a cosmic conflict, indeed *the* cosmic conflict."[33]

The idea of an unfinished war, even a war whose outcome is assured, relies on and supports the already–not yet temporal understanding:

29. Macky, *St. Paul's Cosmic War Myth*. Though not often clustered with apocalyptic interpreters, Macky's views align with the apocalyptic reading of Paul, particularly in understanding that Sin and Death are cosmic powers, that those in Christ are continuing participants in the present age, and that there is an ongoing battle between God and powers hostile to God.

30. See, for instance, de Boer, who influentially claims that a category of Jewish apocalyptic that he terms "cosmological Jewish apocalyptic eschatology" expects that "God will invade the world under the dominion of the evil angelic powers and defeat them in a cosmic war" (*Defeat of Death*, 85). According to de Boer, Paul partakes of this type of apocalyptic thinking.

31. See Scott C. Ryan for an excellent review of scholarship on this matter (*Divine Conflict and the Divine Warrior*).

32. Caird, *Principalities and Powers*, 16.

33. Martyn, "From Paul to Flannery O'Connor," 282. Martyn writes further: Now is "God's apocalyptic war of liberation. . . . The real cosmos, then, is not a harmony, but the scene of struggle . . . [though the] outcome is not in question. In Paul's letters there is never a hint that God will ultimately lose" (283).

Though Beker rarely uses battle tropes, his apocalyptic reading of Paul emphasizes that God's triumph is not yet, though it is imminent. It will be realized at "the end" (*Paul the Apostle*, 367).

Ryan stands in line with the apocalyptic reading: "For Paul, God won the primary battle in the cross and resurrection, but until God's final consummation the war rages on in the present. Paul enlists those now set free from captivity to Sin and Death into God's militia to participate in the ongoing war in the present life" (*Divine Conflict and the Divine Warrior*, 244).

God in Christ initiated a clash between the powers of the old age
and those of new creation; the battle is in process; though already
the victory has arrived, not only do the vanquished suprahuman foes
remain, but they are still aggressively fighting. This interpretative
position understands Paul to conceive of a continuing suprahuman
battle. In fact, however, there is relatively little battle imagery in
Paul. Teresa Morgan rightly notes "the paucity of Paul's references
to Satan and cosmic war" and writes that Paul's focus is "on the
benign irresistibility of God's rule and the life that is to be lived
under *pax dei.*"[34] Moreover, we should expect a significant amount
of such imagery. Jeremy Punt states the obvious: Paul and his communities are "living in the presence of the Roman army."[35] That Paul
refers to his partners as fellow soldiers (for instance, Phil. 2:25) and
uses military terms when speaking about administrative matters is
straightforwardly explained; as Morgan shows, Paul is echoing the
language and style of provincial administrators.[36]

*Paul indeed conceived of a cosmic war between God and inimical
powers, but the apostle is convinced that, through Christ's cross,
resurrection, and exaltation, God won that war.*[37] This is not to
say that Paul conceives of God as unconcerned with Sin, which
still has power in death-time. His conviction that death-time will
be obliterated at the eschaton indicates that Paul believes that God
will not permit Sin's existence forever. Paul's focus, however, is on
the consequences of God's victory for those united with the one
through whom God won that victory. Union with Christ illuminates
the cosmic victory that takes place through Christ. Sin belongs to
the time from which believers are liberated—death-time. Through
avoidance of sinning, those in Christ witness to Sin's impotence.
In life-time, Sin has no power. When believers think or act sinfully
it is not because they are ruled by Sin or because Sin has a partial

34. Morgan, *Being "in Christ" in the Letters of Paul*, 192.
35. Punt, "Paul, Military Imagery and Social Disadvantage," 219.
36. Morgan, *Being "in Christ" in the Letters of Paul*, 174–81.
37. Interestingly, Wasserman sees something similar in the ancient Mediterranean world's
references to divine war: these function to portray a stable cosmos with the supreme deity in
control (*Apocalypse as Holy War*).

hold on them due to the overlap of the ages. It is because they are not acting from their freedom.

Context of Victory

God's victory is the context in which Paul uses military images. Upon union with Christ, believers enter the zone of victory where there is liberation from Sin. Life in Christ is the only place where sinning can be avoided because, in Christ, Sin is dead. Paul acknowledges the continued existence of death-time, even alluding to Christ's continuing defeat of Death (1 Cor. 15:26; as noted, the verb "destroy" is in the present active indicative). This temporality, however, is of no consequence to those joined to Christ. It is God's concern, not theirs. The faithful live exclusively in life-time, in which they are enabled to live from God's victory.

Those in union with Christ are those who may demonstrate God's victory through their God-given capacity as justified people to avoid sinning. *Paul uses battle tropes to describe an ethical as opposed to a cosmological battle.* The cosmological battle between God and anti-God powers has been won. Clearly death-time remains (below I ponder what this says about the nature of God's victory), but that temporality is not believers'. When believers sin, it is not because they are still partially living in the age ruled by Sin[38] but because they give in to the illusory influence of their former enslaver. Though actually free, they do not self-identify as free or act from their freedom.

In light of Christ's resurrection and exaltation, Paul's statement in 1 Corinthians 2:8 that the rulers of this age crucified the Lord of glory reveals God's victory and the rulers' defeat. God's defeated opponents (Sin and Death) have been marginalized and contained in death-time—a form of life in which all of creation existed until God's victory; a form of life ruled by its trajectory toward extinction. This temporality will be completely obliterated at Christ's day.

---

38. Contra Victor C. Pfitzner, who, using Ephesians, writes, "The internal conflict of the believer against sin (Rom 6:12–14) is part of the great cosmic struggle against Satan and the powers of darkness (Eph 6:12)" (*Paul and the Agon Motif*, 163).

Until then, those living life-time can be dead to Sin (Rom. 6:11). Those united with Christ are capable of putting to death the deeds of the body (Rom. 8:13; cf. Col. 3:5).

Paul speaks of the process of being transformed into the glory of the Lord (2 Cor. 3:17–18). This transformation can only happen in Christ. When believers sin, it is not a sign that they still have one foot in the present evil age or that God's battle against Sin is ongoing. The very fact that believers can avoid sinning is a sign of their union with Christ's victory over Sin; they are united with the one who died to Sin (Rom. 6:10). On the other hand, in death-time, Sin is impossible to resist and so sinning is inevitable.[39] It is only by being united with Christ that blamelessness is possible (1 Cor. 1:8). There is no condemnation for those who are in Christ Jesus (Rom. 8:1), both because of God's gift of righteousness and because those united with Christ participate in actualizing that gift by choosing against sinning. They have necessary help from the spirit in this endeavor (8:4–9).

In 1 Thessalonians 5:8, as in Romans 13:12, Paul directs believers to put on defensive armor. This armor is appropriate to "the day," which is incontrovertibly a day of salvation/victory (1 Thess. 5:8–9). The Thessalonian believers are of the day, which is the day of the Lord (5:2), a day when all dead or alive who belong to Christ will bodily join in Christ's exalted existence (4:17) and always be with the Lord. Warfare imagery is here used in the context of the present victory of being able to be of "the day."[40]

The concluded victory is clear from 2 Corinthians 2:14, where Paul speaks of himself and others in Christ being led in God's triumphal procession. Paul sees those united with Christ as captive slaves following behind God's victory march.[41] Peter Macky writes that in this passage Paul portrays believers proclaiming Christ's victory and bringing "the aroma of death to all those who refuse to bow to

---

39. See my comment on Rom. 2:12–16 above.

40. Cf. Thomas R. Yoder Neufeld, who reads this passage as "an invitation for the Thessalonians to see themselves as enjoying the status of the exalted already, now, *prior to*, or better, as *part of* the fulfillment of the eschatological scenario" (*"Put on the Armour of God,"* 91).

41. Cf. Pfitzner: "The normal meaning 'to lead in triumphal procession' must be retained over against the seemingly easier sense 'to cause to triumph'" (*Paul and the Agon Motif*, 162).

his rule."[42] In 2 Corinthians 10:3–6, Paul uses warfare imagery to portray a battle about knowledge. Given that the battle concerns divine knowledge, the war is not waged κατὰ σάρκα ("according to the flesh"): this is not a flesh-and-blood battle but a battle about divine things, using divine power (10:4). It is, however, a battle that takes place in the context of overall victory. This is made clear through a comparison with how availability of divine knowledge is presented in 2 Corinthians 10 and how Paul presents access to knowledge of God in Romans 1:24–28. The Romans passage describes humanity after God has handed them over—presumably to Sin.[43] Humanity's capacity to know was taken away as a result of that handing over— their minds became debased. Romans 1:24–28, then, describes a situation prior to Christ's cross and resurrection. Second Corinthians 10:3–6, on the other hand, describes the situation of those united with the exalted (victorious) Christ; they have access to knowledge of God and are capable of defending that knowledge. Romans 1, then, depicts the circumstance before God's victory in Christ, a circumstance where knowledge of God has become inaccessible. In 2 Corinthians 10, knowledge of God is available because of God's victory. Paul considers it critical for believers to defy misinformation and obstacles to seeing God's victory. A further indication that the battle in 2 Corinthians 10 takes place in the context of victory is Paul's confidence in his ability, and that of others, to destroy strongholds where arguments against knowledge of God reside. This confidence is grounded in Paul's confidence in God's victory. Paul claims that he has weapons that have God's power, capable of defeating error. There are still hostile strongholds, presumably because some Corinthians remain arrogant (10:5) and have not accepted obedience as the right response to God's victory. Paul's certainty

---

42. Macky, *St. Paul's Cosmic War Myth*, 157. Cf. Col. 2:15, which describes the cross as the moment of victory in which God disarmed the principalities and powers, making a public example of them, triumphing over them in Christ. Though the principalities and powers are not annihilated, to be in Christ is to be in victory. Consequently, with Christ believers have died to τὰ στοιχεῖα τοῦ κόσμου. See F. F. Bruce who aligns τὰ στοιχεῖα τοῦ κόσμου with forces that enslave people and from which believers are freed (*Epistles to the Colossians*, 18).

43. Cf. Beverly R. Gaventa, who writes that God handed humanity off "to the anti-God powers," which include Sin ("'God Handed Them Over,'" 122).

that any resistance will be overcome (10:5) is based on his conviction that the battle is won.[44]

Those united with Christ use weapons fit for the victory that is established, especially weapons of righteousness (2 Cor. 6:7). Paul's reference to weapons of righteousness comes shortly after he has spoken of becoming the righteousness of God. God's righteousness is more powerful than Sin. Weapons of righteousness are weapons that have defeated Sin. God's righteousness triumphed over Sin at the cross (Rom. 3:21–26), and so lives lived in faith from the gift of righteousness bestowed as a consequence of God's triumph may avoid sinning. Weapons of righteousness are used in an ethical endeavor. Paul's concern when facing opponents (some of whom are part of the Corinthian church; 2 Cor. 5:20) is to use weapons appropriate to the victory God has achieved. The claim that Paul perceives these opponents to be participants in an ongoing suprahuman battle is an overreach.[45] Paul clearly believes in suprahuman powers and sees Satan as still active. The apostle even implies that false apostles may be Satan in disguise (11:14). Yet, as is clear from the fact that God uses an angel of Satan to instruct Paul in the sufficiency of God's grace (12:1–9), even Satan is subservient to God. God is in control of Satan because God has won the battle. The contest between true and false knowledge is not at once a contest between God and Satan; instead, it is a contest between those who accept their liberation and are obedient to Christ's rule and those who resist the consequences of their liberation. God has won: in Christ, God was reconciling the world to himself (5:19). The goal for those united with Christ is to live from that victory.

Warfare Imagery Is Ethical, Not Cosmological

Union with Christ is a moral journey. Life in Christ is the place where sinning can be laid aside (Rom. 13:12). Believers avoid sinning

---

44. Contra Lisa M. Bowens, who views 2 Corinthians 10–13 as evidence that Paul thinks there is a cosmic battle underway (*Apostle in Battle*).

45. For instance, Bowens, *Apostle in Battle*, 123.

because they can—the battle is won. Having been brought from death to life, believers are capable of putting their limbs/bodies in service to God (6:13). God's victory does not place in servitude those who trust in it. Though the victory itself cannot be lost, individual believers can walk away from it. If they do, it is not because they have one foot in the present evil age but because they do not see or value their liberation from that age.[46]

Paul encourages the Philippians to fight side by side (Phil. 1:27) in the context of stating his commitment to their προκοπήν ("progress") and joy in the faith (1:25), and his exhortation that they lead lives worthy of the gospel of Christ (1:27). This is an ethical battle. Paul Holloway recognizes the "causal relationship between 'joy' and 'progress,'" which moral thinkers such as Seneca describe.[47] Believers are fighting side by side so that their manner of life can be a sign to the opponents of the gospel of Christ. As Stephen Fowl observes, "the faith of the gospel" involves "holding a variety of convictions . . . [and] holding these convictions also entails a variety of practices."[48]

In 1 Corinthians 9:6–7, Paul uses the image of a soldier alongside that of planting a vineyard and tending a flock. He does so in order to make an apology for not taking money from the Corinthians (9:15). Using warfare imagery, Paul commends himself and his coworkers, emphasizing their successes as they enact being "the righteousness of God" (2 Cor. 5:21)—that is, avoiders of sinning. Though Paul and his companions look as though they are dying and punished, in fact, they live and are not killed. They possess everything (6:10). The weapons of righteousness are signs that this is the day of salvation (victory). These weapons are for the purpose of being model ministers (6:3). They further an essential ethical endeavor. This ethical endeavor is nothing less than embodying and demonstrating God's victory over Sin. While this may have cosmological consequences in

46. *Pace* Morgan who thinks that Paul sees the present as a time of jeopardy because "the faithful still live, according to the flesh, in the 'present evil age' as well as being part of the 'new creation'" (*Being "in Christ" in the Letters of Paul*, 238).
47. Holloway, *Philippians*, 100.
48. Fowl, *Philippians*, 63–64.

that it displays God's victory to the powers in death-time, it does not have cosmological purpose: *Paul conceives of believers not as doing God's work of battle but as witnessing to God's victory by living in the exalted/victorious Christ.*[49]

The "armor of light" (Rom. 13:12) is used against the "works of darkness" which Paul describes as orgies, drunkenness, sexual immorality, and so on and which he summarizes as the desires of the flesh (13:12–14). Here, again, warfare imagery is used in an ethical rather than cosmological context. The reason defensive armor is needed is not because believers take part in an ongoing cosmic battle but so that those in union with Christ can protect themselves from the desires of the flesh. I agree with Gaventa that in Romans 6:13 ὅπλα means weapons.[50] I, however, do not think that Paul conceived of these as weapons engaged in fighting an ongoing war to defeat anti-God powers. Rather, Paul uses warfare imagery to emphasize and dramatize his exhortation in 6:11 and declaration in 6:14: the faithful are those who must reckon themselves dead to Sin and alive to God in Christ Jesus; they are those over whom Sin has no power. Believers fight a moral battle within the context of liberation from Sin's power; they do not fight so as to help God defeat the power of Sin.

The fact that believers will be judged (1 Cor. 3:13) confirms the seriousness and essentialness of their acting out of the righteousness they have been given. John Barclay makes this point excellently: "Paul expects the gift [of being granted status as heirs and being given the spirit] to find expression in the practice of believers—and he is not embarrassed to warn them that God will be the judge of that. . . . The final judgment of believers does not at all contradict the good news of the unconditioned gift."[51]

What battle imagery there is in Paul functions ethically. Warfare tropes emphasize the opportunity to struggle against sinning. Fur-

49. Ephesians changes Paul's understanding by portraying believers as those who are struggling against spiritual forces of evil in the heavenly places (6:12). This understanding evidences a different theological and social situation, perhaps one where the threat to the faithful is seen as more sinister and powerful than what Paul conceived.
50. Gaventa, "Rhetoric of Violence," 64.
51. Barclay, *Paul and the Gift*, 441.

ther, battle imagery stresses the necessity of such struggle. We need further note that, more often than not, Paul appeals to his churches to avoid sinning without using battle tropes. His ethical exhortations typically identify sinful behavior and dispositions, and the alternative Christlike behavior and dispositions (e.g., Gal. 5:13–25).

I have proposed that life in Christ's time means life in a temporality in which Christ's past is present. Christ's crucifixion, which defeated Sin's power, is, along with his resurrection, in Christ's present tense. Christ's crucifixion and resurrection defeated Sin's attempt to have power over him and are the condition of his exalted life. Liberation from Sin's power is the condition also of those united with the exalted Christ.

Satan

Paul refers to Satan seven times: Romans 16:20; 1 Corinthians 5:5; 7:5; 2 Corinthians 2:11; 11:14; 12:7; 1 Thessalonians 2:18.[52] Paul also refers to "the god of this age" (2 Cor. 4:4) and "the tempter" (1 Thess. 3:5), references that most interpreters take to be to Satan by another name. Paul presents Satan as an aggressor against God and believers, though one who is under God's control and powerless over believers, should they live from their union with Christ.

Paul regards Satan as ruler of an environment separate from the one under Christ's lordship. Paul claims that the reason his gospel is veiled to those who are perishing is because "the god of this age" has blinded them (2 Cor. 4:3–4).[53] In other words, Satan is in control of those who do not see the glory of Christ in Paul's gospel. The flip side of this is that those who do see the light recognize that Jesus Christ is Lord (4:4–5). Paul describes two environments: one for those blinded by Satan, and another for those in whose hearts God's light has shone so that they have "knowledge of the glory of God in the face of Jesus Christ" (4:6). These two exist at the

---

52. Belial appears in 2 Cor. 6:15.
53. Most commentators understand the phrase "the god of this age" to refer to Satan. See Derek R. Brown for discussion of alternatives (*God of This Age*, 131–34).

same time and explain why some people do not believe his gospel. The statement in 1 Corinthians 5:5 also assumes that there are two environments—one governed by Satan and the other by "our Lord Jesus" (5:4). These two are mutually exclusive: there is life under Satan or life under the lordship of Jesus. Nevertheless, Satan is subservient to the Lord Jesus, for Satan can service the purpose of salvation at the day of the Lord: the handing over of the sexually immoral man is for the destruction of the flesh in order that the spirit might be saved at the day of the Lord. Satan can, in effect, be made to work for God's purposes.

Paul writes that Satan hindered him and his team from coming to the Thessalonians (1 Thess. 2:18). Though Paul blames Satan for obstacles to his mission, Christ is triumphant: Paul is certain of the Lord Jesus's parousia (2:19). Paul is also overjoyed at news of the faith and love of the Thessalonians, which demonstrate their capacity to resist the "tempter" (3:5)—a capacity available only to those delivered from this age and its god (2 Cor. 4:4).

Satan's subservient role is clear when Paul speaks of the angel of Satan, a thorn in the flesh (2 Cor. 12:7), which was given to him and which the Lord would not take away so that Paul could understand that God's grace is sufficient and God's power is made perfect in weakness (12:7–9).[54] God uses a situation initiated by Satan, presumably in the form of a hostile opponent in Corinth,[55] for God's purposes. Paul here, as elsewhere, presents Satan as actively, though ineffectually, seeking to obstruct Christ's rule. As long as those united with Christ choose against Satan, God's victory is manifest.

The victory of God, in which God's power is made perfect in weakness, as epitomized on the cross, means that Paul's acceptance of his weakness in light of God's power neutralizes Satan's messenger's torment (κολαφίζῃ; 2 Cor. 12:7). Though the thorn remains, Paul's assurance that God's grace is sufficient and that his weakness

---

54. *Pace* Lisa M. Bowens, *Apostle in Battle*. I agree with the majority of interpreters that God is the subject of the passive ἐδόθη. As mentioned earlier, I also respectfully disagree with Bowens that this passage indicates ongoing divine warfare (164).

55. See D. Brown for discussion (*God of This Age*, 182–86). I agree with Brown's conclusion that this likely refers to a personal adversary (186).

is how God perfects God's power (12:9) defines the apostle's life. Satan's messenger becomes a means to a more profound experience of Paul's life in Christ. Rather than Satan's messenger serving Satan's ends, it serves God's. Satan is active, but for those in Christ there is no contest: God's victory in Christ means that those united with Christ need neither serve Satan nor engage in combat with him. Paul's stance toward Satan is not conflictual; he does not engage. Paul writes to the Corinthians that in the presence of Christ he offers forgiveness, a forgiveness that thwarts Satan (2:10–11).

Satan has servants, some of whom are false apostles who obstruct and undermine Paul's mission (2 Cor. 11:4). Paul presents himself as unafraid of Satan's power. He positions himself in response to Satan's servants (the false apostles) by boasting in his Jewish heritage (11:22), of the visions and revelations of the Lord he has received (12:1–10), and of his weakness (11:30), which is in truth his strength (12:10). Satan does not have power over Paul; rather, the power of Christ rests on the apostle (12:9). Paul exhorts the faithful to see that Satan need not threaten them. Satan is under God's control and will soon be crushed under believers' feet (Rom. 16:20).[56] Calvin writes that Paul "promises that the Lord will subdue [Satan] and make him to be trodden under foot."[57]

Paul envisions Satan as active in the present evil age and capable of enticing believers to choose against the gifts of the Spirit, such as self-control (see Gal. 5:23). The apostle advises the Corinthians on conjugal matters by warning that Satan is capable of tempting if one partner denies sex to the other. Lack of self-control can lead to yielding to Satan's temptation (1 Cor. 7:5). Satan's activity, however, does not indicate that believers live both under his rule (the present evil age) and in Christ. Rather, those in union with Christ are free to choose the desires of the flesh or the fruit of the Spirit. As mentioned above, life in Christ's victory over Sin is not life in a totalitarian regime: God does not take away freedom of choice or, for that matter, freedom to be tempted by Satan.

56. Since 16:20 is not missing from any manuscripts, it should be taken as part of Paul's letter.
57. Calvin, *Romans and Thessalonians*, 325.

The Nature of God's Victory

Those who disagree with my proposal that Paul thinks that God has won the battle with hostile powers may do so on the basis of an assumption of what God's victory must look like—total annihilation of God's foes. Typically, of course, Christ's cross, resurrection, and exaltation is understood to have *inaugurated* God's victory, a victory that will only be complete at the eschaton when God will be all in all—that is, when no foes are left. I hear Paul claiming, rather, that God's victory over God's foes requires not their destruction but their diminishment. God's extracting those who have faith from the present evil age (Gal. 1:4) and God's establishment of a new creation in Christ diminish the range of the powers of this age. Paul believes that this is enough to accomplish actual freedom from the "law of Sin and Death" (Rom. 8:2).[58]

Further, Paul does not think that the eschaton will complete the victory that those in Christ live. What the eschaton promises to those in Christ is new bodies with which to experience God's victory. *It is for the present evil age and its powers that the eschaton is of significance.* At the end, when Death is destroyed, this age and its powers will be obliterated. Apart from giving them incorruptible bodies, this will not change things for those in Christ. It will, however, make an immense difference for this age and its powers—they will be extinguished. Equally important, and relatedly, the end will liberate creation from bondage to decay. Looked at solely from chronological human time, it might appear as if there is an ongoing battle that will not be complete until the eschaton, when death-time is abolished. Looked at from the perspective of union with Christ, however, the battle is won. Those united with Christ live in Christ's temporality, in which Christ's crucifixion, resurrection, and exaltation exist simultaneously.

This is not already–not yet temporality. The eschaton is at once a revelation of what currently is and the obliteration of death-time. Since, however, liberation from death-time occurs upon union with

58. I have added the capitals in this quotation from the NRSV.

Christ, the eschaton will not change the temporality of believers' existence—at the eschaton they will continue in the life-time they live now. The significance of the eschaton is for those who live apart from Christ, and for creation.

Conclusion

Rather than simply recapitulating, here I ponder matters raised by my reading from the perspective of one personally invested in Paul's ideas, and I conclude by emphasizing a foundational piece of my thinking.

God's Choice of the Cross and Resurrection

We might ponder whether it is because of the cross and resurrection that Paul construes things as he does. God's choice to defeat Sin and Death through the ostensible weakness of the crucifixion of God's own Son, which ends in Christ's exalted life—life that is visible only to faith—discloses a particular kind of victory. It is a victory demonstrated in weakness and surrender, what Paul identifies as love: Christ loved me and gave himself for me (Gal. 2:20). It is a victory perceived only through faith, which itself necessitates weakness and surrender, for faith requires letting go of our own wisdom (1 Cor. 1:18–25, 3:19) and power, abandoning ourselves to Christ, the crucified and risen one (Gal. 2:20).

Paul's conviction that God uses crucifixion and resurrection as the means to accomplish God's victory, and as the revelation of God's victory, may be the foundation of the apostle's conception of God's victory as complete, though currently hidden except to the

159

eyes of faith. God uses means appropriate to the nature of God's capacious love; though God is essentially and fittingly unknowable (Rom. 11:34; 1 Cor. 2:16), God allows for revelation of God's love to those who align themselves with the kind of strange and humble victory achieved in Christ's cross and resurrection. The ones who join themselves to Christ's faith and life perceive the conclusive fact of God's victory over Sin and Death.

God's love precludes a totalizing sort of victory. God's love for those who will not join themselves to Christ and so remain in death-time means that God allows these people to live their lives in the destructive and defeatist environment of death-time.[1] God's victory does not snatch away the illusory temporality that many find comfortable. God's allowance of the continuation of death-time does not signal an incomplete job but rather discloses how God extends God's own life to all of God's creation. The cross and resurrection is the way God offers life-time, and consistent with this is God's choice not presently to extinguish but rather to diminish death-time. God's love in Christ's cross and resurrection is demonstrated in allowing space and time for that love to be rejected.

On the other hand, Paul does not think that non-human creation desires to live in death-time. Non-human creation bears the cost of those who reject or are blind to the offer of life-time. Paul intimates that this grieves the one who subjected creation to emptiness (ματαιότητι; Rom. 8:20). Understanding the subject of τὸν ὑποτάξαντα ("the one who subjected"; 8:20) as God,[2] we can see how Paul describes God's action of subjection as done in awareness that creation was blameless (οὐχ ἑκοῦσα; 8:20).[3] Yet, accomplishing God's victory in a manner consistent with God's love requires that creation itself be subjected while death-time continues. This is not something that pleases God, but given the nature of God's love, it is necessary. In order to live death-time, humans need (subjected) cre-

1. Speaking to an imaginary interlocutor, who is not among those joined to Christ, Paul declares God's strategy as mercifully to delay the day of wrath to give opportunity for repentance (Rom. 2:1–5).
2. Cranfield correctly opines that this participle's subject "can only be God" (*Romans*, 1:414).
3. Cranfield translates this as "not through its own fault" (*Romans*, 1:414).

ation to use/abuse.[4] However, creation's subjection is done in hope (8:20), indicating how precious creation is to God. Though creation may not itself be aware of the fact, the crucible of hope in which it lives its subjection means that it is groaning toward liberation and new life. God subjected creation out of love for all God created. Consequently, while some humans live death-time, using creation destructively,[5] creation is fundamentally enveloped by God's life.

God's victory over Sin and Death is accomplished at Christ's cross and resurrection. This victory opens to humanity the quality and quantity of time that God, Christ, and the Spirit live—what I have termed life-time. Life-time is a kind of time that is unstoppable and brims only with superabundant life. In truth, it is the only real time. God's victory does not, however, obliterate the kind of time that is shaped by Death and Sin and that serves their purposes—a temporality that in truth is non-time. While God's triumph severely diminishes the range of death-time, and announces that it will be obliterated, God's victory allows death-time to continue.

Who Is God's Victory For?

That God allows the ongoing existence of death-time, even in the context of certainty of its extinction, intimates that God's victory is for all. Paul puts it this way: God will be all in all (1 Cor. 15:28). Eventually, there will be no place or time apart from God. (It is to be noted that Paul does not mention an afterlife [hell] apart from God.) Until God is all in all, it is only those who are joined to Christ's crucifixion and resurrection who know this. The faithful live life-time exclusively, although as Paul's exhortations against sinning and his reframing of the meaning of physical death and suffering show, believers do not always recognize the exclusivity of their existence. This is not to say that when believers do not correctly perceive,

4. Robert Jewett writes, "It is the human race that remains responsible for the defacing of the ecosystem" (*Romans*, 514).
5. Sadly, though Paul does not speak to this, those living life-time (Christians) also use creation destructively.

they have slipped from one temporality to another or that they have incorrectly negotiated life in a situation of overlap. It is, rather, a matter of faith—of perceiving what is, even though it is hidden. *Faith is not the exercise of believing in the face of evidence to the contrary but the exercise of recognizing that the evidence itself is an illusion*: dying is in truth not fatal; suffering is in fact subsumed in Christ's resurrection; and sinning is truly an unnecessary and avoidable dead end.

Paul exhorts the faithful to see that they, like him, are found in Christ (Phil. 3:9) and nowhere else. Everything else not only is rubbish but is excluded from life in union with the exalted Christ, who is at once crucified and risen. The challenge of faith is continually to acknowledge the reality and exclusivity of life in Christ. This involves avoidance of sinning, understanding suffering as sharing in the suffering of the resurrected and exalted Christ, and regarding physical death as gain (Phil. 1:21).

Those who do not have this faith also live in an exclusive temporality: death-time. Interestingly, though he will occasionally speak of those who are perishing (2 Cor. 4:3) and of "outsiders" (1 Thess. 4:12), Paul speaks very rarely of such people. Nevertheless, Paul's intense commitment that the gospel be heard signals both his concern for the plight of non-believers and his conviction that they can exit death-time and enter Christ's time. In other words, *Paul believes that God's victory is for all*.

What Difference Does Being a Believer Make?

As mentioned, Paul's conviction that believers are those who live Christ's time has consequences for our understanding of the apostle's eschatology. At the telos, those in Christ will receive bodies like Christ's glorious body, yet now, though their bodies are mortal, they live God's unending time. Unlike creation, including "those who are perishing," they are already released from bondage to corruption. The eschaton is then less important to those in Christ than it is for creation: at the eschaton creation will be released from bondage. The question arises: what is the benefit of being in Christ? That is, if in the end everything that is receives what believers have currently—life in God's time—what difference does being a believer make?

Perhaps Paul would say that the benefit is both epistemic and existential. Those in Christ are those who know that the time of their lives is not an automatic passing away of moments until their bodies die. Believers are those with the knowledge not only that an immensity of glory will be revealed to them but that each breath they take is with and through and because of God's life and love. Those in Christ can be aware that they live Christ's time, which is also God's. This knowledge has an existential power—believers can live in the embrace of transformative hope. Hope for Paul is the capacity through faith to be aware of *what is*. Believers' knowledge that God through Christ shares God's time and life with them means that life now is transfused with the God-given capacity to hope and so to see the glory that is and will be forever. This stupendous gift offers lives of joy. This is clearly a benefit to believers, and it has the power to make believers a benefit to God's creation. Lives lived without fear of physical death, in awareness that sinning is not obligatory and that suffering is in company with Christ, promise to be lives of creative and healing love for all.

Relating to Those Who Live Death-Time

The exclusivity of the two temporalities is not an excuse or demand for the faithful to separate themselves from non-believers. The model of Paul's life is one of engagement with those who do not believe. Clearly the apostle did not think that when he interacted with non-believers he was stepping into death-time. Paul does not separate himself from non-believers, and he understands the sufferings of his missionary work as signs of being in Christ. Paul knows that he is completely joined to the exalted victorious Christ and that his mission is his costly engagement with those who are perishing. They, along with the faithful, are the ones God's victory is for.

Ethical Implications

My proposal that God's victory is complete though death-time continues might be heard to imply that, since God is in control of the
situation, the faithful need not try to make the world a better place.
Paul's exhortations against sinning give the lie to such an implication. And the apostle's description of the conquering embrace of
God's love at the end of Romans 8 offers a vision of a way of being in
a world in which so many are trapped in death-time. The response of
love for all is the only fitting one for those who have been welcomed
into life-time/God's time. As Paul says after presenting his vision of
the telos, "Therefore . . . be steadfast, immovable, always excelling
in the work of the Lord" (1 Cor. 15:58).

Challenges of Perception

Among the challenges this way of reading Paul presents is that of
perceiving human chronological time as enveloped by Christ's non-
chronological time. This perception is available to thought, clearly.
However, whether it is available to human experience is another
matter. Those who have known transcendent experiences of being
in God's presence or who regularly recognize their daily lives as
surrounded by God's love in Christ may find it unproblematic to
perceive their time as surrounded by God's time in Christ. Many,
however, may find it almost inconceivable that the temporality of
their quotidian is not all there is and, likewise, that the sequential
time they experience need not define their time.

Another challenge, alluded to above, is that of perceiving God's
victory as complete even though the obliteration of what I term
death-time has not yet happened. If indeed this is how Paul saw
things, it necessitates, as discussed above, a particular understanding
of how God conquers. It also entails what might be seen as a naive
or overly optimistic view of believers' divinely endowed capacity to
reckon with such a victory. Is the fact that Ephesians introduces the
idea of two ages (albeit, as mentioned earlier, in a complexified way),

and also the idea of fighting a spiritual war, an understandable development or reaction to Paul's conception? After some years of trying to conceive of the life of faith in Paul's terms, did one of his heirs decide that it was pastorally wise to reframe the apostle's vision? Perhaps the writer of Ephesians decided that the idea that believers are completely in Christ, capable of reckoning with suffering, sinning, and their deaths as entirely "in Christ," needed modification. That writer seems to have decided, as have many recent interpreters of the apostle, that it is most pastorally helpful for believers to see their struggles as the result of the continued influence of the present evil age.

If we accept this as the explanation for the difference between Paul and at least one of his heirs,[6] the issue of diversity within the canonical Paul emerges. To some this may be a matter of concern: whose voice is right? However, this variety may also be seen as opportunity. When the idea of two ages becomes a way for Christians to avoid the challenge of living in Christ by blaming their suffering, sinning, and deaths on forces outside Christ, the undisputed Paul summons believers to a deeper vision and experience. Perhaps somewhat in line with Job in this regard, Paul sees that nothing truly contests God and that it is the role of the faithful to embrace, live, and, indeed, celebrate this. On the other hand, when believers reach the limits of their ability to find God's love in the midst of their struggles, those biblical authors who envision an evil age currently at war with God's reign can offer much needed solace. The Bible's variety, in my view, contributes to its transforming power and effectiveness as God's word.

Why Two Kinds of Time Is Not the Same as Two Ages

One of the critical foundations of my reading of Paul has to do with my claim that Paul did not understand Christ and the life of believers

---

6. Interestingly, Colossians goes in another direction. This letter seems to intensify Paul's view; it speaks of Christ's kingdom, it declares that victory was achieved on the cross, and it says that believers are raised with Christ.

in the context of a two-age framework. After having drawn out some
of the implications of such a reading above, it may be clarifying to
restate this foundational piece. I have stated that "death-time" and
"life-time" should not be heard as alternative appellations for the
old and new age. This is the case in part because Paul himself does
not indicate that he thinks in terms of two ages.[7] That is, I avoid the
two ages as an interpretative framework because I think Paul himself
eschewed that framework. On the assumption that Paul would have
been familiar with temporal frameworks involving two (or more)
ages, it is highly noteworthy that the apostle writes of existing in
the present age or of living in Christ but not of life in two ages.
This strongly suggests that Paul avoids shaping his understanding
of God's work in Christ with the framework of ages. Moreover,
interpreters' use of the two-age framework regularly entails two
corollaries that I find to be impositions on Paul's thought. One has
to do with the nature of believers' existence and the other with
eschatology.

Apocalyptic interpreters in particular understand Paul to think
that believers' suffering, their temptation to sinning, and their physical deaths are the result of being under attack from the forces of
the present evil age. As I discuss, however, Paul sees suffering as in
and with Christ, he claims that believers are dead to Sin and consequently capable of avoiding sinning, and he understands that the
physical deaths of those who belong to Christ open the way to a
greater experience of life with Christ. Moreover, the companion to
the prevalent idea of the persistent influence of the present age on
believers is that God's victory is won though the battle continues.
I, on the other hand, see Paul claiming that at Christ's cross and
resurrection, God defeated the powers of this age. The one indication of a continuing battle is 1 Corinthians 15:26, which speaks of
Death's defeat as ongoing, a reference that I take to refer to Christ
keeping Death in a defeated position. Particularly when taken in
light of Paul's consistent presentation of the accomplishment of

---

7. Of course, Paul does not speak of death-time or life-time either. I recognize these to be
heuristic categories.

God's victory at the cross and resurrection, and of my proposal about the apostle's understanding of the nature of God's victory, this one reference might best be heard to indicate Christ's continuous subordination of Death in death-time.

Integrally related to the idea of an ongoing battle is that the role of the faithful is to fight in that battle. Especially among apocalyptic readers, believers are understood to be God's soldiers waging an ongoing battle, the outcome of which is certain but not yet fully accomplished. I, however, hear Paul to say that, when joined to Christ, the faithful live liberated from the present evil age (Gal. 1:4) and that due to God's victory, that age need not concern them. The evil age's most devastating and destructive tools (suffering, sin, and physical death) have been defeated through God's victory and now serve God's purposes in Christ.

This leads to the second corollary of the consensus interpretation: a certain view of eschatology. The majority of interpreters think that the apostle's two-age framework meant that he saw Christ's resurrection as creating both a solution and a problem. The solution is that the new age has come; the problem is that the faithful are not also resurrected. Consequently, the interpretation goes, Paul construed the idea of the overlap of the ages. Paul thereby maintained his temporal framework by modifying it: Christ inaugurates the new age, and the faithful live in it while simultaneously existing in the present evil age. Believers, it is said with great regularity, live in the overlap of the ages.

My reading, on the other hand, proposes that Paul perceived Christ's resurrection as transformative of the cosmos even while the faithful have corruptible bodies. The metamorphosis that occurs through Christ's resurrection guarantees believers' resurrection, not due to their being in the inaugurated-but-certain-to-be-fulfilled new age but because they are in Christ, in whom Death and Sin are conquered. As a consequence of God's work in Christ, there are two separate kinds of temporalities that do not intermingle or overlap: death-time and life-time. Those living life-time are liberated from engagement with the forces of death-time. The evidence of this is that the instruments of death-time (suffering, sinning, and mortality), which are purposed for destruction, have been taken into Christ and transformed in service of God's life.

Christ's cross and resurrection open to humanity the kind of time the exalted Christ lives. Christ lives God's time in which there is only life. Since this is the case, the apostle conceived of those joined to Christ as living exclusively in one kind of time: life-time. To nuance this a bit: those who live life-time live the kind of time they will always live.[8] The event of their resurrection will not accomplish their escape from a situation of temporal overlap. Further, since God's victory is for all, those who presently live death-time (which, like life-time, is an exclusive kind of time) will at the telos also be incorporated into life-time—that is, God's life.

Two final comments about what I find problematic about the two-age interpretative framework are in order. First, it tends to suggest or imply that Paul conceived of the new age as God's ultimate goal. This is clearly not the case, as evidenced by 1 Corinthians 15:28. God's ultimate goal is that God would be all in all. If Paul thinks that this divine "all-ness" is equivalent to the new age, he does not say, and perhaps that is the wise course also for his interpreters.

Finally, the almost incomprehensible idea, so central to Paul, that believers are joined to a divine being (with no reference to this as equivalent to "an age") summons us to humble wonder. It is not that God has finally fulfilled God's promise of providing an alternative age; rather, God has embraced humanity with and within God's own life. The eschatological goal is the revelation of God's Son, who offers humanity God's life-filled endless time—the temporality lived now by those in Christ.

---

8. This is not to say that suffering, sin, and physical death will always continue. When believers' bodies are transformed to incorruptibility, clearly they will no longer physically die or experience the trials of human life. Did Paul think that features entailed by the incarnation—suffering in particular—remain in Christ's own life after God is all in all? He does not say.

Bibliography

Adams, Samuel V. *The Reality of God and Historical Method: Apocalyptic Theology in Conversation with N. T. Wright*. Downers Grove, IL: IVP Academic, 2015.

Agamben, Giorgio. *The Time That Remains: A Commentary on the Letter to the Romans*. Translated by Patricia Dailey. Stanford: Stanford University Press, 2005.

Anselm of Canterbury. *Monologion*. In *S. Anselmi Opera Omnia*. Edited by F. S. Schmitt. Edinburgh: Thomas Nelson and Sons, 1946–61.

Aristotle. *Physics*. Vol. 1, *Books 1–4*. Translated by P. H. Wicksteed and F. M. Cornford. Loeb Classical Library 228. Cambridge, MA: Harvard University Press, 1957.

Athanasius. *On the Incarnation*. Translated and edited by a religious of C. S. M. V. Crestwood, NY: St. Vladimir's Seminary Press, 2003.

Augustine. *The City of God*. Translated by Marcus Dods. Edinburgh: T&T Clark, 1871.

———. *Confessions*. Vol. 1, *Introduction and Text*. Edited by James J. O'Donnell. Oxford: Oxford University Press, 1992.

———. *Confessions*. Translated by R. S. Pine-Coffin. London: Penguin, 1961.

———. *Retractationes*. Translated by Meredith Freeman Eller. "The Retractiones of Saint Augustine." PhD Diss., Boston University Graduate School, 1946.

Barclay, John M. G. *Paul and the Gift*. Grand Rapids: Eerdmans, 2015.

———. Review of *Galatians: A New Translation with Introduction and Commentary*, by J. Louis Martyn. *Review of Biblical Literature* 3 (2001): 44–49.

———. Review of *Paul and the Faithfulness of God*, by N. T. Wright. *Scottish Journal of Theology* 68, no. 2 (2015): 235–43.

Barr, James. *Biblical Words for Time*. Rev. ed. London: SCM, 1969.

Barrett, William. "The Flow of Time." In *The Philosophy of Time: A Collection of Essays*, edited by Richard M. Gale, 354–76. Garden City, NY: Anchor Books, 1967.

Barth, Karl. *Church Dogmatics*. Edinburgh: T&T Clark, 1956–75.

———. "Der Christ in der Gesellschaft." In *Anfänge der dialektischen Theologie*. Edited by J. Moltmann, 1:3–37. Munich: Kaiser, 1962.

———. *The Epistle to the Romans*. Translated by E. C. Hoskyns. Oxford: Oxford University Press, 1977.

Beker, J. Christiaan. *Paul the Apostle: The Triumph of God in Life and Thought*. Edinburgh: T&T Clark, 1980.

———. *The Triumph of God: The Essence of Paul's Thought*. Translated by Loren T. Stuckenbruck. Minneapolis: Fortress, 1990.

Belcastro, Mauro. "The Advent of the Different: Θλῖψις, ὑπομονή, ἐλπίς and the Temporal Disclosure of the Divine Eternity in Paul's Letter to the Romans." *Early Christianity* 10, no. 4 (2019): 481–500.

Berger, Klaus. "'Salvation History': A Theological Analysis." In *Encyclopedia of Theology: The Concise Sacramentum Mundi*, edited by Karl Rahner, 1506–12. New York: Seabury, 1975.

Bevere, Allan R. *Sharing in the Inheritance: Identity and the Moral Life in Colossians*. Journal for the Study of the New Testament: Supplement Series 226. Sheffield: Sheffield Academic Press, 2003.

Bird, Michael. *An Anomalous Jew: Paul among Jews, Greeks, and Romans*. Grand Rapids: Eerdmans, 2016.

Blackwell, Ben C. "The *Greek Life of Adam and Eve* and Romans 8:14–39: (Re-)creation and Glory." In *Reading Romans in Context: Paul and Second Temple Judaism*, edited by Ben C. Blackwell, John K. Goodrich, and Jason Maston, 108–14. Grand Rapids: Zondervan, 2015.

Boakye, Andrew K. *Death and Life: Resurrection, Restoration, and Rectification in Paul's Letter to the Galatians*. Eugene, OR: Pickwick, 2017.

Boccaccini, Gabriele. Introduction to *Paul the Jew: Rereading the Apostle as a Figure of Second Temple Judaism*, edited by Gabriele Boccaccini and Carlos A. Segovia, 1–32. Minneapolis: Fortress, 2016.

Bouttier, Michel. *En Christ: étude d'exégèse et de théologie pauliniennes*. Paris: Presses universitaires de France, 1962.

Bowens, Lisa M. *An Apostle in Battle: Paul and Spiritual Warfare in 2 Corinthians 12:1–10*. Wissenschaftliche Untersuchungen zum Neuen Testament 2/433. Tübingen: Mohr Siebeck, 2017.

Brandon, S. G. F. *History, Time, and Deity: A Historical and Comparative Study of the Conception of Time in Religious Thought and Practice*. Manchester: Manchester University Press, 1965.

Brettler, Marc. "Cyclical and Teleological Time in the Hebrew Bible." In *Time and Temporality in the Ancient World*, edited by Ralph Mark Rosen, 111–28. Philadelphia: University of Pennsylvania Museum of Archaeology and Anthropology, 2004.

Brown, Alexandra R. *The Cross and Human Transformation: Paul's Apocalyptic Word in 1 Corinthians.* Minneapolis: Fortress, 1995.

Brown, Derek R. *The God of This Age: Satan in the Churches and Letters of the Apostle Paul.* Wissenschaftliche Untersuchungen zum Neuen Testament 2/409. Tübingen: Mohr Siebeck, 2015.

Bruce, F. F. *The Epistles to the Colossians, to Philemon, and to the Ephesians.* New International Commentary on the New Testament. Grand Rapids: Eerdmans, 1984.

Brunner, Emil. "The Problem of Time." In *God, History, and Historians: An Anthology of Modern Christian Views of History*, edited by C. T. McIntire, 81–96. New York: Oxford University Press, 1977.

Bultmann, Rudolf. *History and Eschatology.* The Gifford Lectures 1955. Edinburgh: Edinburgh University Press, 1957.

———. "History and Eschatology in the New Testament." *New Testament Studies* 1, no. 1 (1954): 5–16.

———. "The Significance of the Old Testament for the Christian Faith." In *The Old Testament and Christian Faith: A Theological Discussion*, edited by Bernhard W. Anderson, 8–35. New York: Herder and Herder, 1969.

———. *Theology of the New Testament.* 2 vols. London: SCM, 1952.

Caird, G. B. *Principalities and Powers: A Study in Pauline Theology.* Oxford: Clarendon, 1956.

Calvin, John. *The Epistles of Paul the Apostle to the Romans and to the Thessalonians.* Translated by Ross MacKenzie. Edited by David W. Torrance and Thomas F. Torrance. Calvin's New Testament Commentaries 8. Grand Rapids: Eerdmans, 1995.

Campbell, Constantine R. *Advances in the Study of Greek: New Insights for Reading the New Testament.* Grand Rapids: Zondervan, 2015.

———. *Paul and Union with Christ: An Exegetical and Theological Study.* Grand Rapids: Zondervan, 2012.

Campbell, Douglas A. *The Deliverance of God: An Apocalyptic Rereading of Justification in Paul.* Grand Rapids: Eerdmans, 2009.

———. *Framing Paul.* Grand Rapids: Eerdmans, 2014.

———. *Paul: An Apostle's Journey.* Grand Rapids: Eerdmans, 2018.

———. *Pauline Dogmatics: The Triumph of God's Love.* Grand Rapids: Eerdmans, 2020.

———. *The Quest for Paul's Gospel.* London: T&T Clark, 2005.

Chester, Andrew. *Messiah and Exaltation: Jewish Messianic and Visionary Traditions and New Testament Christology.* Wissenschaftliche Untersuchungen zum Neuen Testament 207. Tübingen: Mohr Siebeck, 2007.

Clark, Gordon H. "The Theory of Time in Plotinus." *The Philosophical Review* 53, no. 4 (1944): 337–58.

Collins, John J., ed. *Apocalypse: The Morphology of a Genre. Semeia* 14. Missoula, MT: Scholars Press, 1979.

Cousar, Charles B. Review of *Galatians: A New Translation with Introduction and Commentary*, by J. Louis Martyn. *Review of Biblical Literature* 3 (2001): 42–44.

Craig, William Lane. "God, Time, and Eternity." In *What God Knows: Time, Eternity, and Divine Knowledge*, edited by Harry Lee Poe and J. Stanley Mattson, 75–94. Waco: Baylor University Press, 2005.

Cranfield, C. E. B. *A Critical and Exegetical Commentary on the Epistle to the Romans*. 2 vols. Edinburgh: T&T Clark, 1975–79.

Croasmun, Matthew. *The Emergence of Sin: The Cosmic Tyrant in Romans*. Oxford: Oxford University Press, 2017.

Cullmann, Oscar. *Christ and Time: The Primitive Christian Conception of Time and History*. Translated by Floyd V. Filson. Philadelphia: Westminster, 1950.

———. *Salvation in History*. Translated by S. G. Sowers. New York: Harper & Row, 1967.

Davies, Jamie P. *The Apocalyptic Paul: Retrospect and Prospect*. Eugene, OR: Cascade Books, 2022.

———. *Paul among the Apocalypses? An Evaluation of the "Apocalyptic Paul" in the Context of Jewish and Christian Apocalyptic Literature*. London: Bloomsbury T&T Clark, 2016.

———. "Why Paul Doesn't Mention the 'Age to Come.'" *Scottish Journal of Theology* 74, no. 3 (2021): 199–208. https://doi.org/10.1017/S0036930621000375.

Davies, W. D. *Paul and Rabbinic Judaism: Some Rabbinic Elements in Pauline Theology*. 4th ed. Philadelphia: Fortress, 1980.

Dawson, Christopher. "The Christian View of History." In *God, History, and Historians: An Anthology of Modern Christian Views of History*, edited by C. T. McIntire, 28–45. New York: Oxford University Press, 1977.

de Boer, Martinus C. *The Defeat of Death: Apocalyptic Eschatology in 1 Corinthians 15 and Romans 5*. Sheffield: JSOT Press, 1988.

———. *Galatians: A Commentary*. Louisville: Westminster John Knox, 2011.

———. "Paul and Jewish Apocalyptic Eschatology." In *Apocalyptic and the New Testament: Essays in Honor of J. Louis Martyn*, edited by Joel Marcus and Marion L. Soards, 169–90. 1989. Reprint, London: Bloomsbury Academic, 2015.

Deissmann, G. Adolf. *Die neutestamentliche Formel "in Christo Jesu."* Marburg: N. G. Elwert'sche, 1892.

———. *Paul*. London: Hodder & Stoughton, 1926.

Donfried, Karl Paul. "The Kingdom of God in Paul." In *The Kingdom of God in 20th Century Interpretation*, edited by Wendell Willis, 175–90. Peabody, MA: Hendrickson, 1987.

Downs, David J., and Benjamin J. Lappenga. *The Faithfulness of the Risen Christ: Pistis and the Exalted Lord in the Pauline Letters*. Waco: Baylor University Press, 2019.

Dunn, James D. G. "How New Was Paul's Gospel? The Problem of Continuity and Discontinuity." In *Gospel in Paul: Studies on Corinthians, Galatians and Romans for Richard N. Longenecker*, edited by L. Ann Jervis and Peter Richardson, 367–87. Sheffield: Sheffield Academic Press, 1994.

———. *Romans 1–8*. Word Biblical Commentary 38A. Grand Rapids: Zondervan, 2015.

———. *The Theology of Paul the Apostle*. Grand Rapids: Eerdmans, 1998.

Du Toit, Philip La G. "Reading Galatians 6:16 in Line with Paul's Contrast Between the New Aeon in Christ and the Old Aeon Before the Christ Event." *Stellenbosch Theological Journal* 2 (2016): 203–25.

Eastman, Susan Grove. "Apocalypse and Incarnation: The Participatory Logic of Paul's Gospel." In *Apocalyptic and the Future of Theology*, edited by Joshua B. Davis and Douglas Harink, 165–82. Eugene, OR: Wipf & Stock, 2012.

———. "Christian Experience and Paul's Logic of Solidarity: The Spiral Structure of Romans 5–8." *The Biblical Annals* 12, no. 2 (2022): 233–53.

———. "The 'Empire of Illusion': Sin, Evil and Good News in Romans." In *Comfortable Words: Essays in Honor of Paul F. M. Zahl*, edited by J. D. Koch and T. H. W. Brewer, 3–21. Eugene, OR: Wipf & Stock, 2013.

———. "Oneself in Another: Participation and the Spirit in Romans 8." In Thate, Vanhoozer, and Campbell, *"In Christ" in Paul*, 103–26.

———. *Paul and the Person: Reframing Paul's Anthropology*. Grand Rapids: Eerdmans, 2017.

———. *Recovering Paul's Mother Tongue: Language and Theology in Galatians*. Grand Rapids: Eerdmans, 2007.

———. "Whose Apocalypse? The Identity of the Sons of God in Romans 8:19." *Journal of Biblical Literature* 121, no. 2 (2002): 263–77.

Fagg, Lawrence W. *The Becoming of Time: Integrating Physical and Religious Time*. Durham, NC: Duke University Press, 2003.

Fee, Gordon D. *The First Epistle to the Corinthians*. Rev. ed. New International Commentary on the New Testament. Grand Rapids: Eerdmans, 2014.

Fitzmyer, Joseph A. *Romans: A New Translation with Introduction and Commentary*. Anchor Bible. New Haven: Yale University Press, 2007.

Fowl, Stephen. *Philippians*. Two Horizons. Grand Rapids: Eerdmans, 2005.

Frank, Erich. "The Role of History in Christian Thought." *Duke Divinity School Bulletin* 14, no. 3 (November 1949): 66–77.

Frey, Jörg. "Demythologizing Apocalyptic? On N. T. Wright's Paul, Apocalyptic Interpretation, and the Constraints of Construction." In Heilig, Hewett, and Bird, *God and the Faithfulness of Paul*, 489–532.

Furnish, Victor P. *Theology and Ethics in Paul*. 1968. Reprint, Louisville: Westminster John Knox, 2009.

Gaventa, Beverly Roberts. "The Character of God's Faithfulness: A Response to N. T. Wright." *Journal for the Study of Paul and His Letters* 4, no. 1 (2014): 71–79.

————. "The Cosmic Power of Sin in Paul's Letter to the Romans: Toward a Wide-screen Edition." *Interpretation* 58 (2004): 229–40.

————. *First and Second Thessalonians*. Interpretation. Louisville: John Knox, 1998.

————. "'God Handed Them Over.'" In *Our Mother Saint Paul*, 113–24.

————. *Our Mother Saint Paul*. Louisville: Westminster John Knox, 2007.

————. "The Rhetoric of Violence and the God of Peace in Paul's Letter to the Romans." In *Paul, John, and Apocalyptic Eschatology: Studies in Honor of Martinus C. de Boer*, edited by Jan Krans, Bert Jan Lietaert Peerbolte, Peter-Ben Smit, and Arie Zwiep, 61–75. Novum Testamentum Supplements 149. Leiden: Brill, 2013.

Goff, Matthew. "Heavenly Mysteries and Otherworldly Journeys: Interpreting 1 and 2 Corinthians in Relation to Jewish Apocalypticism." In *Paul the Jew: Rereading the Apostle as a Figure of Second Temple Judaism*, edited by Gabriele Boccaccini and Carlos A. Segovia, 133–50. Minneapolis: Fortress, 2016.

Gorman, Michael. *Cruciformity: Paul's Narrative Spirituality of the Cross*. Grand Rapids: Eerdmans, 2001.

Greig, A. Josef. "A Critical Note on the Origin of the Term *Heilsgeschichte*." *Expository Times* 87 (1976): 118–19.

Griffiths, Paul J. *Decreation: The Last Things of All Creatures*. Waco: Baylor University Press, 2014.

Harink, Douglas. *Paul among the Postliberals: Pauline Theology beyond Christendom and Modernity*. Grand Rapids: Brazos, 2003.

————. "Time and Politics in Four Commentaries on Romans." In *Paul, Philosophy, and the Theopolitical Vision: Critical Engagements with Agamben, Badiou, Žižek, and Others*, edited by Douglas Harink, 282–312. Eugene, OR: Cascade Books, 2010.

Hart, David Bentley. *The New Testament: A Translation*. New Haven: Yale University Press, 2017.

Hawking, Stephen. *A Brief History of Time*. New York: Bantam Books, 1998.

Hays, Richard B. "The Conversion of the Imagination: Scripture and Eschatology in 1 Corinthians." *New Testament Studies* 45 (1999): 391–412.

————. *First Corinthians*. Interpretation. Louisville: Westminster John Knox, 1997.

————. Review of *Galatians: A New Translation with Introduction and Commentary*, by J. Louis Martyn. *Journal of Biblical Literature* 119, no. 2 (2000): 373–79.

Heidegger, Martin. *Being and Time*. Translated by John Macquarrie and Edward Robinson. New York: Harper & Row, 1962.

Heilig, Christoph, J. Thomas Hewitt, and Michael F. Bird, eds. *God and the Faithfulness of Paul: A Critical Examination of the Theology of N. T. Wright*. Minneapolis: Fortress, 2017.

Hengel, Martin. "'Salvation History': The Truth of Scripture and Modern Theology." In *Reading Texts, Seeking Wisdom: Scripture and Theology*, edited by David Ford and Graham Stanton, 229–44. Grand Rapids: Eerdmans, 2003.

Hewitt, J. Thomas. *Messiah and Scripture: Paul's "in Christ" Idiom in Its Ancient Jewish Context*. Wissenschaftliche Untersuchungen zum Neuen Testament 2/522. Tübingen: Mohr Siebeck, 2020.

Hill, C. E. "Paul's Understanding of Christ's Kingdom in 1 Corinthians 15:20–28." *Novum Testamentum* 30 (1988): 297–320.

Hill, Wesley. *Paul and the Trinity: Persons, Relations, and the Pauline Letters*. Grand Rapids: Eerdmans, 2015.

Hodgson, Peter C. *God in History: Shapes of Freedom*. Nashville: Abingdon, 1989.

Hollander, H. W., and J. Holleman. "The Relationship of Death, Sin, and Law in 1 Cor 15:56." *Novum Testamentum* 35, no. 3 (1993): 270–91.

Holleman, Joost. *Resurrection and Parousia: A Traditio-Historical Study of Paul's Eschatology in 1 Corinthians 15*. Leiden: Brill, 1996.

Holloway, Paul. *Philippians*. Hermeneia. Minneapolis: Fortress, 2017.

Hooker, Morna D. *From Adam to Christ: Essays on Paul*. Cambridge: Cambridge University Press, 1990.

———. "Interchange and Atonement." In *From Adam to Christ*, 26–41.

———. "Interchange in Christ." In *From Adam to Christ*, 13–25.

———. "On Becoming the Righteousness of God: Another Look at 2 Cor 5:21." *Novum Testamentum* 50, no. 4 (2008): 358–75.

Hubbard, Moyer V. *New Creation in Paul's Letters and Thought*. Cambridge: Cambridge University Press, 2002.

Hunsinger, George. "*Mysterium Trinitatis*: Karl Barth's Conception of Eternity." In *Disruptive Grace: Studies in the Theology of Karl Barth*, 186–209. Grand Rapids: Eerdmans, 2000.

International Council on Biblical Inerrancy. "The Chicago Statement on Biblical Hermeneutics." 1982.

International Council on Biblical Inerrancy. "The Chicago Statement on Biblical Inerrancy." 1978.

Jackelén, Antje. *Time and Eternity: The Question of Time in Church, Science, and Theology*. Philadelphia: Templeton Foundation Press, 2005.

James, William. "The Perception of Time." In *The Human Experience of Time: The Development of Its Philosophic Meaning*, edited by Charles M. Sherover, 368–83. New York: New York University Press, 1975.

Jenson, Robert W. "Apocalyptic and Messianism in Twentieth Century German Theology." In *Messianism, Apocalypse and Redemption in Twentieth Century German Thought*, edited by Wayne Cristaudo and Wendy Baker, 3–12. Adelaide: ATF Press, 2006.

———. *God after God: The God of the Past and the God of the Future, Seen in the Work of Karl Barth.* New York: Bobbs-Merrill, 1969.

———. *Systematic Theology.* Vol. 2, *The Works of God.* Oxford: Oxford University Press, 1999.

Jervis, L. Ann. *At the Heart of the Gospel: Suffering in the Earliest Christian Message.* Grand Rapids: Eerdmans, 2007.

———. "Christ Doesn't Fit: Paul Replaces His Two Age Inheritance with Christ." *Interpretation* (2022): 1–14.

———. "Peter in the Middle: Gal. 2:11–21." In *Text and Artifact in the Religions of Mediterranean Antiquity: Essays in Honour of Peter Richardson*, edited by Stephen G. Wilson and Michel Desjardins, 45–62. Studies in Christianity and Judaism/Études sur le Christianisme et le Judaïsme 9. Waterloo, ON: Wilfrid Laurier University Press, 2000.

———. "Promise and Purpose in Romans 9:1–13: Towards Understanding Paul's View of Time." In *God and Israel: Providence and Purpose in Romans 9–11*, edited by Todd D. Still, 1–26. Waco: Baylor University Press, 2017.

———. "Reading Romans 7 in Conversation with Post-Colonial Theory: Paul's Struggle Toward a Christian Identity of Hybridity." *Theoforum* 35, no. 2 (2004): 173–93.

———. "Timely Pastoral Response to Suffering: God's Time and the Power of the Resurrection." In *Practicing with Paul: Reflections on Paul and the Practices of Ministry in Honor of Susan G. Eastman*, edited by Presian R. Burroughs, 74–87. Eugene, OR: Cascade Books, 2018.

Jewett, Robert. *Romans.* Hermeneia. Minneapolis: Fortress, 2007.

Jipp, Joshua W. *Christ Is King: Paul's Royal Ideology.* Minneapolis: Fortress, 2015.

Kant, Immanuel. *Critique of Pure Reason.* Translated by F. Max Müller. Garden City, NY: Anchor Books, 1966.

Käsemann, Ernst. "The Beginnings of Christian Theology." In *New Testament Questions of Today*, 82–107.

———. *Commentary on Romans.* Translated and edited by Geoffrey W. Bromiley. Grand Rapids: Eerdmans, 1980.

———. "Justification and Salvation History." In *Perspectives on Paul*, 60–78. Philadelphia: Fortress, 1971.

———. *New Testament Questions of Today.* Philadelphia: Fortress, 1969

———. "On the Subject of Primitive Christian Apocalyptic." In *New Testament Questions of Today*, 108–37.

Keck, Leander. *Christ's First Theologian: The Shape of Paul's Thought.* Waco: Baylor University Press, 2015.

———. *Romans.* Nashville: Abingdon, 2005.

Kümmel, Werner Georg, and Hans Lietzmann. *An die Korinther I–II.* Handbuch zum Neuen Testament 9. Tübingen: Mohr, 1969.

Lambrecht, Jan. "Paul's Christological Use of Scripture in 1 Cor. 15.20–28." *New Testament Studies* 28 (1982): 502–27.

———. "Structure and Line of Thought in 1 Cor. 15:23–28." *Novum Testamentum* 32, no. 2 (1990): 143–51.

Langdon, Adrian. *God the Eternal Contemporary: Trinity, Eternity, and Time in Karl Barth*. Eugene, OR: Wipf & Stock, 2012.

Leftow, Brian. *Time and Eternity*. Ithaca, NY: Cornell University Press, 1991.

Lincoln, Andrew T. *Paradise Now and Not Yet: Studies in the Role of the Heavenly Dimension in Paul's Thought with Special Reference to his Eschatology*. Society for New Testament Studies: Monograph Series 43. Cambridge: Cambridge University Press, 1981.

Longarino, Joseph. "Apocalyptic and the Passions: Overcoming a False Dichotomy in Pauline Studies." *New Testament Studies* 67 (2021): 582–97.

———. *Pauline Theology and the Problem of Death*. Tübingen: Mohr Siebeck, 2021.

Longenecker, Richard N. *Paul, Apostle of Liberty: The Origin and Nature of Paul's Christianity*. Grand Rapids: Eerdmans, 2015.

Löwith, Karl. *Meaning in History: The Theological Implications of the Philosophy of History*. Chicago: University of Chicago Press, 1949.

Macaskill, Grant. *Union with Christ in the New Testament*. Oxford: Oxford University Press, 2014.

Macky, Peter. *St. Paul's Cosmic War Myth: A Military Version of the Gospel*. New York: Peter Lang, 1998.

Mangina, Joseph L. *Karl Barth: Theologian of Christian Witness*. Louisville: Westminster John Knox, 2004.

Marsh, John. *The Fulness of Time*. New York: Harper & Brothers, 1952.

Martyn, J. Louis. "The Daily Life of the Church in the War between the Spirit and the Flesh." In *Theological Issues in the Letters of Paul*, 251–66.

———. "From Paul to Flannery O'Connor with the Power of Grace." In *Theological Issues in the Letters of Paul*, 279–97. Nashville: Abingdon, 1997.

———. *Galatians: A New Translation with Introduction and Commentary*. Anchor Bible 33A. New York: Doubleday, 1997.

———. *Theological Issues in the Letters of Paul*. New York: T&T Clark International, 1997.

Matera, Frank J. *Galatians*. Sacra Pagina 9. Collegeville, MN: Liturgical Press, 2007.

Matlock, R. Barry. *Unveiling the Apocalyptic Paul: Paul's Interpreters and the Rhetoric of Criticism*. Sheffield: Sheffield Academic Press, 1996.

McCormack, Bruce L. "Longing for a New World: On Socialism, Eschatology and Apocalyptic in Barth's Early Dialectical Theology." In *Theologie im Umbruch der Moderne: Karl Barths frühe Dialektische Theologie*, edited by Georg Pfleiderer and Harald Matern, 135–49. Zurich: Theologischer Verlag, 2014.

McTaggart, J. M. E. *The Nature of Existence*. Vol. 2. Cambridge: Cambridge University Press, 1927.

———. "Time." In *Nature of Existence*, 2:9–31.

Metz, Johann Baptist. "God: Against the Myth of the Eternity of Time." In *The End of Time? The Provocation of Talking about God*, edited by Tiemo Rainer Peters and Claus Urban, 26–46. English edition translated and edited by James Matthew Ashley. New York: Paulist Press, 2004.

Minkowski, Eugène. "The Presence of the Past." In *The Human Experience of Time: The Development of Its Philosophic Meaning*, edited by Charles M. Sherover, 504–18. New York: New York University Press, 1975.

Momigliano, Arnaldo. "Time in Ancient Historiography." In *Essays in Ancient and Modern Historiography*, 179–204. Chicago: University of Chicago Press, 2012.

Moo, Douglas. "Paul." In *New Dictionary of Biblical Theology*, edited by T. Desmond Alexander and Brian S. Rosner, 136–40. Downers Grove, IL: InterVarsity, 2000.

Morgan, Teresa. *Being "in Christ" in the Letters of Paul: Saved through Christ and in His Hands*. Wissenschaftliche Untersuchungen zum Neuen Testament 449. Tübingen: Mohr Siebeck, 2020.

———. *Roman Faith and Christian Faith: Pistis and Fides in the Early Roman Empire and Early Churches*. Oxford: Oxford University Press, 2015.

Mullins, R. T. *The End of the Timeless God*. Oxford: Oxford University Press, 2016.

Neufeld, Thomas R. Yoder. *"Put on the Armour of God": The Divine Warrior from Isaiah to Ephesians*. Journal for the Study of the New Testament: Supplement Series 140. Sheffield: Sheffield Academic Press, 1997.

Newman, Judith H. "The Participatory Past: Resituating Eschatology in the Study of Apocalyptic." *Early Christianity* 10 (2019): 415–34.

Newton, Isaac. *The Principia: Mathematical Principles of Natural Philosophy*. Translated by I. Bernard Cohen and Anne Whitman. Berkeley: University of California Press, 1999.

Novenson, Matthew V. *Christ among the Messiahs: Christ Language in Paul and Messiah Language in Ancient Judaism*. Oxford: Oxford University Press, 2012.

Nygaard, Mathias. "Romans 8—Interchange Leading to Deification." *Horizons in Biblical Theology* 39 (2017): 156–75.

Pannenberg, Wolfhart. *Jesus—God and Man*. 2nd ed. Translated by Lewis L. Wilkins and Duane A. Priebe. Philadelphia: Westminster, 1977.

———. *What Is Man?: Contemporary Anthropology in Theological Perspective*. Translated by Duane A. Priebe. Philadelphia: Fortress, 1970.

Pfitzner, Victor C. *Paul and the Agon Motif: Traditional Athletic Imagery in the Pauline Literature*. Leiden: Brill, 1967.

Placher, William C. *Narratives of a Vulnerable God: Christ, Theology, and Scripture*. Louisville: Westminster John Knox, 1994.

Plato. *Gorgias* and *Timaeus*. Translated by Benjamin Jowett. Mineola, NY: Dover, 2003.

Porter, Stanley E. *When Paul Met Jesus: How an Idea Got Lost in History*. Cambridge: Cambridge University Press, 2016.

Punt, Jeremy. "Paul, Military Imagery and Social Disadvantage." *Acta Theologica* 2016, Supplementum 23: 201–24. http://dx.doi.org/10.4314/actat.v23i1s.10.

Radner, Ephraim. *Time and the Word: Figural Reading of the Christian Scriptures*. Grand Rapids: Eerdmans, 2016.

Ramelli, Ilaria L. E. *The Christian Doctrine of* Apokatastasis: *A Critical Assessment from the New Testament to Eriugena*. Boston: Brill, 2013.

Rogers, Katherin. A. "Anselm on Eternity as the Fifth Dimension." *The Saint Anselm Journal* 3, no. 2 (2006): 1–8.

Ryan, Scott C. *Divine Conflict and the Divine Warrior: Listening to Romans and Other Jewish Voices*. Wissenschaftliche Untersuchungen zum Neuen Testament 507. Tübingen: Mohr Siebeck, 2020.

Sanders, E. P. *Paul and Palestinian Judaism: A Comparison of Patterns of Religion*. Philadelphia: Fortress Press, 1977.

Sappington, Thomas J. *Revelation and Redemption at Colossae*. Journal for the Study of the New Testament Supplement Series 53. Sheffield: Sheffield Academic Press, 1991.

Schliesser, Benjamin. "*Paul and the Faithfulness of God* among Pauline Theologies." In Heilig, Hewitt, and Bird, *God and the Faithfulness of Paul*, 21–72.

Schnelle, Udo. *Apostle Paul: His Life and Theology*. Translated by M. Eugene Boring. Grand Rapids: Baker Academic, 2005.

Schweitzer, Albert. *The Mysticism of Paul the Apostle*. Translated by William Montgomery. Baltimore: Johns Hopkins University Press, 1998.

Sellin, Gerhard. *Der Streit um die Auferstehung der Toten: Eine religionsgeschichtliche und exegetische Untersuchung von 1 Korinther 15*. Göttingen: Vandenhoeck & Ruprecht, 1986.

Shogren, Gary Steven. "Is the Kingdom of God about Eating and Drinking or Isn't It? (Romans 14:17)." *Novum Testamentum* 42, no. 3 (2000): 238–56.

Stowers, Stanley K. "Paul's Four Discourses about Sin." In *Celebrating Paul: Festschrift in Honor of Jerome Murphy-O'Connor, O.P., and Joseph A. Fitzmyer, S.J.*, edited by Peter Spitaler, 100–127. Catholic Biblical Quarterly Monograph Series 48. Washington, DC: Catholic Biblical Association of America, 2011.

Stuckenbruck, Loren T. "Posturing 'Apocalyptic' in Pauline Theology: How Much Contrast to Jewish Tradition?" In *The Myth of the Rebellious Angels*, 240–56. Wissenschaftliche Untersuchungen zum Neuen Testament 335. Tübingen: Mohr Siebeck, 2014.

Stump, Eleonore, and Norman Kretzmann. "Eternity." *The Journal of Philosophy* 78 (1981): 429–58.

Tannehill, Robert C. *Dying and Rising with Christ: A Study in Pauline Theology.* 1967. Reprint, Eugene, OR: Wipf & Stock, 2006.

Thate, Michael J., Kevin J. Vanhoozer, and Constantine R. Campbell, eds. *"In Christ" in Paul: Explorations in Paul's Theology of Union and Participation.* Wissenschaftliche Untersuchungen zum Neuen Testament 2/384. Tübingen: Mohr Siebeck, 2014.

Thiselton, Anthony C. "Realized Eschatology at Corinth." *New Testament Studies* 54 (2008): 510–26.

Torrance, T. F. *Space, Time and Resurrection.* Edinburgh: T&T Clark, 1998.

Tuckett, C. M. "The Corinthians Who Say 'There Is No Resurrection of the Dead' (1 Cor 15,12)." In *The Corinthian Correspondence*, edited by R. Bieringer, 247–75. Bibliotheca Ephemeridum Theologicarum Lovaniensium 125. Leuven: Leuven University Press, 1996.

Vielhauer, Philipp. *Oikodome: Aufsätze zum Neuen Testament.* Vol. 1. Münich: Kaiser, 1979.

Von Rad, Gerhard. *Old Testament Theology.* Vol. 2. Translated by D. M. G. Stalker. London: SCM Press, 1975.

Wasserman, Emma. *Apocalypse as Holy War: Divine Politics and Polemics in the Letters of Paul.* New Haven: Yale University Press, 2018.

———. "Paul among the Philosophers: The Case of Sin in Romans 6–8." *Journal for the Study of the New Testament* 30, no. 4 (2008): 387–415.

Watson, Francis. *Paul and the Hermeneutics of Faith.* 2nd ed. London: Bloomsbury T&T Clark, 2016.

Wedderburn, A. J. M. *Baptism and Resurrection: Studies in Pauline Theology against Its Graeco-Roman Background.* Tübingen: Mohr Siebeck, 1987.

———. "Some Observations on Paul's Use of the Phrases 'in Christ' and 'with Christ.'" *Journal for the Study of the New Testament* 25 (1985): 83–97.

Weil, Simone. *Gravity and Grace.* Translated by Emma Crawford and Mario von der Ruhr. New York: Routledge, 1999.

Weima, Jeffrey A. D. *1–2 Thessalonians.* Baker Exegetical Commentary on the New Testament. Grand Rapids: Baker Academic, 2014.

Weiss, Johannes. *The History of Primitive Christianity.* Vol. 2. Translated and edited by Frederick C. Grant. New York: Wilson-Erickson, 1937.

Whitehead, Alfred North. *The Concept of Nature: Tarner Lectures.* Cambridge Philosophy Classics. Cambridge: Cambridge University Press, 2015. https://doi.org/10.1017/CBO9781316286654.

———. *Process and Reality: An Essay in Cosmology (Gifford Lectures 1927–28), Corrected Edition.* Edited by David Ray Griffin and Donald W. Sherburne. New York: Free Press, 1985.

Wolter, Michael. *Paul: An Outline of His Theology.* Translated by Robert L. Brawley. Waco: Baylor University Press, 2015.

Wrede, William. *Paul*. Translated by Edward Lummis. Eugene, OR: Wipf & Stock, 2001.

Wright, M. R. *Cosmology in Antiquity*. New York: Routledge, 1996.

Wright, N. T. *The Climax of the Covenant*. Minneapolis: Fortress, 1991.

———. *The Kingdom New Testament: A Contemporary Translation*. New York: HarperOne, 2011.

———. *The New Testament and the People of God*. Minneapolis: Fortress, 1992.

———. *Paul and His Recent Interpreters: Some Contemporary Debates*. Minneapolis: Fortress, 2015.

———. *Paul and the Faithfulness of God*. Minneapolis: Fortress, 2013.

———. *Paul in Fresh Perspective*. Minneapolis: Fortress, 2005.

Yarbrough, Robert. "Paul and Salvation History." In *The Paradoxes of Paul*. Vol. 2 of *Justification and Variegated Nomism*, edited by D. A. Carson, Peter T. O'Brien, and Mark A. Seifrid, 297–342. Grand Rapids: Baker Academic, 2004.

———. "Salvation History (*Heilsgeschichte*) and Paul: Comments on a Disputed but Essential Category." In *Studies in the Pauline Epistles: Essays in Honor of Douglas J. Moo*, edited by Matthew S. Harmon and Jay E. Smith, 181–97. Grand Rapids: Zondervan, 2014.

Ziegler, Philip G. *Militant Grace: The Apocalyptic Turn and the Future of Christian Theology*. Grand Rapids: Baker Academic, 2018.

Name Index

Adams, Samuel V., 11n46, 11n49, 29n76
Agamben, Giorgio, xxxiv*n*48, 43–45,
  43nn171–77, 44nn178–85, 130n53
Anselm of Canterbury, xxxi,
  xxxi*nn*33–34
Aristotle, xi, xxvi*n*7, xxvii, xxvii*n*10,
  xxvii*n*12, xxviii, xxviii*n*16, 62, 62n1,
  62nn3–4
Athanasius, 107n36, 139n10
Augustine, xxvi, xxvi*n*3, xxvii,
  xxvii*n*11–12, xxviii, xxvii*nn*17–19,
  xxix, xxix*n*20, xxix*n*22, xxx,
  xxx*nn*28–29, 3–4, 63, 63n7, 65,
  65n9, 65nn11–12, 82n14

Barclay, John M. G., ix, x, xi, xxi,
  10n44, 34n115, 152, 152n51
Barr, James, 14, 14n68
Barrett, William, xxvii*n*13
Barth, Karl, ix, x, xvi, xxx, xxx*n*24,
  xxxii, xxxii*nn*41–43, 25–30,
  25nn38–40, 26nn41–49, 27nn51–53,
  27nn55–59, 28nn60–67, 29nn68–76,
  30n77, 41, 41n164, 42n170, 66–68,
  66n19, 67nn20–21, 67n23, 67nn25–
  27, 68n29, 70n33, 88n30, 111n41

Beker, J. Christiaan, 19n2, 32–34,
  32nn96–100, 33nn101–10, 34n111,
  35n118, 36n128, 42n169, 86n24,
  98n11, 105, 105n31, 127n48, 131n56,
  132n58, 135n1, 137n7, 138n8,
  142n21, 145n33
Belcastro, Mauro, 57n30
Berger, Klaus, 3n5
Bird, Michael F., xxxii*n*47
Blackwell, Ben C., 110n39
Boakye, Andrew K., 50, 50n10
Boccaccini, Gabriele, 140n14
Boethius, xxx, xxxi
Bouttier, Michel, 119–20, 120nn14–15
Bowens, Lisa M., 150nn44–45, 154n54
Brandon, S. G. F., xxvii*n*14
Brettler, Marc, xxvii*n*14
Brown, Alexandra R., xx, 21, 21n11,
  136n3
Brown, Derek R., 153n53, 154n55
Bruce, F. F., 149n42
Brunner, Emil, 7, 7n18
Bultmann, Rudolf, ix, xi, 11–13, 11n51,
  12nn52–55, 13n56, 13n58, 13n63,
  28n63, 30, 33, 99n17, 100n19

183

Scripture Index